I0435974

Spring Mountains National Recreation Area
Las Vegas Ranger District
Humboldt-Toiyabe National Forest

2011 Annual Report

*Monitoring and Evaluation for Conserving Biological Resources
of the Spring Mountains National Recreation Area*

May 11, 2012

Prepared by:

*Management and Engineering Technologies
International, Inc. (METI)
8600 Boeing Drive, El Paso, Texas 79925*

*Rocky Mountain Research Station
Grassland, Desert and Shrubland Program
Forestry Sciences Laboratory, Albuquerque, NM*

Primary Contributors

Stephen J. Solem, a Senior Advisor for Natural Resource Planning and Inventory and consultant to METI, Inc. located in Missoula, MT, served as inventory and monitoring program coordinator and as a primary author of this report.

Burton K Pendleton, PhD, a Research Ecologist at the Rocky Mountain Research Station located in Albuquerque, NM, conducted the species status review, orchestrated the analysis and evaluation, and served as a primary author of this report.

Julie A. Woldow, Communication Specialist and consultant to METI, Inc. located in Anchorage, AK, reviewed the report manuscript, provided writer-editor support to the primary authors, participated in the IM Audit and assisted in preparing the IM Audit report.

Marc Coles-Ritchie, PhD, Vegetation Ecologist and consultant to METI, Inc. located in Salt Lake City, UT, provided oversight of the springs inventory program, and analysis and evaluation of the springs data.

Jeri Ledbetter, GIS and Database Specialist and consultant to METI, Inc. located in Flagstaff, AZ, developed the GIS potential habitat models and maps, and springs data summaries. She also served as the Northern Arizona University springs inventory crew leader.

Kevin S. McKelvey, PhD, Research Ecologist at the Rocky Mountain Research Station located in Missoula, MT, served as primary contributor to the genetic analysis and monitoring program.

Joy Berg, a Senior Advisor for Natural Resource Planning and Implementation and consultant to METI, Inc. located in Wisconsin Falls, WI, provided leadership for the Implementation and Monitoring Audit and developed the 2010 IM Audit Report.

Amy Gilboy, an Inventory and Monitoring Specialist and consultant to METI, Inc. located in Fort Collins, CO, assisted during the IM Audit.

Jim Menlove, Ecologist with Interior West Forest Inventory and Analysis program at the Rocky Mountain Research Station located in Ogden, UT, contributed FIA analysis and reporting information.

Carly K. Woodlief, Biological Technician, RMRS. SMNRA Species Database management

Acknowledgements

Staff from the Spring Mountains NRA contributed to accomplishment of inventories and surveys during this past year and development of this report. **James Hurja** provided leadership and coordination, and assistance to the contract team. Numerous staff members assisted in implementing different components of the inventory program and in review of the draft report.

Abe Springer and **Larry Stevens** from NAU were instrumental in updating the Cost Reimbursable Agreement and providing oversight and leadership for the spring inventory program.

Michael Wilson, **Debra Finch**, and **Bill Block**, Science Program Managers for the Rocky Mountain Research Station, provided support and staff assistance for inventory and monitoring and development of this report.

Contents

The 2011 field season represents the first full year of data collection and analysis for all program components outlined in the Spring Mountains National Recreation Area's Comprehensive Inventory and Monitoring Strategy (USDA Forest Service 2008b). This report includes three major sections and appendices:

- Section 2 describes inventory and monitoring design and data collection in 2010 and 2011.
- Section 3 includes an evaluation of information collected from various sources and the SMNRA inventory and monitoring program with respect to ecological context, species conservation, and management interactions.
- Section 4 provides recommendations regarding plans and programs.
- Appendices to the report present data analysis and findings for data collected during 2010 and 2011.

Inventory and Monitoring Data Collection

Forest Inventory and Analysis Plots - Data collection for intensified FIA plots was postponed until 2011 to ensure consistency with changes in the national FIA Field Manual. A total of 91 of 126 scheduled inventory plots were installed by crews from the Rocky Mountain Research Station's Interior West Forest Inventory and Analysis Program. A late start in the field season, threatened government shutdown, and law enforcement/safety issues precluded data collection on 35 sites. These sites will be inventoried in 2012. Work on installing the national FIA plots within Nevada also began in 2011, providing the ability to link SMNRA data to other plots across the state.

Springs Inventory – At the conclusion of the 2011 field season, inventory crews from Northern Arizona University had inventoried a total of 47 spring sites. Crews collected data at 32 sites in 2011. However, inventory of some sites was deferred because of law enforcement/safety concerns and inaccessibility. Many of these sites will be inventoried in 2012.

Genetics Monitoring and Analysis – Collection of genetic material from Palmer's chipmunks across the SMNRA occurred during 2011. This trapping effort augmented 2010 collection efforts in Kyle and Lee Canyon areas located on the eastside of the SMNRA.

Species-Specific and Project Surveys – In 2011, the autecology study of SMNRA butterflies and their host plants was concluded by scientists from the University of Nevada at Las Vegas. Their study identified new information regarding relationships between butterflies and their hosts and the limited habitat for these species within the SMNRA. In addition to this study, few other project surveys were conducted because of the backlog of pending project environmental analyses and decisions. Efforts to load data collected from previous years into NRM-NRIS and to correct geo-reference errors within NRM-NRIS continued.

Implementation/Monitoring Audits – The IM Audits focused on recreation (OHV) management and management of springs/riparian areas on five sites located around the SMNRA.

Data Evaluation

Ecological Context – Information on the potential effects of climate change on species and their habitats within the SMNRA improved substantially during 2011. A climate change vulnerability report for the Humboldt-Toiyabe National Forest was recently published by scientists from the Rocky Mountain Research Station (Howell 2011). This report provides the basis for identifying both mitigation and adaptation strategies for the SMNRA. Analysis of FIA data was delayed because of data migration issues at the new Kansas City data center. FIA data is critical to improving our understanding of the ecological context in which CA species exist. Work is also progressing on an updated map of existing vegetation for the SMNRA using data from FIA plots and other sources. This map will be consistent with the National Vegetation Classification and will provide the basis of comparing existing conditions to historic conditions described by Provencher (2008).

Species Conservation – Genetic analysis of Palmer's chipmunk within the SMNRA provided one of the major findings for 2011. The study documents the presence of a large healthy Palmer's population within the SMNRA. Potential habitat maps for all CA Species were developed using information from the SMNRA Species Reference Database (see Appendix B). A crosswalk between FIA cover types and Land Type Associations used in the Spring Mountains General Management Plan will provide the basis for establishing baseline vegetation information for the SMNRA (see Appendix C). Springs inventory information is beginning to provide a consistent basis for understanding the variation of spring types and their characteristics across the SMNRA (see Appendix D).

Management Interactions – Implementation/Monitoring Audit findings provide important information regarding the effects of management actions and uses on CA Species habitats. Efforts to manage recreation (OHV) use are proving effective, but could be improved using a combination of public information (signing) and trail system development to encourage use in appropriate areas. An evaluation of springs/riparian management practices also concluded that many practices were effective, but required maintenance and monitoring. A framework for developing consistent management responses using a combination of recreation use levels and ecological significance was developed. Springs inventories conducted in 2011 indicate that the effect of wild horses and burros on these sites is extensive; most disturbances noted were on the Westside of the SMNRA.

Recommendations

Forest Plan – Forest Plan and SMNRA General Management Plan (Plan Amendment #4) monitoring requirements need to be updated to reflect a focus on CA Species and improved information and science. This update could be accomplished under the revised Forest Service planning regulations. The need to develop a consolidated version of the Forest Plan and the General Management Plan is also recommended.

Conservation Agreement – Because the Conservation Agreement is being revised, consistency with the revised planning regulations and incorporation of Forest Plan/General Management Plan direction by reference rather than repeating or interpreting Forest Plan/General Management Plan direction were recommended.

Management Activities and Programs – The consistent application and interpretation of Forest Plan/General Management Plan direction, information from the SMNRA Landscape Assessment, and management response frameworks developed during IM Audits were recommended. In addition, new information regarding CA Species (butterflies/host plants, and Palmer's chipmunk) needs to be addressed in ongoing and proposed projects and activities.

Monitoring Program – Evaluation of legacy data sets, new information and more detailed analysis of some monitoring questions used to design the SMNRA inventory and monitoring program identified eight of the 41 monitoring questions that could be dropped and the need to modify one question to include monitoring requirements from the General Management Plan. Improved inventory and monitoring program coordination and authorization of studies and inventories by third-parties within the SMNRA will ensure data collected are available for use, and that third-party research activities don't compromise other resource management objectives, including Wilderness and the Carpenter Canyon Research Natural Area.

Appendices

Appendices to the 2011 Annual Report represent a growing body of information and data regarding CA Species located in the SMNRA. These Appendices include:

Appendix B: Species Fact Sheets and Habitats – Potential habitat maps for all CA Species are included in this appendix along with Species Fact Sheets for Charleston ant, egg milkvetch, rough angelica and Palmer's chipmunk. The Species Fact Sheets and potential habitat maps were developed using information in the SMNRA Species Reference Database. When complete, this **appendix** will be published as a stand-alone document representing the best available science for SMNRA CA Species.

Appendix C: Forest Inventory and Analysis Reports – Includes information for specific monitoring questions that can be developed from intensified FIA data. At the conclusion of the 5-year inventory cycle, a separate report regarding the Forest Resources of the SMNRA will be published.

Appendix D: Springs – This appendix includes an analysis of all springs data collected across the SMNRA. The characteristics of springs, their ecological significance, and restoration priorities will be included in a stand-alone report developed once all known springs have been inventoried.

Appendix E: Management Response Frameworks – Information developed during the IM Audits that can be applied to similar settings within the SMNRA are presented in this appendix. These "frameworks" represent best practices based on a review of design and mitigation practices for different projects within the SMNRA.

1. Introduction

The Spring Mountains National Recreation Area (SMNRA) includes approximately 316,000 acres of National Forest System lands managed by the Humboldt-Toiyabe National Forest in Clark and Nye Counties, Nevada (see Figure 1-1). The Spring Mountains have long been recognized as an island of endemism, harboring flora and fauna found nowhere else in the world. Conservation of the species endemic to and resident in the Spring Mountains is a goal described in the Organic Act for the SMNRA (Public Law 102-63, August 4, 1993).

Management direction for the SMNRA was established in an amendment (USFS 1996) to the Toiyabe National Forest Land and Resource Management Plan (USFS 1986), which is often referred to as the "General Management Plan" (GMP).

In 1998, a Conservation Agreement (USFS 1998) was developed between the Forest Service, US Fish and Wildlife Service and State of Nevada, Department of Conservation and Natural Resources, affirming the parties' commitment to providing long-term protection for the rare and sensitive flora and fauna of the SMNRA. The Conservation Agreement is being revised and updated and is proceeding through the approval process (USFS 2011a). Since the SMNRA's establishment, efforts to conduct inventory and monitoring have contributed to a greater understanding of the species' habitats and status. However, several problems persisted in the approach to monitoring and evaluation, which led to the development of a comprehensive strategy for inventory and monitoring within the SMNRA.

The *Spring Mountains NRA Inventory and Monitoring Strategy* (I&M Strategy) (USFS 2008b) was developed to establish a comprehensive inventory and monitoring program to provide a basis for protecting and conserving resident biological resources. I&M Strategy objectives included:

- Establish a sustainable monitoring and evaluation system with respect to cost over a 10-20 year time horizon.

- Provide high quality data using statistically sound inventory and monitoring methods when possible and appropriate.

- Identify data gaps associated with priority monitoring questions and methods for acquiring needed data.

- Utilize data and information systems that support dynamic and scalable evaluation processes.

- Provide the ability to detect locally- and globally-induced changes in ecological context as well as the ability to focus on species specific information.

Species that are the focus of this monitoring and evaluation effort were identified in the SMNRA Landscape Assessment (ENTRIX, Inc. 2008) and are reflected in the updated Conservation Agreement (CA) (USFS 2011a). Species and their priorities are listed in Table 1-1.

Monitoring questions and their priorities were established by SMNRA leadership and are documented in the I&M Strategy (see Appendix A). Within this document, the order of presentation for monitoring questions is based on the established priority, not numeric order or by resource topic.

Table 1-1: Spring Mountains NRA Conservation Agreement Species List

Tier 1 Species	
Invertebrates	Acastus checkerspot (*Chlosyne acastus robusta*) Spring Mountains dark blue butterfly (*Euphilotes ancilla purpurea*) Spring Mountains dark blue butterfly (*Euphilotes ancilla cryptica*) Morand's checkerspot (*Euphydryas chalcedona morandi*) Mt. Charleston blue butterfly (*Plebejus shasta charlestonensis*) Charleston ant (*Lasius nevadensis*) Spring Mountains pyrg (*Pyrgulopsis deaconi*) Southeast Nevada pyrg (*Pyrgulopsis turbatrix*)
Vascular Plants	Clokey's milkvetch (*Astragalus aequalis*) Egg milkvetch (*Astragalus oophorus var. clokeyanus*) Spring Mountains milkvetch (*Astragalus remotus*) Trianglelobe moonwort (*Botrychium ascendens*) Scalloped moonwort (*Botrychium crenulatum*) Narrowleaf moonwort (*Botrychium lineare*) Moose moonwort (*Botrychium tunux*) Clokey's greasebush (*Glossopetalon clokeyi*)
Tier 2 Species	
Invertebrates	Spring Mountains comma skipper (*Hesperia colorado mojavensis*) Nevada admiral (*Limenitus weidemeyerii nevadae*) Spring Mountains icarioides blue butterfly (*Plebejus icarioides austinorum*) Carole's fritillary butterfly (*Speyeria carolae*) Spring mountainsnail (*Oreohelix handi*) Kyle Canyon mountainsnail (*Oreohelix jaegeri*)
Mammals	Townsend's big eared bat (*Corynorhinus townsendii*) Allen's big-eared bat (*Idionycteris phyllotis*) Palmer's chipmunk (*Neotamias palmeri*)
Reptiles	Western redtail skink (*Eumeces gilberti rubricaudatus*)
Vascular Plants	Rough angelica (*Angelica scabrida*) Charleston Mountain pussytoes (*Antennaria soliceps*) King's rosy sandwort (*Arenaria kingii spp. rosea*) Spring Mountains rockcress (*Boechera nevadensis*) Shortstyle draba (*Draba brachystylis*) Jaeger's draba (*Draba jaegeri*) Charleston Mountain draba (*Draba paucifructa*) Nevada willowherb (*Epilobium nevadense*) Clokey's buckwheat (*Eriogonum heermannii var. clokeyi*) Dwarf greasebush (*Glossopetalon pungens*) Charleston Peak mousetail (*Ivesia cryptocaulis*) Jaeger's mousetail (*Ivesia jaegeri*) Keck's beardtongue (*Penstemon leiophyllus var. keckii*) Jaeger's beardtongue (*Penstemon thompsoniae spp. jaegeri*) Clokey's catchfly (*Silene clokeyi*) Compact chickensage (*Sphaeromeria compacta*) Charleston Mountain kittentails (*Synthyris ranunculina*) Jones' townsend daisy (*Townsendia jonesii var. tumulosa*) Charleston Mountain violet (*Viola purpurea var. charlestonensis*)

Species included in this list are the focus of the Conservation Agreement and Strategy. Species were included because they,

> "...are either endemic to the Spring Mountains or have such a limited or restricted range that the viability of the species depends on the Spring Mountains population(s). For the purposes of prioritization of proactive conservation actions when resources are limited, the signing agencies grouped species into two categories, either Tier 1 or Tier 2. Tier 1 species are the highest priority for proactive conservation when resources are limited; Tier 2 species are a priority when additional resources are available. (USFS 2011a, page 4)."

The I&M Strategy identified species addressed in the CA as either Species of Concern or Species of Interest (SOC/SOI) and did not include all species listed in the 2011 revision of the Conservation Agreement. As a result, references to SOC/SOI from the I&M Strategy have been replaced with the term "CA Species" which refers to the species listed in Table 1-1. Additional species have been added to Table 1-1 based on the revised CA.

The SMNRA inventory and monitoring program was initiated in June 2010. This is the second annual report and describes the cumulative analysis and evaluation of data collected during 2010 and 2011 and builds on the analysis completed in 2010 (Solem et. al. 2011). The annual report is organized into the following sections:

- **Section 2** – Describes the initial inventory and monitoring data collection design and subsequent modifications made in 2010 and 2011, data collection completed, and modifications and program plans for 2012;

- **Section 3** – Presents analysis and evaluation of inventory and monitoring data collected during 2010 and 2011 with respect to the conservation of biological diversity for selected species within the SMNRA by assessing information regarding ecological context, species conservation, and management interactions; and

- **Section 4** – Provides recommendations for changes in the Forest Plan, Conservation Agreement and Strategy, management activities or programs, and the inventory and monitoring program.

Detailed data summaries and analyses are included in the Appendices. At the conclusion of the first five-year inventory and monitoring cycle, these appendices will be published as stand-alone documents, therefore each appendix has a separate listing of literature cited.

2. Data Collection Methods, Accomplishments and Plans

Inventory and monitoring systems established in the I&M Strategy consist of multiple systematic sampling methods, species-specific surveys, genetic analysis, and structured observations. The inventory and monitoring component designs and relationships are summarized in Table 2-1.

Table 2-1: Inventory and Monitoring Program Design Summary

Program Component	Inventory and Monitoring Design
Intensified Forest Inventory and Analysis (FIA) Program	In keeping with initial objectives to provide long-term, cost-effective monitoring, inventory will focus on plant communities using an intensified FIA grid rather than attempt prohibitively expensive individual species sampling for all plant CA Species. The base FIA program will be: (1) Extended to include sampling vegetation in non-forested areas, (2) Intensified to focus on specific ecological settings by increasing the plot ratio to 7 times the base grid, and (3) Reduced from 10 years to 5 years between re-measurement to accelerate collection of data useful for monitoring trends and conditions affecting ecological context. Information on known butterfly host and nectar plants, invasive species, and CA Species lists will be incorporated into data collection procedures.
Springs/Riparian Inventory	Springs and associated riparian areas provide important habitats for a number of CA Species, in addition to other species unique to spring/riparian settings. Inventory and monitoring of springs and riparian areas will focus on these sites because of the high density of CA Species, sensitivity of these areas to disturbance by multiple sampling/inventory crews, and the cost of multiple site visits. Inventory of all known springs using a common inventory protocol over a five-year cycle will provide a baseline for all springs and allow for comparison of information between springs. Data collected will allow design of more intensive surveys of a sub-set of the springs within the SMNRA.
Genetic Analysis and Monitoring	The primary use for genetic analysis is to address questions of population health and structure. Taxonomic questions can be addressed on an opportunistic basis, taking advantage of the GenBank database, once that database has been sufficiently populated with congener species to allow clarification of taxa below the species level (sub-species and varieties). Collection of genetic material will be accomplished in conjunction with other monitoring methodologies.
Species-Specific Surveys and Monitoring	In those instances where ongoing inventory and monitoring of individual species is underway, those efforts will continue. Over time a "bridge" between individual species methods and integrated monitoring via FIA and the Riparian/Springs protocol could result in the cessation of monitoring for some individual species. As data from FIA and the integrated springs/riparian monitoring become available, potential habitats for these and other species can be identified and species-specific surveys conducted with greater efficiency.
Implementation and Monitoring (IM) Audits	IM Audits review consistency of implementation with NEPA documentation and contracts or implementation instructions and the effectiveness of design and mitigation measures. Priorities for activities or projects to be audited are based on the ability of management to influence the outcome, risk, and uncertainty associated with project or activity effects on CA Species. IM Audits are focused on the identification of adjustments that can be made for the audited project/activity and when possible applied as improvements in future project design or mitigation measures.

The following subsections include the following discussions regarding each of the inventory and monitoring program components: (1) a summary of the initial design, (2) modifications made and 2010 and 2011 accomplishments and (3) modifications and data collection planned in 2012, including coordination items discussed with SMNRA staff and leadership.

a. Intensified Forest Inventory and Analysis

The Forest Inventory and Analysis (FIA) program serves as the nation's census of forested lands. It uses a grid from which to select sample locations and a system of sampling panels to sample across years. Plots are composed of sub-plots designed to collect information for numerous data elements. The system employs an annual sampling scheme to provide annual updates useful for monitoring trends. Extension of the base grid into non-forested areas and increasing the number of samples would be required to provide appropriate data accuracy for the SMNRA.

Ancillary and regionally specific monitoring protocols have been developed for use in conjunction with standard FIA protocols to focus on both individual and groups of species. The grid-based system is valuable for detecting changes in ecological context, either globally or locally induced, and for developing inferences on both ecological sustainability and species' habitat relationships. An important feature of this system is the resulting high data quality and statistical reliability.

The intensification of the base FIA program is a principle component of the overall inventory and monitoring program for the Spring Mountains National Recreation Area. FIA provides the rigor and recurrent sampling framework necessary to develop information needed to effect adaptive management-based changes thereby promoting species conservation. This is the primary reason for selecting FIA as the foundation for subsequent evaluation and analysis.

Initial Design

The FIA intensification for the SMNRA is designed to address the need for data necessary to monitor trends within an ecological context as well as data useful for developing habitat relationships and improving information on CA Species occurrence. The Design Tool for Inventory and Monitoring (DTIM) was used to match information needs associated with individual monitoring questions to FIA data collection protocols and analysis reports. Using existing estimates of sampling errors, DTIM estimates the number of sample plots needed to provide acceptable results.[1]

Since the initial design of the program, modifications have been made to accommodate crew safety and to coordinate program implementation with changes in the national FIA Field Guide. These modifications are described and documented chronologically.

The intensified FIA program for the SMNRA includes the following principal modifications to the base Interior West FIA protocols:

1) **Increased sampling intensity** - To achieve acceptable statistical accuracy, the plot density within the SMNRA will be increased on all lands by a factor of 7 times the standard FIA sampling grid density. This means approximately 350 additional plots would be located across the SMNRA using FIA protocols, resulting in roughly 7 plots for every 6000 acres.

2) **Procedures applicable to SMNRA needs** - Sampling procedures and species lists for this survey are specifically designed to gather information on species identified as CA Species. All plots would be

---

[1] An electronic copy of preliminary data entered into DTIM was provided to the SMNRA as a separate document.

sampled according to Interior West-FIA (IW-FIA) standard protocols. These include national FIA "core" protocols, and standard IW-FIA regional components that also measure downed woody material, understory plant cover, and presence of invasive species.

3) **Extension into non-forested lands** - FIA normally samples vegetation only on forested plots. On the SMNRA all plots will be sampled for vegetation and downed woody material, regardless of land use/land cover.

4) **Shorter re-measurement cycle** - Shortening the timeframe for re-measurement from the standard 10 years to 5 years compresses the rate of collecting baseline information providing a basis for monitoring the ecological context for individual species evaluations and broad ecological trends.

5) **Collection of genetic material for analysis** – At the time the I&M program was designed it was thought that all plant species listed in Table 1-1 were appropriate for genetic monitoring and would be found in conjunction with implementation of the intensified FIA program. These assumptions were not correct and modifications to the program have been made as described below.

2010 Modifications and Accomplishments

Field data collection was deferred in 2010 to accommodate changes during late 2010 to the *National FIA Field Manual* (USFS 2010) regarding protocols for understory species and invasive species.

Analysis of FIA data collected in 1997 on the base grid (51 forested plots) was used to construct data tables to address monitoring questions originating from Forest Plan standards or monitoring items. This effort identified a number of analytical issues regarding different definitions of size class breaks, criteria for defining "old growth," and an inconsistency between the vegetation cover classifications used in the Forest Plan and those used by the IW-FIA program. More information is available in the *2010 Annual Report on Monitoring and Evaluation for Conserving Biological Resources of the Spring Mountains National Recreation Area* (Solem et. al. 2011).

2011 Modifications and Accomplishments

There were 126 plots scheduled for completion during the 2011 field season. These included the plots in the 2010 and 2011 inventory panels. During the threatened government shutdown and subsequent Agency-wide restrictions on travel budgets in late spring, several weeks of fieldwork were lost. As a result, low-elevation plots could not be visited during the projected flowering window for CA Species. Sampling of these low elevation plots will occur in the 2012 field season. In addition, some plots were inaccessible due to hazardous conditions associated with law enforcement activities. Completion of these plots is currently scheduled to occur during the 2012 field season.

In all, 91 plots were completed. Several CA Species were identified on some of the plots, as well as numerous butterfly host/nectar plants. Genetic material was not collected during the 2011 inventory program given the need to complete the equivalent of two year's worth of plots during the field season.

In November 2011, a post-season de-briefing with SMNRA and I&M program personnel identified coordination improvements, which have been addressed and incorporated into 2012 program plans.

2012 Program Plans

The 2012 inventory panel has 63 plots. In addition to these, crews will attempt to finish the 35 non-sampled plots from the 2011 field season, for a total of 98 plots. Inventories will be scheduled to visit plots at the time of year when the CA Species are most likely to be flowering.

2012 Program Coordination Items and Modifications

Discussion with SMNRA staff identified the following coordination items and modifications to the 2012 program:

CA Species Occurrence Information - In reviewing CA Species occurrence data on FIA plots it was noted few observations are actually being recorded on plots. In 2011, notes from the field crews identified CA Species occurrences off the plots and provided notes of these observations and locations. FIA crews will be asked to record CA Species observations during transit to and between inventory plots during the 2012 field season. These observations and locations will be provided to the SMNRA at the conclusion of the field season.

Collection of Genetic Material – The collection of CA Species genetic material during the FIA plot inventory was dropped from last year's program because of the need to complete two panels of inventory within a single year. Based upon low frequency of CA Species occurrence and the lack of existing genetic "discovery" work for plants, no genetic material will be collected during 2012 FIA inventory.

Crew Access in Recreation Sites – Recreation site construction will be occurring in the Kyle and Lee Canyon areas this summer. Access to and through these areas and developed sites will need to be coordinated with SMNRA staff.

Willow Creek Road – A private landowner has threatened to close the Willow Creek Road and there may be access problems or law enforcement issues that could limit crew access. FIA crews should coordinate with SMNRA staff when planning to access plots via this route.

Training – Several of the SMNRA staff were interested in monitoring the FIA crew training to become familiar with the data collection procedures and approach if the training were to occur in the Las Vegas area. Participation by SMNRA staff is welcome and scheduled dates and training locations will be provided to the SMNRA. SMNRA staff are also welcome to accompany a crew to an actual field plot, especially early in the season when it is likely to be FIA crews conducting the work instead of contractors.

Dispatch Notification – The upcoming season is shaping up to be dryer than normal and additional emphasis should be placed on monitoring fire conditions, weather, and checking in with dispatch so crew locations are known.

Inventory and Analysis Data

Data collected in 2010 and 2011 are being loaded into the National FIA Database and will also reside in the NRM-NRIS FSVeg application for use by SMNRA staff.

Analysis of inventory data relative to monitoring questions identified in the I&M Strategy is located in Appendix C.

Figure 2-1: Intensified FIA Inventory Plots to be Inventoried in 2011 and Planned in 2012

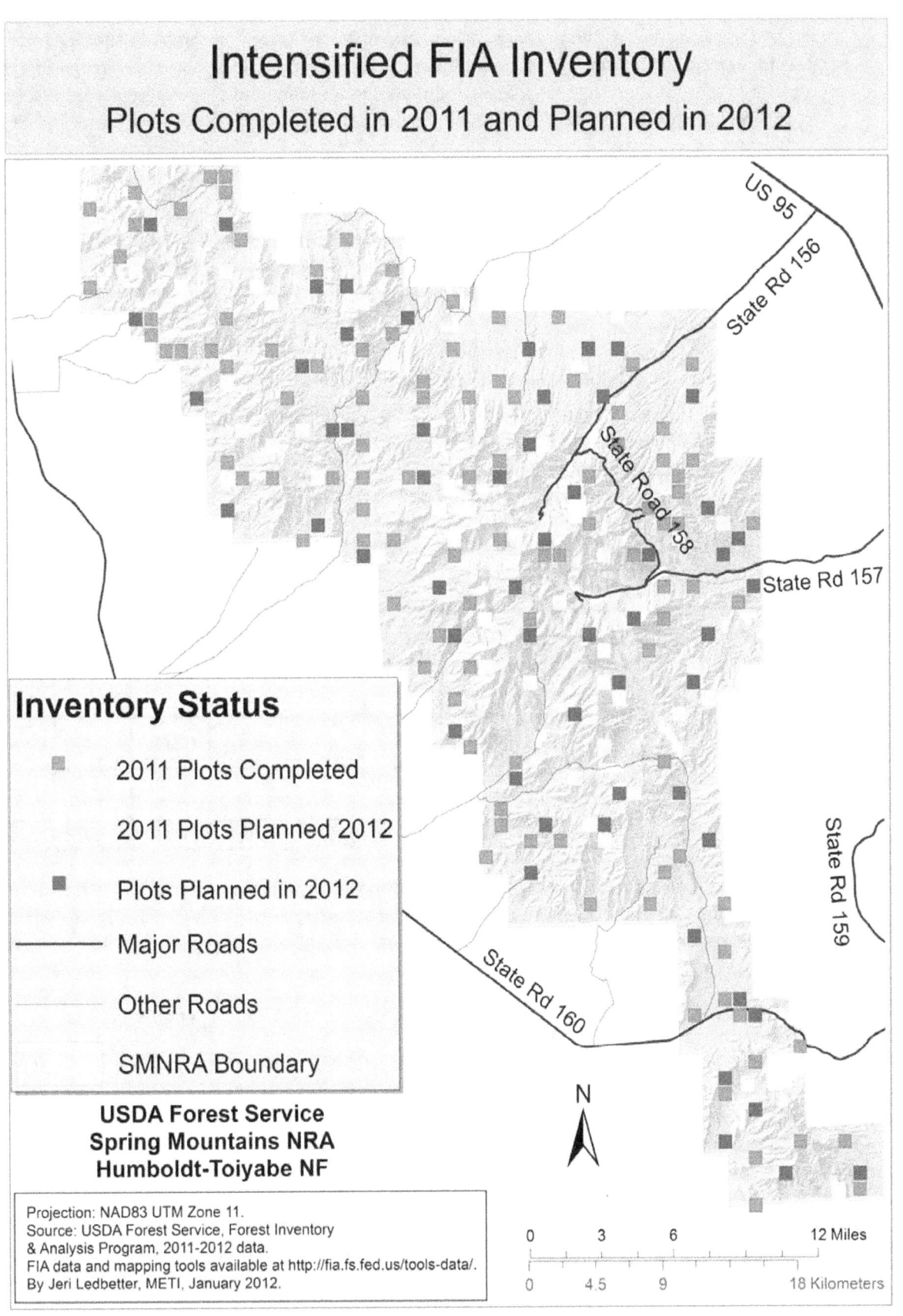

b. Springs and Riparian Area Inventories

Springs and riparian areas within the Spring Mountains National Recreation Area (SMNRA) provide habitats for and sustain a disproportionate number of species compared to uplands. Recognizing the importance of these sites to the sustainability of many species identified as CA Species, the SMNRA Inventory and Monitoring Strategy (USFS 2008b) focused additional attention on these areas.

Initial Design

The SMNRA landscape analysis (ENTRIX, Inc. 2008) identified 149 known springs and associated riparian areas within the NRA. Since the initial design of the program, modifications have been made to accommodate crew safety and to minimize travel and access costs by sampling "clusters" of springs. These modifications are described and documented chronologically.

1) **Sampling Program** - A 5-year sampling program is paired to the FIA re-measurement cycle to assist in the collection and compilation of SMNRA-wide baseline data as soon as possible.

   The sampling program for the SMNRA used a "list frame with a random start" to develop a systematic (stratified random) sampling schedule. The primary factor considered during the development of the sampling schedule was a balanced geographic representation across the four 4th code hydrologic units (or HUC) within the SMNRA.

Table 2-2: Initial Sampling Schedule – Number of Sites by 4th Code Hydrologic Unit (HUC)

Region	HUC-4 Name	HUC-4	CY10	CY11	CY12	CY13	CY14	Total
Lower Colorado	Las Vegas Wash	15010015	11	11	12	11	11	56
Great Basin	Sand Spring – Tikaboo Valleys	16060014	4	3	3	4	3	17
	Ivanpah-Pahrump Valleys	16060015	14	14	14	14	14	14
California	Upper Amargosa	18090202	2	1	1	1	1	6
		Total	31	29	30	30	29	149

2) **Protocols and procedures for the SMNRA** - Inventory will be accomplished using the national *Forest Service Groundwater Dependent Ecosystems Level II Inventory Field Guide* (USFS, 2011b) with additional data elements for the SMNRA. Additional data collection focuses on CA Species and known host and nectar plants for butterflies.

3) **Quality Assurance/Quality Control (QA/QC)** - Key aspects of QA/QC procedures include:

   a. Training in the use of the protocol would be provided to all crew members and supervisors.
   b. Data would be collected using field forms and transferred to a Microsoft (MS) Access database for eventual migration to the FS NRIS database. Spot checks of data entry on the field forms and data transfer to the MS Access database would be performed and noted as part of the QA/QC process.
   c. To evaluate observer variability and accuracy in applying the protocol, a minimum of two sites would be re-sampled. The evaluation of observer variability will indicate the level of accuracy associated with data collection and may identify needs for modifying the national protocol components or instructions.

4) **Species identification** - Collection of specimens for identification followed accepted procedures for collection. SMRNA and RMRS staff will conduct species identification.

5) **Collection of genetic material** - This effort was designed to support the genetics analysis program. Collection of genetic material for analysis will include springsnails and plant species listed in Table 1-1 associated with springs and riparian environments was planned.

2010 Modifications and Accomplishments

A Cost Reimbursable Agreement (9/2/10) between Northern Arizona University (NAU) and the SMNRA of the Humboldt-Toiyabe National Forest was established in September of 2010. This not only utilized the expertise of NAU staff and students in conducting spring and riparian inventories, but also provided teaching opportunities for NAU staff involved in the SMNRA inventory effort.

Training for NAU and SMNRA staff was conducted from September 7-9, 2010 and included an office review of methods and procedures for the *Groundwater Dependent Ecosystems (GDE) Level II Field Guide*. Field training for NAU and SMNRA staff was provided by the national team developing the GDE inventory field guides and included a site visit to Mack's Spring. Training included methods for collection of genetic material and collection of samples for identification.

The NAU survey team conducted spring inventories were during September 11 to 13 and October 20 to 30, 2010 using the Forest Service Groundwater Dependent Ecosystems Level II Inventory Field Guide. Of the 31 springs scheduled for inventory during 2010, 16 were not inventoried because they were not a spring or they were on private land. For safety reasons, the team did not inventory Rose's Spring as planned for 2010, and that site was moved to the 2011 schedule. Of the scheduled springs, 14 were inventoried and assessed, as well as 2 new springs found by the NAU team, and 3 springs from a future year (2013) -- because the survey team was near those somewhat difficult-to-reach sites it made sense to inventory them. Therefore the total number of springs inventoried in 2010 was 19 (see map in Figure 2-2 and list in Appendix D-1).

On-site quality control and quality assurance during site visits was provided by Marc Coles-Ritchie (METI, Inc). Spot checks of data entry and GDE database entry was accomplished by Jeri Ledbetter (NAU survey team leader).

The NAU survey team provided recommendations regarding crew safety and operations to SMNRA staff at the conclusion of the 2010 season. These recommendations were approved and used to develop the 2011 field program.

2011 Modifications and Accomplishments

Recommendations, such as for safety and travel efficiency, identified by the NAU survey crew in 2010 were incorporated into the 2011 field work plans. Based upon the NAU team's recommendations, the inventory sample schedule was adjusted to allow for crew safety determinations, inclusion of new springs, and sampling of spring "clusters" in situations where access is difficult and time consuming. This recommendation was approved by the SMNRA and NAU was directed to prepare a survey plan for future years that used the "cluster" approach while maintaining a balance of sampling across the four hydrologic units used in the original sampling design.

Spring inventories were conducted by the NAU inventory team from July 23 to August 8 and September 6 to 14, 2011. The survey team visited a total of 32 sites during these two field efforts and used the national *Groundwater Dependent Ecosystems Level II Inventory Field Guide* to inventory 28 of those sites. One site that could not be sampled due to hazardous weather in 2010 was sampled in 2011. Of the springs visited, 6 were dry, likely due to seasonal variability in flow. Two sites were determined to be secondary emergences from sites upstream and therefore were not inventoried. Six previously unmapped and unnamed springs were identified and inventoried.

The crew was unable to reach several springs on the 2011 inventory schedule: two at the top of a steep cliff; two with private ownership that the crew was not permitted to visit; two that the SMNRA requested not to be surveyed due to law enforcement security concerns; and four that the crew could not reach because of the very poor quality of roads. In place of these, the crew surveyed springs that were scheduled for future years, or that they discovered during 2010 and 2011 surveys.

2012 Program Plans

The NAU inventory team will conduct inventories of 30 sites during 2012. The field schedule will be designed to conduct sampling at the time of year when the species of concern and interest are most likely to be flowering. The NAU team has scheduled inventories to occur during the following time periods:

May 21 – June 3: Low elevation sites
June 23 – July 3: High elevation sites
September: Remaining sites if needed

Program Coordination Items and Modifications

Discussions between NAU inventory teams and SMNRA staff identified the following coordination items and modifications to the 2012 program:

Supplemental Springsnail Collection for Genetics Analysis – During all subsequent surveys springsnails should be collected for genetic analysis. Supplemental springsnail collection will need to occur at springs known to have springsnail populations that are not being inventoried in 2012.

Noxious vs. Invasive Species List – Definitions and lists of what constitutes an invasive or noxious species should be provided to NAU crews so the species can be noted in the spring inventories.

CA Species Observations – Observations of CA Species or butterfly nectar and host plants made by the NAU survey crew should be noted and provided to the SMNRA using procedures similar to those discussed during the FIA presentation.

Riparian Surveys - Opportunities to conduct surveys in the riparian areas associated with the 4 perennial streams within the SMNRA will be identified and, if possible, they will be completed using the draft national *Riparian Vegetation Monitoring Technical Guide*, which will establish a link to the spring inventory data because the same protocols are used.

QA/QC and Resampling – Marc Coles-Ritchie (METI, Inc.) and Abe Springer (NAU) are providing QA/QC during the course of each inventory year. One item that has not been accomplished as part of QA/QC, is resampling of a spring site previously sampled to provide an estimate of sampling error. Opportunities to accomplish this during 2012 will be identified and discussed with the NAU survey crew.

Inventory and Analysis Data

Each year a detailed report of work accomplished has been prepared by the NAU inventory team and provided to the SMNRA under the terms of the Cooperative Agreement. In addition, a report for each site surveyed has been provided to the SMNRA (see Appendix D-2.2 for an example) and inventory data have been entered into the national GDE database. Appendix D-2 lists the attributes included in the site report and an example of a report that can be generated from the national GDE database.

Appendix D-4 provides an analysis of data collected relative to those monitoring questions involving springs.

Figure 2-2: Springs Inventories Completed in 2011 and Planned in 2012.

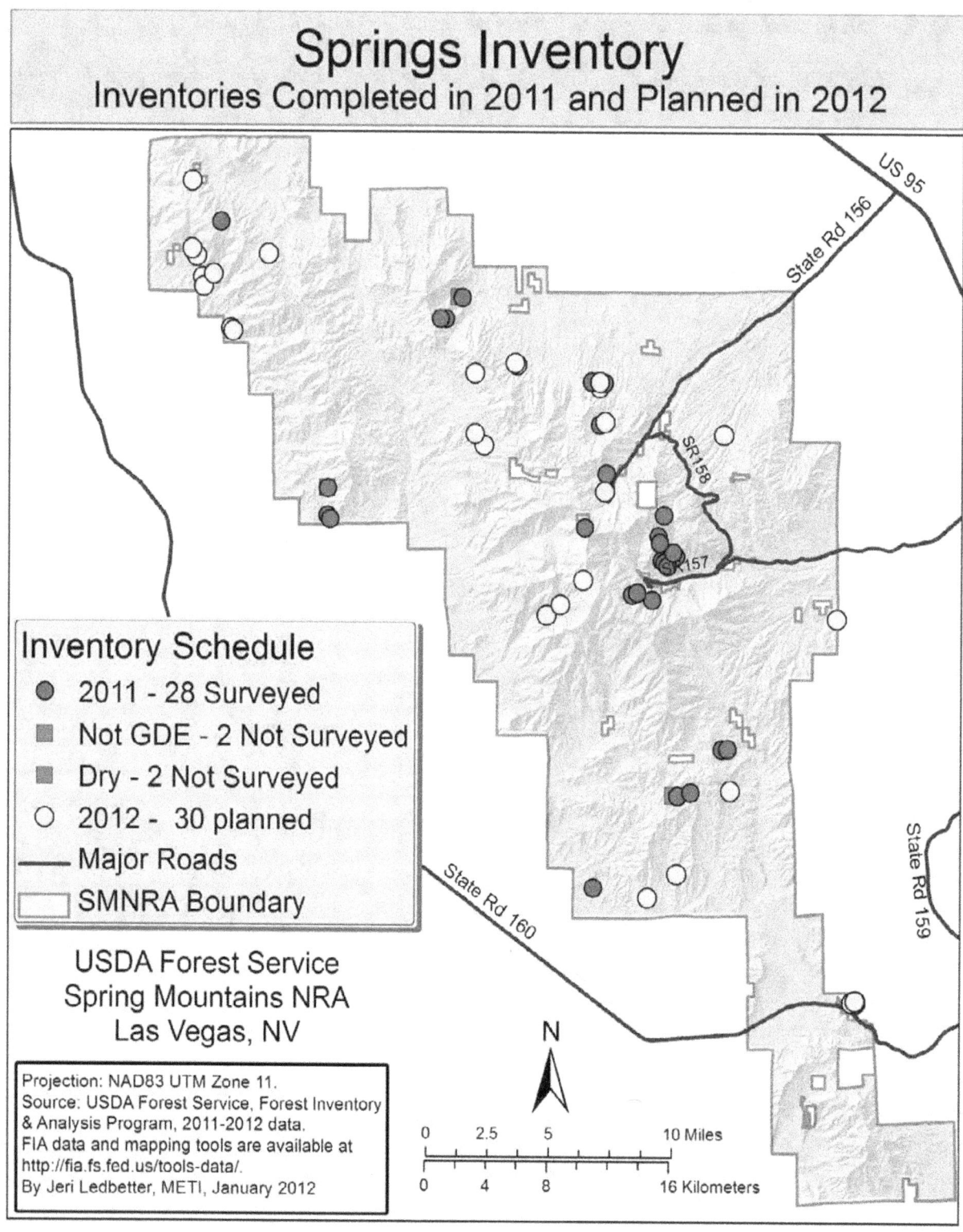

c. Genetic Monitoring and Analysis

Genetic monitoring uses individual genetic differences to infer population attributes such as size, structure, migration, and population of origin (for immigrants). These metrics are related to studies of phylogeny, which uses genetic differences to determine relationships between species. For phylogeny, one is looking for genetic differences that are fixed within a species but differ between species. For genetic population monitoring, one is looking for genetic differences that occur among individuals.

Genetic monitoring requires completion of three analysis stages. For species that have been previously genetically monitored, the first stage is "discovery," in which interesting areas of DNA are located and analyzed, and inexpensive assays developed to identify differences using samples of the species being investigated. The second stage involves collecting samples from the target population's range. During the third stage genetic assays developed during discovery are applied to collected materials and population metrics are derived. The advantages of genetic monitoring over direct population monitoring lie in the greatly reduced sampling required, as well as in the ability to evaluate important population attributes that are generally not accessible through other methods. Coarse-scale genetic analyses such as analyses to identify species (e. g. to separate morphologically cryptic species) or sub-species can generally be performed using areas of mitochondrial DNA that are common to most organisms. For species that have not been previously genetically monitored, however, population level analyses will generally require some level of discovery prior to analysis. However, this process does not need to delay sample collection; samples, once stabilized, can endure years of storage. Monitoring for change can be done after the fact, a property unique to DNA monitoring.

<u>Initial Design</u>

Priorities for genetic analysis and assumptions made during development of the I&M Strategy resulted in the initial program design described in the following section. Since development the basis for many of the assumptions have changed and modifications have occurred in both priorities for genetic analysis and in plans for the collection of genetic material. Changes in program priorities and rational are documented chronologically.

1) **Genetic analysis priorities** – Species prioritized for genetic monitoring and analysis include CA Species for which genetic analysis will be most beneficial, as depicted in Table 2-3.

Table 2-3: Genetic Analysis and Monitoring Species Priorities

Genetics Priority Group 1	Palmer's chipmunk (*Neotamias palmeri*) Acastus checkerspot (*Chlosyne acastus robusta*) Spring Mountains dark blue butterfly (*Euphilotes ancilla purpurea*) Morand's checkerspot (*Euphydryas chalcedona morandi*) Mt. Charleston blue butterfly (*Plebejus shasta charlestonensis*)
Genetics Priority Group 2	Spring Mountains pyrg (*Pyrgulopsis deaconi*) Southeast Nevada pyrg (*Pyrgulopsis turbatrix*) Clokey's milkvetch (*Astragalus aequalis*) Egg milkvetch (*Astragalus oophorus var. clokeyanus*) Spring Mountains milkvetch (*Astragalus remotus*) Trianglelobe moonwort (*Botrychium ascendens*) Scalloped moonwort (*Botrychium crenulatum*) Narrowleaf moonwort (*Botrychium lineare*) Moose moonwort (*Botrychium tunux*) Jones' Townsend daisy (*Townsendia jonesii var. tumulosa*)

Of the species identified for genetic monitoring, the only one for which genetic studies exist on a similar population is the chipmunk. Thus, for Palmer's chipmunk, the discovery phase was less intensive than for the rest of the species listed; for those species, discovery will need to begin with virtually no prior knowledge.

2) **Collection of genetic material** - Obtaining genetic samples if the organism is "in hand" is almost always fast and easy, and samples can be stored compactly. Materials to stabilize sample DNA are generally very inexpensive; animal and plant tissues can be dried by placing them in air-tight dessicant-filled vials. If genetic samples can be obtained opportunistically while doing other surveys, the costs of sample acquisition are generally trivial.

3) **Sample distribution** - Genetic surveys should be spatially distributed, but otherwise many of the representative sampling rules do not apply. For each location where the organism is found, there is virtually never a reason to collect more than 30 samples. These 2 attributes, ability to preferentially sample and the need to collect relatively few samples at each location, greatly enhance the ability to obtain adequate samples for monitoring when the organisms are rare or very clumped in distribution. For this same reason, samples obtained through other non-standard mechanisms are generally useful.

4) **Sample collection and management** – Genetic samples are stored in envelopes, labeled with the location, date, and species name, and stored in desiccant for future analysis. Collection locations should be identified on the envelope and each sample should be identified by a four letter species abbreviation (Genus/species), the date of collection, and the collector's initials.

5) **Analysis and reporting** -Analysis and reporting of results is facilitated by an agreement with the RMRS Wildlife and Terrestrial Habitat and Grassland, Shrubland, and Desert research programs. Genetics analysis results will be posted in GenBank. Summary reports as well as published research will be prepared.

2010 - 2011 Accomplishments

The first year of implementation included providing an overview of data collection procedures for crews involved in the inventory and monitoring program. Genetic sampling and analysis were conducted in association with spring inventories and a trapping program was completed for Palmer's chipmunk.

Springsnails were observed at five springs and genetic material was collected at four of those sites. Plant genetic material associated with spring inventories was collected at three sites for three plant species. Samples were archived and stored at the SMNRA office and have been provided to the RMRS Wildlife Genetics Lab for analysis.

Palmer's Chipmunk - The goals of this study were to 1) verify the range of Palmer's chipmunk, 2) determine whether it co-occurs with the Panamint chipmunk, and if so where, 3) determine the population structure of Palmer's chipmunk across the Spring Mountains, specifically looking for the presence of isolated sub-populations, and 4) look for signs of potential hybridization between the two species.

The sampling was broken into two phases. In the first season (2010), the goals were 1) to develop an effective approach to trapping Palmer's chipmunks, 2) develop genetic markers that allow analysis of population structure in Palmer's, and 3) develop nuclear DNA markers that discriminate Palmer's from Panamint chipmunks. Using DNA markers to distinguish the two species of chipmunk would allow reliable species identification without the need for extra genetic tests. In the second season (2011) the goals were to sample across the extent of the Spring Mountains to determine the range and population structure of Palmer's chipmunks. With this broader sample the SMNRA could evaluate the degree to which the two species overlap and look for signs of hybridization.

The results of the genetic analysis for Palmer's chipmunk have been summarized in a separate report (McKelvey et.al. 2012), which will be published in a regional journal in the near future. Key findings from the report include:

- Palmer's chipmunks appear to be limited to higher elevation areas in the central portion of the Spring Mountains. In this sample, no Palmer's were found at elevations below 7500 feet or 2300 m, and for those three sites where both Panamint and Palmer's chipmunks were collected, the differentiation between Palmer's and Panamint appears to be elevational, closely approximating 2300 m.

- It appears the Panamint chipmunks are not limited to the piñyon-juniper forests, but extend into the lower elevation ponderosa pine forests as well. The two chipmunk species, however, do not appear in the same areas: where samples were mixed, Panamint chipmunks were caught at the lower grids exclusively, Palmer's chipmunks at the upper ones. This may suggest that elevation, rather than habitat, better defines the limits between these species.

- Within the high elevation area where Palmer's chipmunks exist (>2300 m; 7500 ft), populations of Palmer's chipmunk appear to be relatively well mixed, with low levels of spatial structuring. None of the populations appears to be isolated.

- Given the presumed long isolation of Palmer's from other closely related species, the well mixed nature of the population, and the lack of any signs of recent bottlenecks, it is reasonable to assume that the population is relatively close to the drift-mutation equilibrium.

Figure 2-3: Palmer's Chipmunk Genetic Sampling Locations

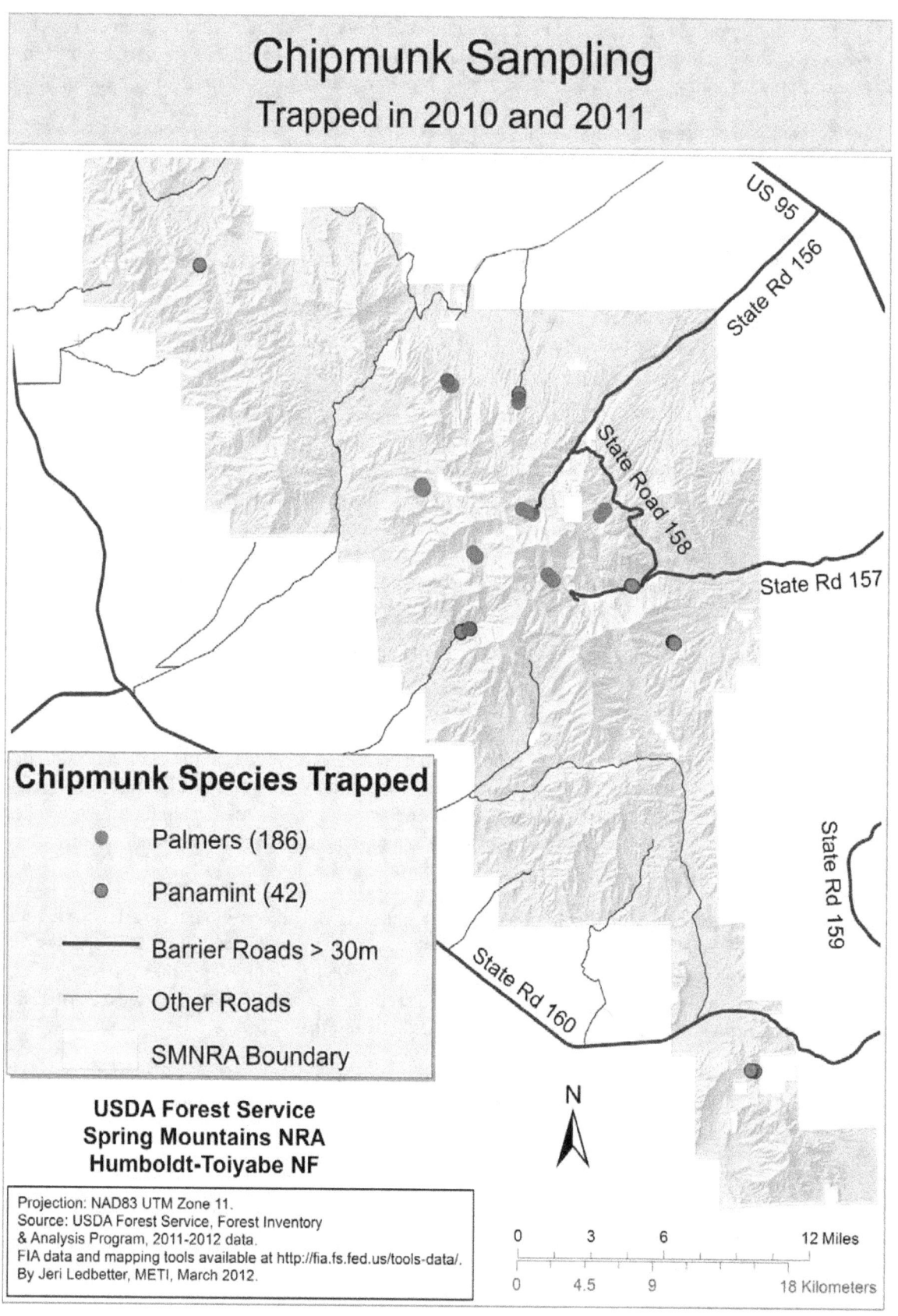

Chipmunk Sampling
Trapped in 2010 and 2011

US 95

State Rd 156

State Road 158

State Rd 157

State Rd 159

State Rd 160

Chipmunk Species Trapped

- Palmers (186)
- Panamint (42)
- Barrier Roads > 30m
- Other Roads
- SMNRA Boundary

**USDA Forest Service
Spring Mountains NRA
Humboldt-Toiyabe NF**

Projection: NAD83 UTM Zone 11.
Source: USDA Forest Service, Forest Inventory
& Analysis Program, 2011-2012 data.
FIA data and mapping tools available at http://fia.fs.fed.us/tools-data/.
By Jeri Ledbetter, METI, March 2012.

N

| 0 | 3 | 6 | 12 Miles |

| 0 | 4.5 | 9 | 18 Kilometers |

2011 Program Modifications

The rationale for species selected for genetic analysis in the different priority groups listed in Table 2-3 were not well documented. The following summarizes the rationale associated with these priority groups:

Genetics Priority Group 1

Palmer's chipmunk was selected early on in the I&M Strategy because out of all CA Species it was the only one with sufficient genetic discovery information to proceed with little or no cost.

Butterflies were the next group in Priority 1 based on their overall status and the work that was being set up with UNLV at the time the I&M Strategy was being developed. The UNLV study provides opportunities for collection of genetic material and recently has confirmed the need to verify the existence of subspecies of the Spring Mountains dark blue butterfly.

Genetics Priority Group 2

Springsnails (Spring Mountains pyrg (*Pyrgulopsis deaconi*) and Southeast Nevada pyrg (*Pyrgulopsis turbatrix)),* because of the collection being done by NAU and their status were determined to be the next priority. Collection of enough genetic samples during the 2010 and 2011 surveys was expected to serve as the foundation for genetics analysis of springsnails in 2012.

Milkvetches were included in this group using similar rationale. Efforts by FIA crews and crews conducting species-specific and project surveys were seen as the mechanism for collecting genetic material. As it is turning out, concerns regarding FIA's ability to collect enough genetic samples are playing out (see Solem, et.al. 2011. page 16, item 2). As a result, this places a greater emphasis on the collection of genetic material using a variety of collection opportunities for these species as opposed to a specific collection program.

Moonworts, like the springsnails, were included because of they would likely be collected during the NAU springs surveys. NAU has collected few samples, but given the 2012 -2013 survey programs, can be requested to survey and collect genetic samples at all sites in addition to the standard inventory procedures.

Jones' Townsend Daisy was added to this priority group based upon the limited information regarding this species and the potential to determine its status using genetic analysis.

The resulting genetic analysis program priorities developed in 2011 included:

2010-2011 - Expanded spatial sample for Palmer's chipmunk and complete the genetic analysis.

2012-2013 - Initiate work on the springsnails and coordinate with UNLV on collection of genetic materials for butterflies to support subspecies differentiation and comparison to species outside the SMNRA. In 2012 collect additional genetic samples of butterflies and springssnails to ensure adequate spatial representation. Complete genetics analysis in 2013.

2013-2014 - Initiate work on the moonworts and milkvetches. Collect additional genetic samples to ensure spatial representation and complete analysis in 2014.

2012 Program Modifications and Program Plans

Discussion with SMNRA staff identified the following coordination items and modifications to the 2012 program plans and the focus of future years:

2012-2013 Program Focus - Since the priorities developed in 2011 were established, additional sources have been reviewed regarding the availability of baseline genetic "discovery" information for plant species. Also, a petition to list two sub-species of the Spring Mountains dark blue butterfly (*Euphilotes ancilla*) under the provisions of the Endangered Species Act has been filed with the FWS. Springsnails resident within the SMNRA have also been petitioned for listing.

As a result SMNRA leadership determined that during these years the scope of the genetics analysis program should be focused on those species petitioned for listing in order to provide a foundation for developing appropriate species conservation measures.

Spring Mountains Dark Blue Butterfly - Discussions with principal investigators for the University of Nevada – Las Vegas (UNLV) autecology study, Fish and Wildlife Service, RMRS scientists, and SMNRA staff identified the need to not only conduct genetic analysis to determine the ability to identify sub-species of the Spring Mountains dark blue butterfly (*Euphilotes ancilla*) but should also address whether their primary host plant *Eriogonum umbellatum* could be investigated.

A detailed study plan for this investigation is being prepared by UNLV and RMRS staff and will be reviewed by the FWS and approved by SMNRA staff prior to implementation. In summary, the approach, which is described in greater detail in the study plan, includes two efforts:

- In conjunction with an autecology study being conducted by UNLV, samples will be collected during 2012 across the known habitat range of the Spring Mountains Dark Blue Butterfly (*Euphilotes ancilla*) to provide the basis for determining species differentiation and genetic divergence of *E. a. purpurea* from *E. a. cryptica*. Two sub-species are believed to occur based on distinctly different emergence and egg-laying time periods.

- There is significant variation among varieties of the primary butterfly host plant, *Eriogonum umbellatum*. Six varieties have been collected in or near southern Nevada, but only three, var. *juniporinum*, var. *subaridum*, and var. *versicolor* have been documented in the Spring Mountains. Seeds from these varieties and any other varieties encountered will be collected and cultivated in common gardens at Washington State University in Pullman, Washington, and the Plant Materials Center maintained by the USDA Agricultural Research Service in Los Lunas, New Mexico, to document phenological and morphological differences between the varieties. The working hypothesis is that the butterfly subspecies lifecycles correspond to early and late flowering varieties of *E. umbellatum*. Genetic analysis can then be conducted using samples from common garden plants once genetic discovery has been completed and a decision to proceed with this genetic analysis has been made.

Springsnails - Samples are being collected as a component of the springs inventory program using a stratified random sampling design. Samples collected in 2010 and 2011 have been collected from four of the five sites where springsnails were observed and have been provided to the RMRS Wildlife Genetics Lab for analysis. Surveys conducted in 2012 could provide additional samples for analysis. Supplemental collection may need to be scheduled from known populations that have not been surveyed by NAU.

Genetic analysis will focus on the ability to apply genetic discovery information for mollusks to these species. Once the ability to use these markers has been verified, occurrence information will be used to identify sites where supplemental springsnail collection should occur during the 2013 field season.

2013-2014 Program Priorities - The lack of genetics "discovery" for plant species warrants changes to the genetics program priorities. Current and anticipated program funding cannot support the cost of conducting this phase of analysis. As an alternative, the use of common gardens as an approach for studying the phenology of these species and to support future genetic analysis should be considered after experience with this approach for *Eriogonum* is evaluated.

Another option for these program years is to focus on (1) additional butterfly species using the experience from 2012 as a foundation and (2) recommended follow-up sampling and analysis for Palmer's chipmunk. The focus of the 2013-2014 program will be re-visited during next year's program coordination meeting.

Inventory and Analysis Data

Genetics analysis results will be posted to GenBank and published in regional or local journals as separate reports.

d. Species-Specific Surveys

Species-specific surveys[2] and surveys conducted in association with project or activity analysis provide valuable information for understanding part of an individual species' life history and occurrence within the SMNRA. Additional information is needed to build a comprehensive understanding of species life history and the ecological context in which the species exists.

Initial Design

In addition to surveys conducted in association with projects and monitoring programs, five individual species monitoring efforts were underway within the SMNRA a decade prior to or were being initiated at the time the I&M Strategy was developed. They include:

- Monitoring the stability of three alpine plant species communities known to provide habitats for several CA Species, in partnership with The Nature Conservancy.
- Monitoring for egg milkvetch, in partnership with The Nature Conservancy.
- Monitoring for rough angelica, in partnership with The Nature Conservancy.
- Monitoring of Palmer's chipmunk, conducted by the US Geological Survey.
- A study conducted under contract by University of Nevada, Las Vegas (UNLV) to monitor butterflies and study their ecology within the SMNRA.

The I&M Strategy included recommendations listed in Table 2-4 for ongoing species-specific surveys.

---

[2] The term survey as used in this document is a structured investigation to determine species occurrence and distribution using potential habitat parameters to define the survey area as opposed to a statistically designed sampling scheme.

Table 2-4: Ongoing Species-Specific Survey Recommendations

Species/Group	Recommendations
Alpine plant communities	Based upon monitoring trends for the alpine plant communities and the ability to use intensified FIA to accomplish the same trend monitoring with greater statistical accuracy, this effort should be completed, data evaluated and results published.
Rough angelica	Evaluate existing occurrence data with GIS analysis tools to determine potential habitat. Potential habitat with limited occurrence data should be surveyed during program years 1-3. If all potential habitats have sufficient occurrence data to validate habitat relationships, this effort should be completed and data evaluation results published.
Egg milkvetch	Evaluate existing occurrence data with GIS analysis tools to determine potential habitat. Potential habitat with limited occurrence data should be surveyed during program years 1-3. If all potential habitats have sufficient occurrence data to validate habitat relationships, this effort should be completed and data evaluation results published.
Charleston ant	Evaluate the taxonomic status through consultation with the appropriate expert(s). If the taxonomic status is confirmed, determine potential habitat with GIS analysis tools. Survey the previous collection sites and potential habitats and determine if it is extant in the SMNRA. If a population is confirmed, monitoring can be implemented.

Funding was recommended to remain constant during the first three program years and focused on the accomplishment of the tasks described above. Data evaluation may identify additional monitoring questions that should be considered for these species as a result of the analysis and evaluation described in Section 3. In later program years, funding is expected to increase to reflect additional species surveys that can be more effectively designed and implemented using the ecological context data generated by the FIA and spring inventory and monitoring programs.

1) **Survey program priorities** – Candidates for individual species monitoring (Table 2-5) were selected based upon current knowledge and concerns regarding their population trends. Several species have documented declines in population numbers, and all have significant knowledge gaps with regard to life history and distribution.

Table 2-5: Species-Specific Survey Priorities

Species Survey Priority Group 1	Palmer's chipmunk (*Neotamias palmeri*) Acastus checkerspot (*Chlosyne acastus robusta*) Spring Mountains dark blue butterfly (*Euphilotes ancilla purpurea*) Morand's checkerspot (*Euphydryas chalcedona morandi*) Mt. Charleston blue butterfly (*Plebejus shasta charlestonensis*) Charleston ant (*Lasius nevadensis*) Rough angelica (*Angelica scabrida*) Egg milkvetch (*Astragalus oophorus* var. *clokeyanus*)
Species Survey Priority Group 2	Clokey's greasebush (*Glossopetalon clokeyi*) Western redtail skink (*Eumeces gilberti rubricaudatus*)

2) **Survey methods and protocols** – Many protocols and methods for monitoring rare plants and animals have already been developed and published in peer reviewed publications. These methods have the statistical rigor that *ad hoc* methods often lack. In keeping with the

philosophy of the SMNRA I&M Strategy, previously developed and tested published methodologies should be the choice for individual species monitoring.

3) **Analysis and reporting** – Species-specific surveys are conducted to establish a baseline for trend analysis and to refine potential habitat models and identify habitat relationships. ArcGIS Spatial Analyst or the TEUI Geospatial Toolkit can be used to link species occurrence data from all monitoring sources.

4) **Data management** – All monitoring efforts, including individual species monitoring, will be entered into FS corporate databases, including NRM-NRIS-Terra and the Threatened, Endangered and Sensitive Plant (TESP) database (USFS 2008a, USFS 2008b).

5) **Collection of genetic material for analysis** – All of the plant species listed in Table 1-1 were thought to be appropriate for genetic monitoring. As noted previously, these assumptions proved to be incorrect and as a result collection of genetic materials for all CA plant species has been deferred until a sufficient genetic "discovery" foundation exists.

2010 and 2011 Accomplishments

Information on program accomplishments and plans in this section are presented by the type of survey and species or groups of species rather than separated by year. In some cases information gathered prior to 2010 is included to provide a comprehensive discussion for each species. Since the I&M strategy was developed, priorities for surveys have evolved and emphasis has changed. The following describes these changes by survey purpose.

Project Survey Areas

Project survey areas and species-specific surveys conducted from 2005 to 2009 are shown on Figure 2-4. Survey categories included on this map include:

Features – Inventories of roads, trails, fences and other infrastructure and facilities
Riparian – Surveys of species associated with riparian areas
Terrestrial – Surveys for terrestrial species associated with uplands
Threatened, Endangered, and Sensitive (TES) Plants – General survey areas for R4 Sensitive, CA Species, and plant species included in the Multi-Species Habitat Conservation Plan (MSHCP) for Clark County, NV, not specific transect or observed locations.

Although a limited number of project surveys and species-specific surveys were conducted in 2010 and 2011, the results have not been entered into the NRM-NRIS database and cannot be displayed. Therefore, Figure 2-4 is provisional pending compilation of project survey information.

Figure 2-4: Species-Specific and Project Surveys

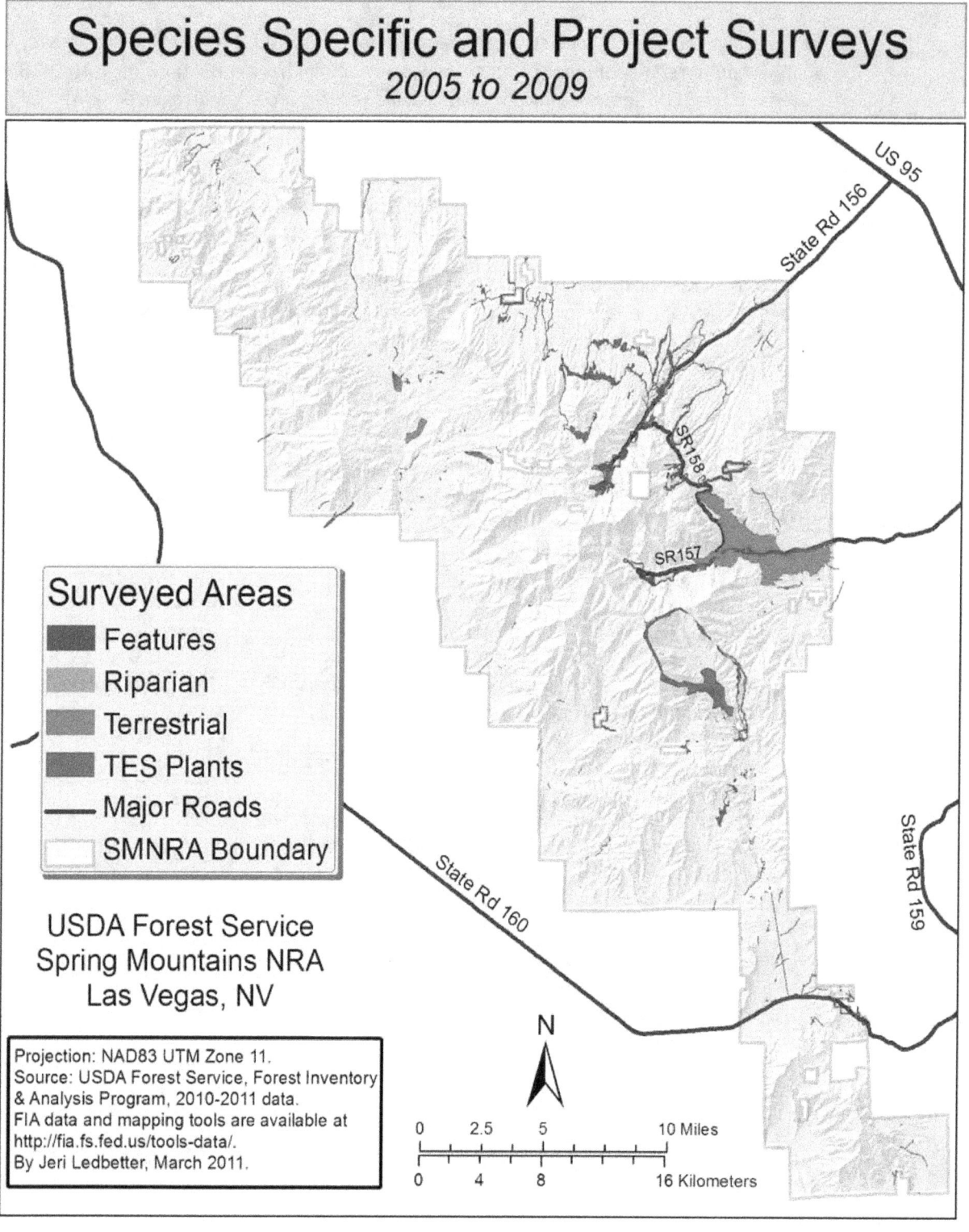

Species Specific and Project Surveys
2005 to 2009

Surveyed Areas

- ■ Features
- Riparian
- Terrestrial
- TES Plants
- — Major Roads
- □ SMNRA Boundary

USDA Forest Service
Spring Mountains NRA
Las Vegas, NV

Projection: NAD83 UTM Zone 11.
Source: USDA Forest Service, Forest Inventory
& Analysis Program, 2010-2011 data.
FIA data and mapping tools are available at
http://fia.fs.fed.us/tools-data/.
By Jeri Ledbetter, March 2011.

N

| 0 | 2.5 | 5 | | 10 Miles |
| 0 | 4 | 8 | | 16 Kilometers |

US 95
State Rd 156
SR158
SR157
State Rd 160
State Rd 159

Species-Specific Surveys or Monitoring

The role of individual or multiple species surveys is important in developing information necessary to address overarching questions related to CA Species occurrence, trend, and status. Equally important is that these surveys be conducted within a framework that allows for the development of information of sufficient data quality (known accuracy and precision) to identify and support changes in species management or proposed management actions.

Rather than de-emphasize individual species monitoring, in later phases of the inventory and monitoring program it may be necessary to <u>increase</u> the amount of effort devoted to these surveys. However, individual species-specific surveys must be conducted using a statistically valid sampling design.

Charleston Ant

Determining the distribution and abundance of *Lasius nevadensis* will require sampling during the mating flight, and should include traps to capture dispersing winged queens, as well as ground searches to observe emergence of alate individuals, and to locate colonies and workers. Sampling should be conducted across the range of suitable habitats throughout the SMNRA. Initially, traps should be placed in grid-fashion across suitable habitat to identify presence of the species. If *L. nevadensis* is found, then ground searches can be conducted to locate colonies that can then be studied to determine habitat requirements of associated species (root aphids and scales, as well as tree and shrub species on which the scale/aphids rely for food) (Pendleton2012a).

Charleston Ant Safaris - Charleston Ant Safaris were initial steps in the process of re-locating the Charleston ant and were conducted with the following objectives in mind:

- Develop community outreach to provide a citizen science opportunity for children and adults.
- Determine the timing of ant mating flights at the original collection site of *Lasius nevadensis*.
- Review available literature on *Lasius nevadensis* and develop a plan for resolving the status of *L. nevadensis*.
- Make the first effort to collect *Lasius nevadensis* since 1954.

2009 Charleston Ant Safari - The Charleston Ant Safari was a successful collaboration between the RMRS and the SMNRA (Pendleton 2012a). Events were held on July 17th, July 25th, and August 15, 2009. The Charleston Ant Picnic was held July 25th to commemorate the 55th anniversary of the discovery of the Charleston Ant. Approximately 50 people attended the picnic. Over 100 people, including 37 children, attended at least one day of the safari, and many attended on more than one day.

On July 17, 2009, two individuals of one species of alate ants were collected. On the 25th through the 28th of July, 2009, at least eight species of alate ants were collected. On August 15, 2009, very few alate individuals were observed. These collections demonstrate that a mating flight occurs during the same timeframe as when Cole collected *L. nevadensis* 55 years ago.

2010 Charleston Ant Safari – More than 50 volunteers attended the 2010 Charleston Ant Safari (Pendleton 2011). They participated in a science discussion, a search and collection of ant specimens, art activities, and games. The morning activities were followed by the 2nd annual Charleston Ant picnic. The worker specimens collected are still being examined, but winged specimens of *Lasius nevadensis* were not collected in 2010. Locating ants in 2010 was more difficult due to the layer of chippings from a fuels reduction treatment done at the only known location of the Charleston ant. The depth of the wood chips was within the prescription, but mating flights observed in 1954 were only observed coming from soil with a low amount of litter (Cole 1956). 2010 plans to erect traps to collect winged alate specimens of the Charleston ant were cancelled due to unanticipated budget restrictions.

2011 Charleston Ant Safari – The 2011 Charleston Ant Safari was held July 20, 2011, with approximately 30 participants. The Ant Safari was one of two Spring Mountain Science Safari events held during the summer of 2011. The other safari, the Pollinator Safari, was held at Lower Lee Meadow on August 16th and was attended by 35 people. Following the Ant Safari, collected ant specimens were sorted and potential *L. nevadensis* specimens were sent to the RMRS Albuquerque Laboratory for examination. Additionally, Dr. Larry Stevens of the Museum of Northern Arizona, while accompanying the spring inventory crew, collected specimens in July that have been prepared and sent to Harvard University for identification. Results are pending.

2012 Charleston Ant Safari – The fourth annual Charleston Ant Safari is planned for late July 2012. The format for the Spring Mountains Science Safaris has been standardized over the last three years and has been very successful. Each safari includes a science discussion, science activity (ant collection is the science activity for the ant safari), games, and an art activity. This year we will explore additional search and collection methods.

Information derived from the SMNRA Species Reference Database was used to identify habitat characteristics described in the Charleston ant species fact sheet and to develop potential habitat map displayed in Appendix B—6.

Alpine Plant Communities

Baseline studies for the three High Elevation Plant Communities were conducted in 1998 and 1999 (Nachlinger 2000b). The Biological Monitoring Plan for the three communities, bristlecone pine woodlands (2900-3450 meters), alpine and riparian spring-fed plant communities (2550-3150 meters) and the alpine herbaceous plant community (3350-3632 meters) was written by Nachlinger (2000a). Many CA Species are found in these three communities.

The objective of this study was to describe the natural patterns and the variation in the Spring Mountain high elevation communities, with a focus upon monitoring the health of these biologically important communities. Visitor use monitoring was an important component of the monitoring effort. Detailed objectives for each community monitored are listed in Nachlinger (2000a)

The methodology used included: One macroplot with ten associated transects was located in the herbaceous community. Two macro plots were located in the bristlecone pine community and two smaller macro plots were located in the riparian spring-fed community. Modified Whitaker plots were set up in the herbaceous and bristlecone macro plots. Sampling methodology for the Whitaker plots was the same for all long-term studies reported in this section. Qualitative sampling and photo points were used to sample springs and riparian macroplots, with a goal of reducing disturbance caused by the sampling effort. All of the data collected under the alpine plant community study are being compiled and analyzed. The evaluations of this study are reported in a separate report (Pendleton 2012b)

Information derived from the species data base and these studies was used to identify habitat characteristics, which were then used to develop the potential habitat maps displayed in Appendices B-13, 26, 30, 31, 35, 37, 40, and 41

Rough Angelica

In the mid-nineties, Rough angelica was a T&E candidate species and long-term studies were initiated to determine it's appropriate listing status. The most detailed analysis of this species' status was completed 15 years ago by Nachlinger and Combs (1996a). Work by Walker (2005) provides an update.

Nachlinger and Combs (1996a) produced a Biological Monitoring Plan for this species. The design included 2 macroplots of unequal size, one at Mary Jane Falls trail site and the second at Stanley B Spring. The objective of the monitoring was to detect population changes at both sites , and to monitor community composition and visitor use. Seedling numbers were monitored at Mary Jane. Monitoring methods included photo points, visitor counts, 35 rectangular 1x20 meter quadrats at Mary Jane, and 10 rectangular 0.5x4 meter quadrats at Stanley B.A modified Whitaker plot was installed in each macroplot to quantify community composition.

Rough angelica occurs in a variety of ecosystems at elevations from 1128 to 3500 meters. The wide elevational range and the number of communities this species inhabits are not typical of most rare species. A map and species fact sheet for Rough angelica is included in Appendix B. The Rough angelica long-term study data have been compiled, the statistical methods evaluated, and the implementation of the monitoring protocol evaluated. The results of the evaluation are reported in a separate report (Pendleton 2012b).

Information derived from these studies and other published literature was used to identify habitat characteristics as described in the species fact sheet and to develop the potential habitat map, displayed in Appendix B-25.

Egg Milkvetch

Smith (2001) produced a very comprehensive evaluation of the state of knowledge for this species. As described in this evaluation, egg milkvetch exhibits broader habitat tolerances than many rare species and inhabits a variety of ecosystems at elevations between 2070-2690 m. Smith (2001) and Anderson (1998) provide baseline location data upon which new location data, study and survey data collected during the last nine years, and the I&M program data can be added.

Nachlinger and Combs (1996b) produced a Biological Monitoring Plan for the species and a study based on that plan began in 1996. Two macroplots of equal size were established at the Bonanza Trail and Bristlecone Trail (one macroplot at each site). The monitoring objectives and data collection design was the same as that used for Rough angelica at Mary Jane Falls Trail.

Long-term study data for egg milkvetch has been compiled, the statistical methods evaluated, and the implementation the monitoring protocol evaluated. The results of the evaluation are reported in a separate report (Pendleton 2012b).

Information derived from these studies was used to identify habitat characteristics as described in the species fact sheet and to develop the potential habitat map displayed in Appendix B—10.

Butterfly Studies

There have been a number of butterfly studies conducted in the SMNRA and funded by the Forest Service and other government agencies. University scientists conducted a number of studies that are included in the published literature. The first study conducted for the Forest Service was completed in 1997 (Weiss and others 1997). Subsequent studies by Boyd, along with several collaborators, made significant contributions to the knowledge base of Spring Mountain butterflies

(Boyd and Murphy 2008, Boyd 2005, Boyd and Austin 2000, Boyd and Austin 1999). There are still knowledge gaps which need to be filled in order to fully understand the life history and distribution of the 9 butterfly species listed in table 1-1. A study in initiated in 2010 by Thompson (Thompson and Garret 2011) is designed to fill in some of these knowledge gaps. Objectives of their study are given as follows:

> "The research was focused on the autecology, life history, and population biology of five subspecies of butterflies identified as priorities for conservation in the Spring Mountain National Recreation Area (SMNRA). The goal of this research was to establish basic autecological information about endemic subspecies of the SMNRA, recommendations for management of butterfly habitat, and methods for habitat restoration. The five focal taxa of interest were: Mt. Charleston blue (Plebejus (Icaricia) shasta charlestonenesis; Austin 1980), Spring Mountains dark blue (Euphilotes ancilla pupura and E. a. cryptica; Austin et al. 2008), Morand's checkerspot (Euphydryas anicia morandi), and Spring Mountains Acastus checkerspot (Chlosyne acastus robusta). In additon, autecological information was collected on four additional taxa as time permitted: Plebejus (Icaricia) icarioides austinorum, Limenitis weidemeyerii nevadae, Speyeria carolae, and Hesperia comma mojavensis."

2012 Program Plans

SMNRA staff identified the following project and species-specific surveys for the upcoming season:

- Clark Canyon project proposal surveys
- Nesting and other surveys associated with mitigation measures for ongoing projects
- Surveys for rough angelica, including suspected habitats on the west-side of the SMRNA
- Monitoring plots for milkvetch required in the Forest Plan/GMP
- Surveys within the boundaries of the Las Vegas Ski and Snowboard Resort

Program Coordination Items and Modifications

Discussion with SMNRA staff identified the following coordination items and modifications to the 2012 program:

NRIS Survey and CA Species Occurrence Data – Survey locations and boundaries and observed CA Species locations are needed to facilitate completion of the habitat characteristic models and accuracy assessments of potential habitat models.

Species Survey Sampling Design and Implementation - Long-term monitoring studies of rough angelica (Angelica scabrida), egg milkvetch (Astragalus oophorus var. clokeyanus) and the alpine plant communities were initiated in cooperation with the Nature Conservancy in 1996. They have been evaluated for: 1) sampling design, 2) adequacy of sample size, 3) implementation of monitoring protocols, and 4) study results. The results of this evaluation are presented in a separate document (Pendleton 2012b.

e. Implementation/Monitoring Audits

Implementation/Monitoring Audits (IM Audits) provide a low cost opportunity to observe, evaluate, and make corrections in project planning, design, and implementation via a structured review process that provides a foundation for identifying corrective actions. The purpose of these audits is to facilitate organizational learning and continuous improvement.

Organizational learning and continuous improvement is facilitated through incorporation of the Plan-Do-Check-Learn cycle established in Environmental Management Systems (ISO 2007). Figure 2-5 is adapted from this process.

Figure 2-5: Implementation/Monitoring Audit Process

Implementation/Monitoring Audit Process

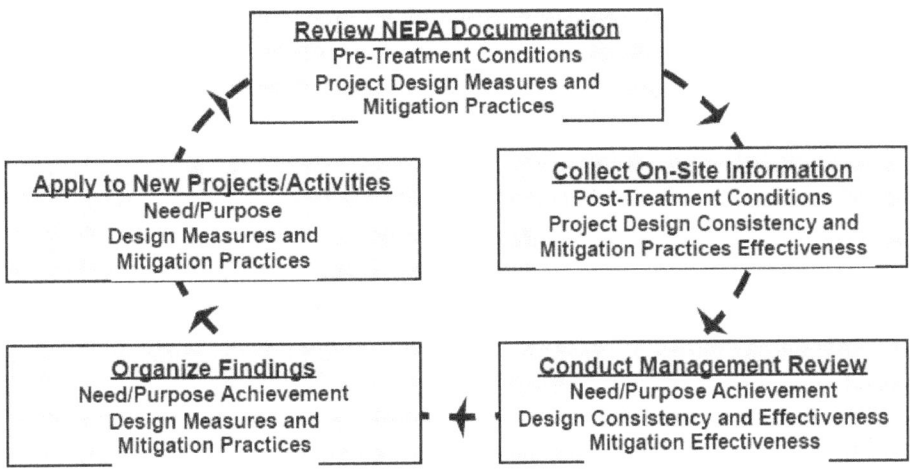

Initial Design

Project and activity areas are selected to address those monitoring questions where a qualitative assessment of conditions has been determined to be sufficient to address the issue, as determined by SMNRA leadership. Specific projects and activities audited are selected by SMNRA leadership (Deputy Forest Supervisor or SMNRA Manager/District Ranger). Management actions must be substantially complete or completed before conducting the IM Audit.

Since the initial design of the audit program, audit priorities were adjusted because management actions have not been taken that could be audited for many of the activities and projects identified for 2011 and 2012. Modifications are described and documented chronologically.

1. **Audit priorities** - The SMNRA I&M Strategy set priorities for evaluating projects and activities using the Implementation and Monitoring Audit Program. Table 2-6 shows the initial projects and activities to be addressed during the first three years of the program.

Table 2-6: Initial Implementation/Monitoring Audit Priorities

2010	2011	2012
• Mechanical hazardous fuel reduction projects • Wildland fire suppression and restoration	• Mechanical hazardous fuel reduction projects • Wildland fire suppression and restoration • Recreational climbing effects on cliff-dwelling CA Species • Cumulative effects on riparian areas and springs • Wildland fire recovery • Wildland fire suppression techniques and recovery	• Mechanical hazardous fuel reduction projects • Wildland fire suppression and restoration • Recreational climbing effects on cliff-dwelling CA Species • Cumulative effects on riparian areas and springs • Wildland fire recovery • Wildland fire suppression techniques and recovery • OHV management practices • Recreational caving effects on CA Species

2. **Audit procedures** –Planning is expensive and time-consuming – the results should be worth it. The audit process begins with a review of the completed (implemented) project's NEPA, planning, and implementation documents. This allows reviewers to step back and look at a completed cycle of planning/doing. Audit procedures include the following basic steps:

a. **Review NEPA Analysis and Documentation**

b. **Collect On-Site Information/Implementation** – This phase of the audit process involves on-site examination of results and a comparison with the desired outcomes described in NEPA documentation examined in the first step.

c. **Conduct Management Review** – Results of the document review and on-site information phases are presented to SMNRA leadership with the focus on project design consistency and mitigation practice effectiveness and identification of audit results to projects currently being planned.

d. **Organize Findings/Prepare Audit Report**

e. **Apply to New Projects/Activities** – This phase of organizational learning and improvement focuses on the application of audit findings and recommendations to ongoing and proposed projects and activities (see Appendix E).

f. **Review of audit procedures** - It is useful to take a conscious look at how audits are conducted; whether there are useful findings; and whether or not those findings make a difference in future planning, project implementation and, ultimately, improved conditions on the ground. A structured evaluation of the IM Audit program is conducted to determine whether to make adjustments in future audits.

2010 Modifications and Accomplishments

The first round of IM Audits was conducted on projects selected by the Deputy Forest Supervisor during a three-day workshop held October 19-21, 2010. Participants included the line and staff personnel involved in the planning and implementation of future hazardous fuel reduction treatments and wildland fire suppression efforts.

Hazardous fuel reduction treatment activities were analyzed and approved by the District Ranger in the Spring Mountains Hazardous Fuels Reduction Project EA, Decision Notice, and FONSI on December 20, 2007. At the time of the 2010 IM Audit, these treatments were nearly complete, providing the audit team the opportunity to evaluate areas where treatments were in progress as well as those where treatment had been completed. Many of the same participants were involved in suppression of and restoration after the Cathedral Wildland Fire, which had also been selected for the 2010 IM Audit. This wildland fire was partially located within the same area as some of the hazardous fuel reduction treatments in Kyle Canyon, although the fire took place before the treatments were completed.

The *2010 Implementation and Monitoring Audit Report* (METI 2011) documents the findings of the IM Audit workshop, addresses the implementation and effectiveness of wildland fire suppression and restoration strategies and techniques used in the Cathedral Wildland Fire, and the design features and mitigation measures employed in the hazardous fuel reduction treatments in Kyle Canyon, Deer Creek, and Lee Canyon. The report includes specific recommendations regarding future hazardous fuel reduction proposals.

An evaluation of audit procedures and effectiveness was conducted in conjunction with the management review held on January 12, 2011. SMNRA leadership and staff were supportive of the overall approach and endorsed its use in 2011.

2011 Modifications and Accomplishments

The second round of IM Audits was conducted on projects selected by the Deputy Forest Supervisor during the management review held on January 19, 2011. Five sites listed below were selected for an analysis of a range of conditions and practices and their effectiveness over time. Decision documents reviewed ranged from a project file for West Mud Springs from the 1980's to a 2010 Decision Memo for actions at Cold Creek.

The *2011 Implementation and Monitoring Audit Report* (METI 2012) documents audit findings and addresses the implementation and effectiveness of riparian, springs, and recreation management strategies at West Mud Springs, Cold Creek, Willow Creek/Spring, Carpenter Canyon, and Mountain Springs/Rainbow Mountain Wilderness. The report concludes with draft frameworks for addressing springs/riparian management and motorized recreation management.

An evaluation of audit procedures was conducted in conjunction with the management review held on January 19, 2012. SMNRA leadership and staff were supportive of the audit approach and endorsed its continued use in 2012.

2012 Modifications and Program Plans

In 2012, the IM Audit will address a series of monitoring questions associated with construction and reconstruction of developed recreational facilities and the management of those facilities. During the January 19, 2012 closeout meeting and March 15, 2012 inventory and monitoring program coordination meeting, discussion with SMNRA staff identified the following coordination items and modifications to the 2012 program:

Site Selection – Program funding in 2012 will limit the field portion of the IM Audit to one day. Analysis of the monitoring questions addressed at potential sites identified concerns with the value of including some sites in the IM Audit. As a result, the following sites were selected for the 2012 IM Audit:

- Lee Meadows restoration and recreation management (LMRR)
- Reconstruction of the Kyle Canyon Picnic Area (KCPA)
- Reconstruction of Cathedral Picnic Area (CPA) and fuel reduction actions within the project area.

Table 2-7 identifies potential monitoring questions to be addressed at each site.

Table 2-7: 2012 IM Audit Focus Areas by Site

Monitoring Questions	2012 Audit Sites		
	LMRR	KCPA	CPA
Soil and Water Conservation Best Management Practices			
MQ 56 – Are soil and water conservation practices being implemented and are they effective?	X	X	X
MQ 57 – Are soil disturbing activities creating excessive sedimentation or soil loss?	X	X	X
MQ 51 – How effective is riparian fencing in protecting springs and riparian areas? What thresholds warrant this level of mitigation?	X		
MQ 59 – Is recreation use or grazing by wild horses/burros or recreational livestock impacting bank stability?	X		
Recreation Site/Use Design and Management Practices			
MQ 3 – How do recreation activities affect CA species and habitats? Which types and locations of recreation activities are having more substantial effects on CAS species and habitats?	X	X	X
MQ 8 How effective are efforts to reduce recreation effects to riparian and spring areas?	X		X
MQ 16 – How can the effects of existing recreation developments and uses be managed to minimize effects on CA species and their habitats? What are the effects of concentrated uses and their overlap with CA species and their habitats?		X	X
MQ 18 – What are the direct and cumulative effects of woodcutting and gathering on CA species and their habitats?	X		X
MQ 5 – How effective are efforts to manage motorized recreation (OHV) and limit other uses to the protection and conservation of CA Species and their habitats?	X		
Invasive Species Prevention and Control			
MQ 41 – What are the most effective methods of treatment of high priority invasive species? Are there specific thresholds of infestations at which treatments are no longer effective?	X	X	X
Wildland Fire and Fuel Management			
MQ 36 – What actions can be taken to reduce wildland fire occurrences (severity) resulting in unwanted type conversion or unacceptable environmental effects?		X	X
MQ 31 – How effective are design features and mitigation measures associated with mechanical fuel treatments in protecting/conserving CA species habitats?		X	X

Project Records – All records for the selected projects should be provided to Joy Berg, METI team leader, directly or via "Dropbox" by June 15 to allow adequate time for review by the IM Audit team. Documents needed include: NEPA documents, contracts, force account instructions, agreements (e.g., Great Basin Institute), and Contracting Officer's Representative and project leader notes.

2012 IM Audit Schedule and Dates – The 2012 IM Audit will occur over a three-day period. The first day involves document review and will be scheduled in the afternoon. The field portion will occur on the second day, followed by a closeout discussion on the morning of the third day. Selection of specific dates will occur as program and meeting schedules are evaluated.

Figure 2-6: 2011 and 2011 Implementation/Monitoring Audit Sites

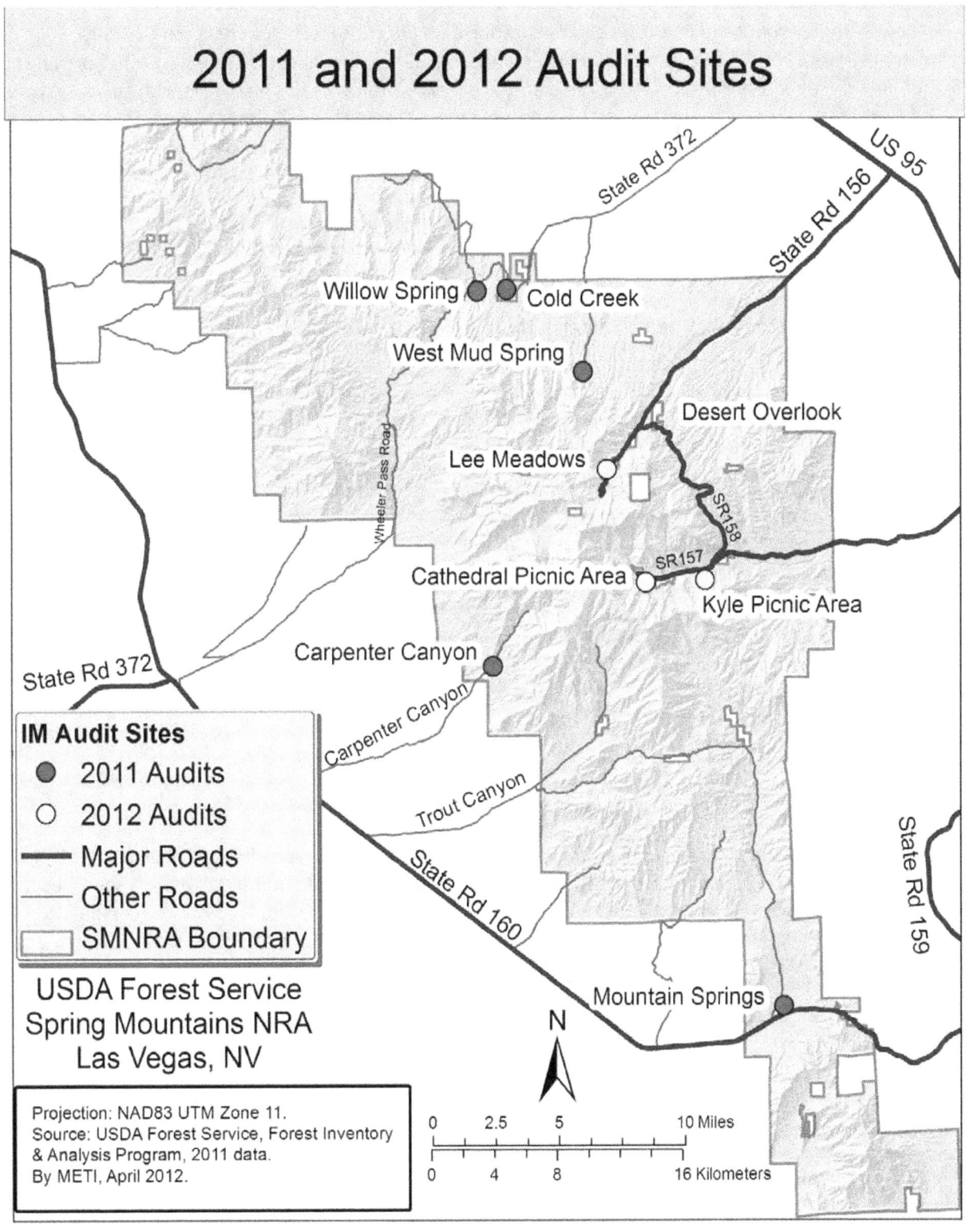

2011 and 2012 Audit Sites

3. Data Analysis and Evaluation

Analysis and evaluation of inventory and monitoring data are critical components of the adaptive management cycle. Data and information generated from inventory and monitoring activities provide a foundation for addressing monitoring questions. This evaluation provides managers with an understanding of relationships between conservation actions (or inaction) and desired outcomes. It also provides the basis for identifying and determining the need for changing land and resource management plan components, the CA and supporting conservation strategy, programs, projects or activities, or the monitoring program.

For the purposes of this effort, analysis and evaluation are focused on the conservation of CA Species within the SMNRA. In addressing this goal, it is important to understand the ecological underpinnings of the I&M Strategy (see Figure 3-1).

Figure 3-1: Ecological Underpinnings of the Inventory and Monitoring Strategy

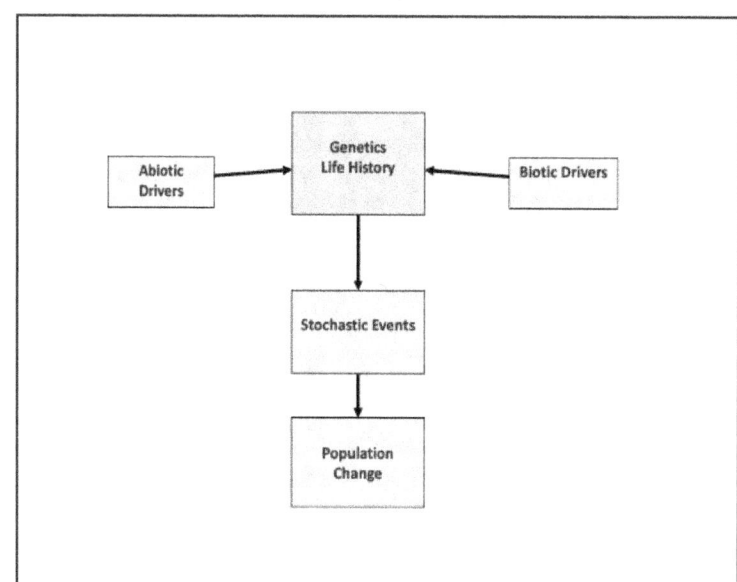

Population trends (net change in the number of individuals in a population) are determined by factors acting at a number of scales. Examples of fine scale would include the square centimeter where a seed lands, den locations and species interactions in a meter square plot. Larger scales would include the community, migration corridors, and ocean temperature patterns. Fine-scale patterns often cannot be understood without knowledge of global and regional processes.

In many cases, regional and landscape-scale forces can swamp the fine-scale forces that determine population dynamics. Factors that influence population change, both fine and large-scale, may be either biotic (biological factors) or abiotic (physical factors). These factors (drivers) influence a population's genetic structure and life history through differential mortality and reproduction. For rare species with limited population sizes, random (stochastic) events, both biotic (e.g. ungulate grazing pattern) and abiotic (e.g. tornado path) factors, can have an enormous impacts on net population change. The SMNRA inventory and monitoring program collects both biotic and abiotic data at multiple scales. The combined data set provides information on species' population dynamics necessary to support an adaptive management approach to conserving and sustaining the ecological and species diversity of the SMNRA.

These ecological concepts can be described in terms of six basic outcomes, each with a specific monitoring focus and affiliated monitoring questions. Outcomes are analyzed and evaluated in three groups: (1) ecological context, (2) species conservation, and (3) management interactions. The monitoring focus and specific monitoring questions associated with each analysis and evaluation group are described in Table 3-1.

Table 3-1: Analysis and Evaluation Monitoring Question Groups

Analysis and Evaluation Group	Outcomes	Monitoring Focus	Monitoring Questions[3]
Ecological Context	Ecological Context	Are changes in ecological context occurring that may affect species distribution or population sustainability?	29, 30, 33, 34, 49, 50, 53, 40, 42, 45, 44, 25, 23,
Species Conservation	Species Occurrence	Where do CA Species occur within the SMNRA?	32, 35, 36, 38, 4, 3, 17, 37, 1, 16, 24, 28, 26, 27, 18
	Habitat Relationships	How do individual species relate to their habitats?	
	Population Sustainability	How well distributed and robust is the population of individual species?	
Management Interactions	Implementation Consistency	Are the design measures and mitigation measures related to CA Species specified in the project or activity management NEPA decision implemented?	31, 33, 38, 8, 39, 5, 7, 9, 51, 59, 43, 56, 57, 55, 41
	Design Measure and Mitigation Practice Effectiveness	How effective are the design measures or mitigation practices in achieving desired results with respect to CA Species conservation?	

Effectively addressing the outcomes associated with many monitoring questions will require information from several inventory and monitoring sources. Similarly, the interpretation and analysis of data collected by different inventory and monitoring components will support analysis and evaluation with respect to each of these outcomes as illustrated in Table 3-2.

Table 3-2: Relationships between Ecological Outcomes and I&M Program Components

Outcomes	Intensified FIA	Springs Riparian	Genetic Monitoring	Species Surveys	IM Audits
Ecological Context	X	X			
Species Occurrence	X	X		X	
Habitat Relationships	X	X	X	X	
Population Sustainability			X		
Implementation Consistency					X
Design/Mitigation Effectiveness					X

Data from these programs, combined with existing datasets, provide the basis for analysis and evaluation and development of recommendations for the conservation of biological resources in the SMNRA.

Data analysis and discussions in the following subsections are organized under each of the monitoring focus items described in Table 3-1. Data used to support these analyses are provided by the inventory components listed in Table 3-2 for each of the outcomes associated with the monitoring focus items.

---

[3]Monitoring questions are listed in priority order as identified in the SMNRA I&M Strategy (USFS, 2008), see Appendix A.

a. Ecological Context

> **Monitoring Focus** - Are changes in ecological context occurring that may affect species distribution or population sustainability?

Species included in the CA inhabit ecosystems whose stability is affected by a number of drivers. The SMNRA is currently affected by a novel set of drivers that these systems have not previously experienced. The primary disturbance processes discussed below have significantly affected the flora and fauna of the SMNRA. The springs/riparian and FIA monitoring will provide data on invasive species and tree cover loss to insects and disease, and fire. The SMNRA, in partnership with the National Park Service, monitors invasive species. Individual wildland fire occurrences and effects are documented and monitored by SMNRA staff. This large data set will provide the basis for monitoring the ecological context of the CA species and their habitats.

Primary disturbance processes or drivers of importance affecting ecological context of the SMNRA include:

Climate Change

Climate influences all of the disturbances discussed in this section. For example, drought induces bark beetle susceptibility in conifers and precipitation and drought contribute to fire frequency and severity. Climate changes that have the most potential impact on Spring Mountain ecosystems include:

- Drought and changes in precipitation patterns can result in a cascade of ecosystem changes
- Changes in plant phenology can potentially lead to a decoupling of pollinator lifecycles with the availability of pollen and nectar resources
- Higher temperatures, particularly winter night time temperatures that limit species elevational ecotone limits, and the lack of snow retention at higher elevations
- Increased CO_2 levels may differentially affect vegetation community dynamics, plant phenology, and below-ground nutrient cycling

Climate models predict a rapid rate of climate change in southern Nevada (Rehfelt et al. 2006), particularly at lower elevations. While the rate of change may be somewhat slower at higher elevations (Loarie et al 2009), shifts in ecotones upward are predicted, e.g. a shift in the blackbrush/pinyon-juniper ecotone (Esque et al 2009) and bristlecone pine movement into the alpine community (Clark County Nevada 2008).

Forest Service managers have dealt with climate issues since the beginning of the agency. The challenge we now face is managing forests during a period when climates are changing at an extremely rapid rate. Management guidance is available from Forest, Region and Washington offices. Howell (2011) prepared a climate change vulnerability report for the Humboldt-Toiyabe National Forest (http://www.fs.usda.gov/land/htnf/landmanagement). It is a comprehensive look at the projected effects of climate change on the forest. The report provides a synopsis of paleo-climates, present climate, and realized and projected impacts of climate upon forest ecosystems. The climate change and forest management section of the report provides a brief primer of management during an era of climate change.

Region 4 has also posted guidelines on its webpage (http://fsweb.r4.fs.fed.us/climate/index.shtml) for incorporating climate change components into the project planning process. The Washington office has a very active climate change group led by Dr. David Cleaves that provides information to help facilitate management of our forests and grasslands during an era of changing climate.

The SMNRA maintains a network of climate monitoring stations. The data collected at these stations provide the context for examining changes in ecosystems and CA species' populations given that climate is an overarching driver of ecosystem change. The climate data collected will be a valuable asset to the I&M analysis process. (James Hurja 2011).

Wildland Fire Exclusion – Departure from Vegetation Range of Natural Variability

Many of the ecological settings within the SMNRA are fire-adapted ecosystems (Provencher 2008) and have been affected by fire exclusion as a result of wildland fire suppression. The role of wildland fire within the SMNRA is not well documented or understood. An analysis of fire history in the Spring Mountains has not been conducted. There have been numerous large fires throughout the area, which can be used to improve knowledge of fire behavior under different burning conditions. Understanding fire's history and behavior under different conditions helps managers effectively and efficiently manage future wildland fires and provides insight regarding the role of fire within the communities supporting CA Species.

Information on wildland fire effects in community types represented in the SMNRA has been the focus of recent research conducted under the auspices of the Joint Fire Sciences Research Program. Of particular note are Pinyon-juniper studies conducted by RMRS scientists (Chambers et al. 2005; Rau et al. 2012).

The Fire Effects Information System (FEIS) maintained by the Rocky Mountain Research Station's Fire Modeling Institute, located in Missoula, MT, contains current information regarding fire effects on vegetation, soils, hydrology and other resources. Information regarding the effects of fire exclusion in different community types is also available from the FEIS.

An important reference point in understanding the ecological context of the SMNRA is the analysis of the range of natural variability for biophysical settings of the SMNRA developed by Provencher (2008). Table 3-4 displays the percentage of area within each of the biophysical settings by seral stage or transition stage used in the LANDFIRE vegetation dynamics modeling.

Existing vegetation conditions by biophysical setting and similar vegetation transition stages was estimated as part of the LANDFIRE calibration process for the SMNRA. This information was developed during a workshop conducted in February 2009, but has only been validated by local knowledge and photo-interpretation. Unfortunately, data developed by Provencher do not use the same biological setting classes as those used by LANDFIRE, so a direct comparison cannot be made between historic and current vegetation using a common typology. Maps of existing vegetation developed for the SMNRA use a different classification system and map legend, again making the comparison of historic vegetation patterns and composition to existing vegetation difficult.

Table 3-4: The Range of Natural Variability for Biophysical Settings of the SMNRA

Biophysical Setting		Natural Range of Variability					
Code [a]	Name	A [b]	B	C	D	E	U
1019	Pinyon-Juniper Woodland	5	5	25	65	0	0
1020	Subalpine Limber-Bristlecone Pine Woodland	15	15	70	0	0	0
1052	Mesic Montane Mixed Conifers	10	30	15	35	10	0
1054	Ponderosa Pine Woodland	10	9	20	60	1	0
1061	Seral Aspen	25	50	15	9	1	0
1062	Curlleaf Mountain Mahogany Woodland	10	15	10	20	45	0
1079	Black Sagebrush	15	40	20	25	0	0
1082	Blackbrush	25	75	0	0	0	0
1104	Mogollon Chaparral	10	90	0	0	0	0
1126	Montane Sagebrush Steppe	20	50	15	10	5	0
1143 [c, d]	Alpine Fell-Field	5	95	0	0	0	0
1145	Subalpine-Montane Mesic Meadow	5	40	55	0	0	0
1145wm [c]	Subalpine-Montane Wet Meadow	5	40	55	0	0	0
1154	Montane Riparian	25	55	20	0	0	0
1155washes	Warm Desert Riparian Systems-Washes	25	75	0	0	0	0

a. Landfire core code that is not preceded by the two-digit map zone identification
b. Standard LANDFIRE coding for the 5-box vegetation model: A=early-development, B = mid-development, open; C = mid-development, closed; D = late-development, open; E = late-development, closed; and U = uncharacteristic.
c. Biophysical settings not in the original map zone 13 of LANDFIRE.
d. Initially coded as 1144, alpine tundra, by Spatial Solutions. Alpine fell-field (1143) was initially identified by NatureServe and LANDFIRE, but not included in the last biophysical setting maps by LANDFIRE.

Maps of existing vegetation developed for the SMNRA by Nachlinger and Reese (1996) use a different classification system and map legend, making the comparison of historic vegetation patterns and composition to existing vegetation difficult. Unfortunately, data developed by Provencher do not use the same biological setting classes as those used by LANDFIRE, so again a direct comparison cannot be made between historic and current vegetation using a common typology.

A new existing vegetation/cover type map of the SMNRA is being developed using the recently updated National Vegetation Classification (FGDC 2011) and available plot information. The map and supporting information will be available in 2012. Tabular information for existing vegetation types that can be directly compared to Provencher's data will also be available. These data can be used to evaluate and quantify departure from historical patterns, placement of current vegetation/cover upon the historic variability continuum, and provides a baseline for evaluating climate-induced changes to vegetation.

Insects and Disease

Plant and animal disease vectors are sensitive to temperature, rainfall, and humidity. Climate changes affect host/pathogen systems, and projected climate change may intensify disease outbreaks (Harvell et al. 2002).

Bark Beetles and Rusts

Bark beetle and rust in conifers are of greatest concern (Breshears et.al. 2009) in the Spring Mountains as plant communities migrate upward in elevation. Warmer winter temperatures may also allow an increased number of pathogenic insects to overwinter and increase the intensity of future outbreaks. Plants and pathogens that have been previously separated by distance may come into contact (Desert Research Institute 2008). The potential for large-scale die-offs of key species and the consequences for ecosystems can be illustrated by the recent widespread mortality of pinyon, *Pinus edulus*. In 2002-2003, 40-80% of pinyons in a four-state region died following prolonged drought and unusually high temperatures (Breshears et al. 2005). Regional mortality of key species has the potential to rapidly alter vegetation composition and associated ecosystem properties for decades.

The Humboldt-Toiyabe 2011 Aerial Insect Disease Detection Survey (http://www.fs.usda.gov/Internet/FSE_DOCUMENTS/stelprdb5349313.pdfcitation) found a limited number of trees with indications of insect damage. Less than 210 ponderosa pines, in 15 total locations, exhibited signs of bark beetle damage. Less than 30 true firs, the total in two locations, were damaged by fir engraver beetles. Given the large forested area of the SMNRA, these numbers do not indicate that a significant insect problem existed at the time of the 2011 survey.

Subsequently during 2011, SMNRA and I&M staff have observed large numbers of newly infected trees within the Kyle and Lee fuel treatment areas.

Bat White-Nose Syndrome

White-nose syndrome (WNS), a disease of bats caused by the fungus *Geomyces destructans,* was first discovered on the east coast of the United States in 2006 and has rapidly moved south and west across the US. The FWS reported in January of 2012 that more than 5.5 million bats have died from the disease in the eastern United States. White-nose syndrome is a disease of hibernating bats and is spread by bat-to-bat contact and from infected cave environments. Fungal spores can also be transported by individuals and caving equipment. In February 2011, the USFWS issued decontamination recommendations for cavers and their equipment (www.fws.gov/whitenosesyndrome). They have also developed guidelines for cave closure in order to limit the spread of the disease.

As of 2012, the closest report to SMNRA of suspected white-nose syndrome is from western Oklahoma. The Conservation Agreement lists two bat species, and if the rapid westward spread of the disease continues, development of contingency plans for the management of caves and their associated bats within the SMNRA is warranted. During the last year, WNS management plans have been developed by the FWS for New Mexico and Wyoming. In May 2011, the Northern Region of the Forest Service began considering potential restrictions for caves and abandoned mines in order to contain the spread of WNS. A program on the Humboldt-Toiyabe National Forest has been initiated to close public access to abandoned mines, many of which provide bat habitat.

Invasive Species

Drought can increase the susceptibility of ecosystems to invasion by nonnative species, especially with elevated levels of CO_2 (Smith et al. 2009). Prolonged drought can result in increased frequency and severity of fires, creating openings for rapid colonization by invasive herbaceous species. Invasive species generally produce large quantities of seed with effective dispersal capability, allowing rapid population expansion and migration to new areas. Invasive species may replace native species as vegetation shifts in response to climate change. Early germinating annuals, such as cheatgrass and red brome, can displace later-germinating native species by depleting the soil moisture necessary for their germination and growth. Streams, roads, and trails are corridors for rapid spread of invasive species.

There are a large number of non-native plant species in the SMNRA. Clokey (1951) reported few weed species in 1935, but as roads were constructed and recreational activity increased so did the number of nonnative plant species. Nachlinger and Reese (1996) documented 31 species of nonnative plants in or adjacent to their plots. Glenne (2003) compiled a list of 120 nonnative plant species in the SMNRA and adjacent BLM land. The Weed Sentry program recorded and mapped invasive species along roadways in the SMNRA from 2004-2009. This information is compiled in a geo-database on file at the SMNRA.

In the future, weed surveys will be conducted by SMNRA staff and information will be added to the database. Of particular concern are: the invasive brome species, which compete with native species and alter fire cycles; perennial rye grass, planted for post fire restoration; and salt cedar, which is extremely problematic at springs and other moist habitats (ENTRIX, Inc. 2008). The SMNRA has a contract for the survey/monitoring of invasive species. The contract also includes eradication services for newly discovered infestations and other control and containment activities.

Desirable Non-Native/Introduced Species

Five species of nonnative wildlife – wild horses, burros, elk, chucker partridge, and the Lahontan cutthroat trout – are resident within the SMNRA and pose documented or potential impacts on CA species and SMNRA ecosystems. These species are managed by other state and federal agencies. Wild horses and burros are managed by the BLM under the Free Roaming Wild Horses and Burro Act. Elk, Lahontan cutthroat trout and chuckar partridge were introduced and managed by the Nevada Department of Wildlife (NDOW) to provide hunting and fishing opportunities.

Wild Horses and Burros

Wild horses and burros are managed as self-sustaining populations of healthy animals, with the goal of maintaining a balance with other multiple uses, including providing critical habitat for focal, threatened and endangered species. The appropriate management level (AML) for the three jointly managed horse management areas (HMA) listed in Table 3-5, which surround the SMNRA, is presently 147 wild horses and 146 burros. All of the herd management areas for the Spring Mountains, together, make up the herd management area complex (HMA).

Table 3-5 - AML and Population Summary for the Spring Mountains Complex

HMA/WHT	AML		Population Estimate	
	Horses	Burros	Horses	Burros
Red Rock	50	50	21	201
Johnnie	47	21	85	573
Wheeler / Spring Mountains	50	75	268	126
Total	147	146	374	900

ENTRIX, Inc. 2008

The Spring Mountains HMA covers a total of 671,625 acres and includes both BLM public lands and National Forest System lands. The AML represents the maximum number that can graze without damaging the range. There is a history of disturbance caused by excess numbers of horses and burros, with moderate to high levels of disturbance from wild horses and burros documented at six springs surveyed in the Spring Mountains NRA in 1995 (USFS 1998). Annual population increase since 2006 is estimated to be 17 to 20 percent for wild horses and 20 percent for burros, a fact that makes maintenance of appropriate population size challenging. As a result, disturbances to vegetation at spring sites have limited time for recovery before herd numbers again exceed target levels.

In January 2007, a roundup resulted in the capture of 368 horses and 400 burros from the Johnnie and Wheeler HMAs, of which approximately 75 horses and 37 burros were released back into the Spring

Mountains. Despite this roundup, the BLM estimates that numbers were still above sustainable levels, with the next herd gather scheduled for 2013 (James Hurja, personal communication 2012).

Wild horses and burros consume herbaceous vegetation and some parts of woody vegetation in a wide variety of vegetation types, with use concentrating at spring/seeps in the SMNRA. Excessive use of grasses and forbs decreases the regeneration capability of these plants, resulting in decreased forage availability with successive years. Ground disturbance caused by trampling, particularly in areas surrounding sensitive springs and seeps, creates conditions favorable to invasive non-native species such as cheatgrass or red brome, or noxious weeds such as knapweed or perennial pepperweed. These weedy species out-compete native species, altering ecosystem function (BLM 2011, Cummings 2010, ENTRIX,Inc. 2008).

AMLs for wild horse and burro numbers are based on an estimated seven percent of available water and forage resources, which is intended to reduce, but does not eliminate, the potential for overgrazing and soil compaction.

There were no gatherings of wild horses and burros on the HMA's in and around the SMNRA during 2011, and the estimated populations remain above the AML's listed in Table 3-5. The next gather is scheduled for 2013 and will provide updated population estimates for these HMA's. Increased ground disturbance, spring degradation and CA species impacts are correlated with increased animal numbers

Elk

First introduced in 1935 with subsequent releases in the 1980s, elk populations within the SMNRA were estimated at 246 in 1996 but subsequently declined to 130 in 2009. Reasons cited for the decline include increased recreational and off-road-vehicle (ORV) use within the herd unit area, habitat degradation caused by excessive numbers of horses and burros, and extended periods of drought. An aerial survey, conducted in 2010, observed only 122 elk, and population estimates for 2011 approximate those observed in 2010 (NDOW 2011).

Elk cause some degree of trampling disturbance through use of springs and seeps as water sources. Grazing of herbaceous vegetation also has the potential to impact CA species. In 2009, the level of reproduction was not deemed sufficient to sustain the population (Cummings, 2010, ENTRIX, Inc. 2008). Alpine environments in the SMNRA did not evolve with large ungulate grazing and elk may negatively impact alpine CA species (Howell 2011).

Lahontan Cutthroat Trout

The Lahontan cutthroat trout occurs only in Carpenter Canyon on the West side of the SMNRA (ENTRIX, Inc. 2008). It is not known to occur elsewhere on the Spring Mountains, and it is managed for recreational fishing by NDOW. Impact of this introduction on stream flora and fauna is unknown. Since its introduction in the 1970s the population has become self-sustaining, but there is not any information on population numbers. NDOW regulations permit a daily limit of 2 trout from Carpenter Creek in Carpenter Canyon.

Chuckar Partridge

The chuckar partridge was introduced to the Spring Mountains as a game bird by the Nevada Department of Wildlife. During most of the year, their diet consists of seeds and leaves of grasses and forbs. In the spring, germinated seed and insects are additions to their diets. However, insects do not make up a large portion of the adult chuckar's diet (Christensen 1996). It is not known if chuckars consume enough seed of plants listed in Table 1-1 to affect those plant's populations.

Monitoring Question Analysis and Evaluation

Table 3-6 presents the analysis and findings developed based upon existing data, data collected in 2010 and 2011, and legacy data for those monitoring questions related to ecological context (see Table 3-1). The order of presentation corresponds to the priorities established by in the SMNRA I&M Strategy (see Appendix A).

Table 3-6: Analysis and Evaluation of Monitoring Questions Related to Ecological Context

Monitoring Question 29 - How does current wildland fire management affect CA Species and habitats compared to historical fire patterns? What are the consequences of wildland fire on CA Species and their habitats?
The role of wildland fire in the SMNRA has been influenced by fire exclusion leading to significant differences between current vegetation composition and historic patterns. Fire Regime/Condition Class mapping indicates a large portion of the SMNRA is vulnerable to fire intensities that will significantly impact ecological function and site conditions, in some instances delaying recolonization of sites and delaying successional patterns. The effect of climate change on fire patterns within the SMNRA cannot be determined without an improved baseline understanding of fire behavior for recent large fire events.   • Fire Regime/Condition Class distribution on the SMNRA identifies a significant departure from historic conditions in some vegetation types and a high risk of fire intensity that may severely affect ecological function (Provencher, 2008).   • CA Species are vulnerable to significant impact from wildland fire. Fire intensity is of primary concern (Condition Class). Historic vegetation patterns and seral stages are not reflected in current vegetation composition, affecting the availability of potential habitats for some CA Species.   • With respect to the management of wildland fire, the 2010 IM Audit identified the need to analyze major fire events and conditions to improve understanding of recent fires and their behavior on the landscape. This information is essential to determining an appropriate suppression response.

Monitoring Question 30 - How do we restore fire dependent ecosystems where it has been excluded? What are the consequences of wildland fire suppression?
TNC's evaluation (Provencher, 2008) of historic vegetation and departure of existing vegetation from this baseline provides information needed to address this question and concludes that there are significant departures from historic conditions, affecting resiliency of these systems from disturbance events, possibly affecting CA Species and their habitats.   • Treatment of hazardous fuels in areas with values at risk must be completed to allow effective use of wildland fire for resource benefits (2010 IM Audit).

Monitoring Question 33 - How effective are fuels treatments in restoring fire to its natural role in the environment?
The 2010 IM Audit identified that hazardous fuel treatments were providing protection to people and property. Without these treatments being completed, the use of wildland fire to restore natural conditions is limited in certain areas. Additional treatments are needed to provide adequate protection of values at risk in Kyle and Lee Canyons and other portions of the SMNRA.   • Treatment of hazardous fuels in areas with values at risk must be completed to allow effective use of wildland fire for resource benefits (2010 IM Audit).

Monitoring Question 34 - How can we maintain the appropriate amounts of wildland fire to maintain healthy ecosystems?
The 2010 IM Audit identified that hazardous fuel treatments were providing protection to people and property. Without these treatments being completed, the use of wildland fire to restore natural conditions is limited in certain areas. Additional treatments are needed to provide adequate protection of values at risk in Kyle and Lee Canyons.   • Treatment of hazardous fuels in areas with values at risk must be completed to allow effective use of wildland fire for resource benefits.

Table 3-6: Analysis and Evaluation of Monitoring Questions Related to Ecological Context (Cont.)

Monitoring Question 49 - Where are springs, fen, and streams distributed and how are baseline conditions, including water quality and yield being affected?

A map of springs sampled and those scheduled for sampling is presented in Appendix D-1.1. During the first two years of sampling (2010 and 2011) approximately 40% of the springs of the SMNRA have been surveyed. A list of spring sites visited and the 47 springs sampled to date is provided in Appendix D-1.2. Analysis of data collected at the spring sites in 2010 and 2011 are presented in Appendix D 3.2.

- Hydrology: Flow was measured at 42 sites (89% of those surveyed). The median flow was 0.17 L/second, with a range of 0.002 to 103 L/second. At the other sites there was either no discernible flow or the flow was diffuse and could not be measured. Other hydrologic data, including water quality data, are presented in Appendix D 3.2.
- Soil: Most of the spring sites had rocky substrate and little soil development. Only four sites had what appeared to be peat development, which might be considered fen-like, although it was generally small and would probably not meet all the criteria of a fen. Additional information on the soils data are presented in Appendix D 3.2.
- Fauna: Deer were observed most frequently (over 40% of sites in both years). Other frequently observed terrestrial vertebrates were: horse, elk, northern flicker, scrub jay, Clark's nutcracker and hummingbird (species not recorded). Many other species, particularly birds, were observed at a lower percentage of sites. The most frequently observed aquatic macroinvertebrates were caddisflies (order *Trichoptera*, family *Limnephilidae*); flatworms (class *Turbellaria*); mayflies (order *Ephemeroptera*, family *Baetidae*); damselflies (order *Odonata*, family *Coenagrionidae*); midges (order *Diptera*, family *Chironomidae*). It is noteworthy that springsnails (genus *Pyrgulopsis*, family *Hydrobiidae*) were found at 5 of 47 (11%) of springs, suggesting that those springs have remained perennial for a very long time, and that the water quality has not changed significantly in centuries or longer. Additional data on fauna are presented in Appendix D 3.2.
- Vegetation: Data on vegetation are summarized in Monitoring Questions 50 and 53, as well as in Appendix D 3.2.
- Disturbance and Management: The most common disturbances were associated with animals (presumably horses, elk and deer), which resulted in trails, trampling, grazing and browsing of vegetation, and various ground disturbances. Other commonly observed disturbances were fire, water extraction, vehicle trails and tracks, and tree cutting.

Monitoring Question 50 - What is the current riparian vegetation composition, structure and pattern associated with springs, fens, and streams?

Most sites were dominated by wetland and facultative vegetation, as indicated by the prevalence index below 3 at 66% of sites. The prevalence index is a measure of the abundance of wetland vegetation, on a scale where "1" would be entirely wetland vegetation and "5" would be entirely upland vegetation. The other 34% of sites were dominated by facultative and upland species, which could be a concern given that these are spring sites.

A few sites had very little vegetation, which could be a result of disturbance from animals.

The vegetation data for each site were compared to riparian vegetation community types described in Weixelman et al. (1996) and in Manning and Padgett (1995), which resulted in the following categorization of the vegetation.

A summary of the vegetation of the 47 springs surveyed in 2010 and 2011 is presented in Appendix D 3.2

- The most commonly observed plant community types were the: *Rosa woodsii* community type (described in Weixelman et al. 1996) at 12 sites; the *Dodecatheon jeffreyi* community type (described in Manning and Padgett 1995) at 9 sites; and the *Salix lasiolepis/Rosa woodsii* Community Type (described in Weixelman et al. 1996) at 6 sites.
- 12 sites did not fit a community type described in Weixelman et al. (1996) or Manning and Padgett (1995) and were informally called the *Baccharis sergiloides* community type, the *Jamesia americana/Dodecatheon redolens* community type, or the *Vitis arizonica* community type.
- Seven sites had little or no vegetation (many were very small sites).

Table 3-6: Analysis and Evaluation of Monitoring Questions Related to Ecological Context (Cont.)

Monitoring Question 53 - What is the ecological status of riparian areas?

Information from the spring surveys that can be used to address the ecological status of associated riparian areas includes: vegetation composition, vegetation condition, faunal species presence, invasive species of flora and fauna, introduced plant species cover, the abundance of wetland vegetation (using the prevalence index), and the amount of bryophyte cover. A high ecological status will generally include the vegetation composition anticipated for the site, vegetation that is healthy and vigorous, faunal species anticipated for the site, a low amount of introduced plant species cover, an abundance of wetland plant species (low prevalence index), and some bryophyte cover.

Disturbance is a natural part of some springs ecosystems, and many riparian plants can tolerate or even thrive in the presence of natural forms of disturbance. Excessive disturbance, as can occur with anthropogenic activities, can impede recovery of native wetland plants (and bryophytes), and can enable establishment of introduced species. Disturbance from animals (particularly horses) was observed at over 80% of spring sites. Summaries of disturbances are presented in Appendix D 3.2, as well as in the discussions for monitoring questions 40, 45, 57, and 59.

A more complete assessment of ecological status could be performed using the plant species cover values for each site to evaluate the ecological status in relation to the expected vegetation for the environment of each site.

If possible, inventory of riparian conditions at the four perennial streams within the SMNRA will be accomplished in 2012.

Data used to address this question are presented in Appendix D 4.1.

- 68% of sites had vegetation composition as expected as well as healthy and vigorous vegetation, based on the responses to the management indicator questions.
- 66% of sites had the anticipated faunal species, based on the response to the management indicator question.
- 64% of sites did not have invasive species of flora and fauna established, based on the response to the management indicator question.
- Introduced plant species cover averaged 2.6% and the median cover was 0, based on vegetation sampling data.
- The prevalence index average and median value was 2.4, which is based on the cover data from vegetation sampling. This is a measure of the abundance of wetland vegetation, on a scale where 1 would be entirely wetland vegetation and 5 would be entirely upland vegetation. 66% of sites were primarily wetland and facultative vegetation (prevalence index below 3). The other sites were dominated by facultative and upland vegetation (prevalence index of 3.0 to 4.1). More wetland vegetation would probably be associated with high ecological status.
- Bryrophytes (mosses) are non-vascular plants that include species with characteristics that allow them to thrive in wet soil conditions. Bryophytes are vulnerable to human disturbance and to changes in hydrology (Tousignant and Brisson 2010). The SMNRA sampling data indicate that bryophyte cover averaged 7.6% and the median was 2.7%. The majority of sites had at least some bryophyte cover, which is a good sign, although it is not clear what the cover should be for SMNRA sites in good ecological status. A study by Nachlinger and Reese (1996) found comparable bryophyte cover for spring community types of the SMNRA: 10% for *Dodecatheon redolens*[4]-*Aquilegia formosa* Series; 2.4% for the *Rosa woodsii var. ultramontana* Association; 0.7 for the *Baccharis sergiloides* Association; and 1.6% for the *Jamesia americana/Petrophytum caespitosum-Ivesia jaegeri* Association. In other regions some wetland and riparian community types have higher bryophyte cover: the *Carex luzulina* Plant Association described by Crowe and Clausnitzer (1997) for eastern Oregon had an average of 54% bryophyte cover (that community type was selected because it was the community type with the highest cover of *Dodecatheon jeffreyi*, which is similar to *Dodecatheon redolens [aka, Primula fragrans] of the SMNRA*). A riparian classification for Utah by Padgett et al. (1989) had multiple communities with greater than 20% cover of bryophytes.

---

[4] This species is also described as *Dodecatheon jeffryi*

Table 3-6: Analysis and Evaluation of Monitoring Questions Related to Ecological Context (Cont.)

Monitoring Question 40 - What is the current trend (distribution and abundance) of invasive species?
Invasive species data collected by the NPS is not entering the SMNRA data stream. Steps are being taken to assure these data are part of the NRM-NRIS database for the SMNRA. FIA data collection will provide information to address this question. Springs inventory data indicate the presence of non-native vegetation at spring sites (see Appendix D 3.2) and tamarisk or saltcedar was observed at one spring site (see Appendix D 3.2). • Insufficient data available in NRM-NRIS to generate findings. • Vegetation sampling in 2010 and 2011 only showed one spring site with an invasive plant species: saltcedar (*Tamarix ramosissima*). • Responses from the management indicator tool indicated that 36% of sites had invasive species of flora and fauna established. That response may have been based on the presence of introduced plant species (observed at 39% of sites) rather than invasive species. The field crew may not have distinguished between introduced (nonnative) and invasive (a designation made by each state) species.

Monitoring Question 45 - Do wild horses adversely affect the habitats of some CA Species?
The annual population of wild horses increased approximately 18% since 2006 and 20 percent for burros, a fact that makes maintenance of appropriate population size difficult. Wild horses and burros typically use the herbaceous and woody vegetation in a wide variety of vegetation types with use concentrating at spring/seeps in the SMNRA. Excessive use of forage decreases the regeneration capability of these plants, resulting in a decrease in the ability of the vegetation to stabilize soil and prevent erosion. In addition, the horses and burros trample vegetation and disturb the ground, particularly in areas surrounding sensitive springs and seeps, which creates conditions favored by invasive or non-native species such as cheatgrass or red brome, or noxious weeds such as knapweed or perennial pepperweed. These weedy species can out-compete native species, further reducing native vegetation diversity. Insufficient data have been collected on the uplands to accurately characterize and identify site-specific effects from wild horses and burros on CA Species. Wild horses were likely a significant component of disturbances noted at springs, because horses and evidence of horses were observed at many sites. Therefore, wild horses and burros have likely had adverse effects on habitat for CA species at springs. Additional data are presented in Appendix D 3.2. • Horses were observed at 40% of spring sites in 2010 and 2011. Animal trails were observed at over 80% of sites; grazing at over 60% of sites and trampling at almost 60% of sites. • 84% of springs inventoried have been adversely affected by herbivory based on responses to the management indicator question "Herbivory is not adversely affecting the site." An examples of adverse impacts listed in the field guide is: where "Native or nonnative ungulates have caused excessive removal of vegetation, abnormally low height (including hedging of shrubs) or cover of vegetation, or major changes in species composition."

Monitoring Question 42 - What role should wildland fire play in areas with invasive plant species? What are the consequences and threats from invasive species that typically follow fire such as cheatgrass in lower elevations?
Information from the Fire Effects Information System can serve as a foundation for understanding the consequences of invasive species following wildland fire. • If more detailed information is required to understand these relationships, consider reframing the question as a research proposal or fire synthesis need for submission to the Joint Fire Sciences Program, the Southern Nevada Agency Partnership, or to the Rocky Mountain Research Station (Fire and Fuel Program and/or Terrestrial Wildlife Program).

Monitoring Question 44 - What are the consequences of climate change and drought on CA Species and their habitats?
Insufficient data have been collected. FIA and springs monitoring over a sufficient time frame is required. • Insufficient data and climate models are available to generate findings specific to CA Species.

Table 3-6: Analysis and Evaluation of Monitoring Questions Related to Ecological Context (Cont.)

Monitoring Question 25 - Are the landscapes being managed within a range of variability that promotes resiliency for CA Species and their habitats? Have ecological systems been altered – therefore, affecting CA Species and their habitats?
TNC's evaluation (Provencher, 2008) of historic vegetation and departure of existing vegetation from this baseline provides the information needed to address this question, and concludes that there are significant departures from historic conditions affecting resiliency of these systems from disturbance events, possibly affecting CA Species and their habitats. • In some instances, the objectives of the interagency hazardous fuel treatment program complement efforts to restore vegetation composition, structure, and distribution to historic conditions. In others, these objectives are in conflict with the Conservation Agreement's strategy because of the overriding need to protect people and property and other values at risk, including habitats for some CA species where resulting fire intensity will significantly alter site conditions. • Wildland Fire Management Plan direction for the SMNRA does not exist and should properly reflect the objectives, standards and guidelines in the General Management Plan which provide for the use of wildland fire for resource benefit. - Identify areas where Fire Management Units 2 and 3 apply within the SMNRA and incorporate this information into WFDSS. - Identify species habitat values-at-risk for inclusion in WFDSS based upon potential habitat models and occurrence data. • Review of the climate change literature and evaluation of climatic conditions needed to maintain ecological communities in their current elevation zones indicate that returning to historic distribution is unlikely, regardless of management actions.

Monitoring Question 23 - What are the effects of air quality on vegetation?
A review of air quality research in Southern Nevada is underway (USGS and others). FIA will collect information on ozone damage to lichens that can provide data on air quality effects to vegetation. • Insufficient data are available to generate findings.

Ecosystems providing habitats for plant and animals of the SMNRA are affected by a number of drivers, including climate, fire, insect and disease, and invasive or introduced species. Data collected through FIA and SMNRA monitoring programs provide the basis for characterizing current habitat parameters and evaluating the effects of these drivers on population dynamics of CA Species.

Of equal importance to monitoring current and future ecological conditions is an understanding of the current range of habitat variability within SMNRA community types, and how composition of community types differs from historic conditions. LANDFIRE models provide some insight into the range of natural variability of these communities and the degree of departure from historic conditions. Existing data are being applied to the monitoring questions developed in the I&M Strategy. Answers to most monitoring questions will require the additional data generated by the I&M program over subsequent years through FIA and springs inventories, genetic studies, and surveys and studies of individual CA Species. An evaluation of the departure of existing vegetation composition from historic conditions can be conducted once the new existing vegetation map is available.

b. Species Conservation

As outlined in the CA (USFS 2011a, page 3), many of the CA Species have been identified for protection because little is known about species distribution, life history, and their response to management and drivers of ecosystem change. During the past decade, numerous studies and investigations have been conducted to address these concerns. A perpetual issue facing parties to the CA has been the organization and access to the best available science and current data for supporting species conservation management decisions. Data and information issues related to species conservation are being addressed on two fronts:

Species Reference Database - Life history, research and studies

The SMNRA I&M Strategy recommended development of a Species Reference Database or library containing all published and unpublished information for each of the CA Species, accessible in a digital format to all SMNRA staff, and maintained with current information. The Species Reference Library was initially established in the spring of 2008 using the R-4 Planning, Appeals, and Litigation MS Access Database as a framework. Initial entries into the MS Access database were made using a literature search conducted by the RMRS. Ongoing work by RMRS and SMNRA staff during 2011-2012 has located a number of reports and documents not previously included in the Species Reference Database. The published literature for the CA Species dated 2009-2012 is also being added to the species database and work will continue to add unpublished information found in SMNRA files.

The available information is under evaluation and a synthesis document, the **species fact sheet**, is being prepared for each CA species. Examples of the species fact sheet format for selected species are included in Appendix B. Species status fact sheets summarize the best available science on each species and, when used with potential habitat maps and models of habitat characteristics, provides a detailed overview of the biology, distribution and status of each CA species. Species fact sheets and habitat maps will be updated as new information becomes available. An establishment and maintenance record is included as part of the species fact sheet.

Natural Resource Information System – Survey areas and occurrence data

The Forest Service maintains the Natural Resource Information System as an application within the Natural Resource Manager (NRM-NRIS). NRM-NRIS is supported by a national management organization that follows standards developed by the Federal Geographic Data Committee and provides standardization across different program organizations within the agency. Generation of data summaries, analyses, reports, and map products are supported through the NRM-NRIS Output tools: Enterprise Data Warehouse (EDW), Geospatial Interface (GI), and I-Web User Views. The EDW provides read-only, historical, and aggregated data using design that provides snapshots of the transactional (editable) data repository. Benefits of the EDW include availability of outputs for general use, a variety of formats for data delivery (e.g., reports, maps, raw and summarized data), and data at national spatial extents. Users access the EDW through various database connection methods including standard ArcMap, the GI, and, in the future, web services.

As noted above, occurrence and survey area data have been included in a number of reports and documents prepared by and for the SMNRA. This information is not in a standard format and has not been compiled into data sets for each species. The compilation and standardization of all available location data in NRM-NRIS is ongoing. Once this process is complete, potential habitat models can be constructed for all of the CA Species using known location data and site characteristics of those locations.

Monitoring Focus – Where do CA Species occur within the SMNRA?

Systematic distribution surveys have not been conducted for CA Species. The I&M program focuses on filling this and other CA Species information gaps. Once survey areas and occurrence data are loaded into NRM-NRIS, maps depicting species occurrence and tabular information can be prepared. This information can then be used in a variety of ways to inform management decisions and better understand where CA Species occur within the SMNRA.

Species Status

Agency policy and criteria for the classification of species as threatened, endangered, candidate, or sensitive are well documented in FS directives (FSM Chapter 2670 and FSM1920/FSH 1909.12) and are the primary source used for classification determinations for species that fall within the scope of the CA for the SMNRA. (see Section 4b-1).

Species fact sheets for selected CA species are presented in Appendix B and represent the best available science for each species. As information on species status is developed and compiled in Appendix B, all species can be evaluated against the agency classification criteria and a determination of the species' status can be documented. As new information is accumulated, the status of a species can be updated using best available information and science.

The NatureServe fact sheets for CA Species do not, in most cases, contain all available information, and have not been updated for over 10 years. Species status fact sheets being developed as part of this effort will be provided to NatureServe and the Nevada Heritage Program. If there is a discrepancy between the status determination documented in the species status sheet report and the Nature Serve status, a request to update the species status will be forwarded to Nevada Heritage Program/Nature Serve by SMNRA staff. This information will also be entered into the NRM-NRIS TES Database application.

> **Monitoring Focus** – How do individual species relate to their habitats?

The primary knowledge gap for all species listed in the CA is distribution within the SMNRA ecosystems. CA Species habitat relationships will be developed using two complementary approaches that allow for improvement over time as life history information becomes available and information on species occurrence improves. The combination of these two modeling techniques will be used in generating future potential habitat maps with known levels of accuracy and a more complete description of habitat traits and biophysical relationships. Figure 3-1 illustrates the relationships of these modeling processes, the data and information used to develop the models, and their potential application.

Figure 3-1: SMNRA Habitat Model Development Process

SMNRA Habitat Model Development Process

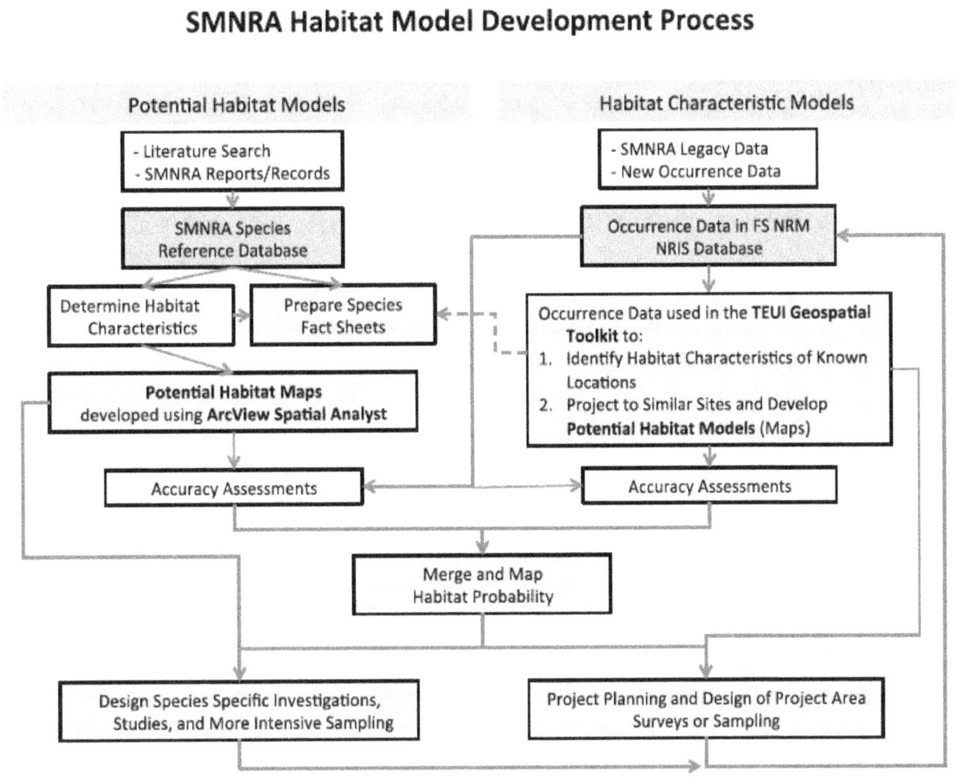

Potential Habitat Modeling

The Species Reference Database provides information about how CA Species relate to their habitats and life history information and also provides insight into the abiotic and biotic forces that determine the species distribution. From these references, habitat characteristics such as elevation range, aspect, soils, etc. can be inferred and used to develop models of potential habitats for individual species using Spatial Analyst, which is a standard ArcGIS analysis tool. Appendix B contains preliminary habitat models for all CA Species, except springsnails, which are located at known spring sites.

The accuracy of habitat modeling can be estimated using occurrence data as a basis for comparing predicted to actual habitat. As occurrence data improves as a result of data collected by the intensified FIA program, project and species specific surveys, and springs inventory program, the accuracy of these habitat models can be assessed.

Habitat Characteristic Modeling

Modeling of habitat characteristics relies upon observed locations to generate habitat characterizations and to map their locations. The TEUI Geospatial Toolkit is used to conduct this analysis. The program uses GIS information to characterize observed locations and generate a potential habitat map, which classifies the SMNRA landscape as to the probability of a CA Species occurring at that location.

As more location and habitat data is collected, the accuracy of the characteristic habitat map improves. The intensified FIA program will produce the first systematic inventory of the entire SMNRA and will provide information occurrence data that will significantly enhance the ability to identify habitat characteristics. Habitat characteristic models will be developed once data accuracy issues regarding species occurrence locations are resolved within NRM-NRIS and, at this point, have been deferred until 2012.

When species occurrence data accuracy issues within NRM-NRIS are resolved and habitat characteristic modeling using the TEUI Geospatial Tool Kit are complete, species status determinations can be reviewed with this improved understanding of how individual species relate to habitats found within the SMNRA.

Monitoring Focus – How well distributed and robust is the population of individual species?

FIA data, previous and ongoing studies data, potential habitat maps, project surveys, and the Species Reference Database, when examined in total, provide the information needed to address the above management question. The sum of this information dictates, when compared against the criteria, the status of the CA Species (see criteria above). The status (T&E, candidate or sensitive) provides the direction for any future monitoring, studies or surveys that are needed for continued adaptive management of CA species. The FIA data provides a statistically sound and robust data set, which will be used to track ecosystem changes and ecotone shifts that may affect CA species.

TES and candidate species are the first priority for species-specific studies. Sensitive species with significant knowledge gaps would be the next priority for individual species studies. This is particularly true if there is so little known about the species that there may not be confidence in the validity of its conservation status (for example, the Charleston ant or other little-known species).

The ultimate measure of species robustness is a heterogeneous gene pool (see Section 2.c). For example, a species with wide distribution across the SMNRA, not genetically isolated from subpopulations and having a heterogeneous gene pool would warrant a lower conservation status priority than a species with a restricted distribution, low population numbers and a homogeneous gene pool. Species listed for genetic analysis in Table 2-3 have been reevaluated in light of recent literature reviews. There is not sufficient background information in the various genetic databases to permit cost effective analysis of most CA plant species. The genetic analysis of Palmer's chipmunk is complete, and the butterflies and springsnails are the next species groups scheduled to undergo genetic analysis.

Monitoring Question Analysis and Evaluation

Table 3-7 presents the analysis and findings developed based upon existing data, data collected in 2010 and 2011, and legacy data for those monitoring questions related to species conservation (see Table 3-1). The order of presentation corresponds to the priorities established by in the SMNRA I&M Strategy (see Appendix A).

Table 3-7: Analysis and Evaluation of Monitoring Questions Related to Species Conservation

---

Monitoring Question 32 - What are the effects (positive/negative) on CA Species habitats from mechanical fuel treatments?

Chipping and mastication depths were identified in the 2010 IM Audit as potentially causing adverse effects to some Tier 1 CA Species. This disposal method was used to avoid effects to Palmer's chipmunk, a Tier 2 CA Species.

- Decisions to implement design or mitigation measures for CA Species should consider the relative risk to different species using the tiered approach described in the CA. Risks to Tier 2 CA Species should generally not outweigh those to Tier 1 CA Species.
- Wood chips from the fuel reduction treatments act as a mulch which inhibits the emergence of many species (including CA species). Mitigation (creating openings in the chip layer) at locations with known or potential habitats for CA Species is possible, but may be cost prohibitive. Monitoring data on the USGS pre-treatment plots can be used to assess effects and provide a basis for remedial treatment design, if warranted.

Monitoring Question 35 - What effects has wildland fire had on the conditions in key CA Species habitats and should these and other areas be protected from wildland fire?

These relationships cannot be determined at this time; insufficient data are available to construct accurate potential habitat maps.

- Insufficient data are available to generate findings.

Monitoring Question 36 - What actions can be taken to reduce wildland fire occurrences (severity) resulting in unwanted type conversion or unacceptable environmental effects?

Existing and confirmed Fire Regime/Condition Class Mapping (Provencher 2008) indicates where fire intensity will be severe enough to compromise ecological function. This information will need to be intersected with potential habitat maps. These relationships cannot be determined at this time; insufficient data are available to construct accurate potential habitat maps.

- Insufficient data are available to generate findings.

Monitoring Question 38 - What wildland fire suppression strategies and techniques can be used to minimize impacts to CA Species?

The 2010 IM Audit assessed the effectiveness of Minimum Impact Suppression Techniques (MIST) used for the Cathedral Wildland Fire and concluded that these techniques were effective in minimizing ground disturbance effects to potential CA Species habitats. Use of MIST techniques is required in Wilderness but not for the balance of the SMNRA.

- Consider use of MIST as a standard practice within the SMNRA to provide mitigation of suppression actions when direct or indirect attack is selected as an appropriate suppression strategy.

Monitoring Question 4 - Are recreational climbing activities affecting CA Species plants in cliff areas or disrupting roosting areas for CA Species bats and other nesting CA Species?

No data collected in these locations. Volunteer programs are being investigated to determine if users can be of assistance in gathering observational data.

- Insufficient data are available to generate findings.

Monitoring Question 3 - How do recreation activities affect CA Species and habitats? Which types and locations of recreation activities are having more substantial effects on CA Species and habitats?

Potential habitats for CA Species were mapped using information in the Species Reference Database and are displayed in Appendix B. Modeling of potential habitats will be improved once soil type issues between the Nye and Clark County soil surveys are resolved and species occurrence location data in NRM-NRIS are validated are made available for analysis.

- Intersecting potential habitat maps with recreation use areas and their footprints from the Landscape Assessment or from the NRM-Infra database can be used to address this issue at an NRA-wide scale.
- Individual project proposals can also be evaluated using these habitat models to identify potential concerns, design or mitigation needs, and site-specific survey requirements.

Table 3-7: Analysis and Evaluation of Monitoring Questions Related to Species Conservation (Cont.)

Monitoring Question 17 - What are the consequences of distributing recreation use outside presently developed canyons and increasing disturbance in previously undisturbed areas? Are there CA Species habitats where recreation impacts to habitat should be avoided?
Potential habitats for CA Species were mapped using information in the Species Reference Database and are displayed in Appendix B. Modeling of potential habitats will be improved once soil type issues between the Nye and Clark County soil surveys are resolved and species occurrence location data in NRM-NRIS are validated are made available for analysis. • Intersecting potential habitat maps with areas where redistribution of recreation use is anticipated can be used to address this issue at an NRA-wide scale. • Areas providing potential habitat for multiple species can be identified using the habitat models to identify areas where redistribution of use is not advisable. • Individual project proposals can also be evaluated using these habitat models to identify potential concerns, design or mitigation needs, and site-specific survey requirements.

Monitoring Question 37 - What is the rate of wildfire recovery on burned species? Is there a difference in recovery time for high vs. low intensity?
Information from the Fire Effects Information System can serve as a foundation for understanding fire effects. Fire Regime/Condition Class estimates fire intensity as a departure from historic conditions and characterizes fire effects in terms of impact to ecological function. Information relative to both aspects of this monitoring question has been developed as part of the Fire Surrogate Studies supported by the Joint Fire Sciences Program. Studies specific to the Humboldt-Toiyabe National Forest are being conducted and results published by Rocky Mountain Research Station scientists located at the Reno Laboratory.

Monitoring Question 1 - What are the effects and impacts of dispersed recreation uses, including OHVs to CA Species and their habitats?

The focus of the 2011 IM Audit only addressed the component of this monitoring question associated with the management of motorized use, specifically off-highway vehicle (OHV) use.
 	
The Motorized Trail Designation Project (2004) and Motorized Vehicle Use Map (USDA Forest Service 2009) established the framework for managing motorized recreation use within the SMNRA. These decisions reflect the standards and guidelines established in the Forest Plan/GMP, however the IM Audit has identified several areas where the implementation of these decisions have (1) not been fully implemented as designed, (2) not been maintained, or (3) program emphasis is not assuring compliance with established restrictions.
 	
Key factors in managing motorized recreation use include:
• <u>Understanding the Distribution and Ecological Significance of CA Species Habitats</u> – Information on CA Species habitats and their distribution are important factors in managing recreation use. This information needs to be considered in conjunction with the timing associated with key life history events. Information being developed as part of the I&M Strategy will address these needs by providing current life history information and potential habitat models.
• <u>Visitor Education, Information and Signing</u> – Establishing and maintaining visitor information for motorized recreation is a difficult task requiring constant attention. The IM Audit identified the following programmatic recommendations listed in Section 3 of the IM Audit Report to address concerns identified.
    ○ Revision of the MVU Map
    ○ Wilderness Portal Management and Signing
    ○ Travel Management Signing
    ○ Partnerships and Visitor Education
• <u>Route Closure and Restoration Practices</u> – As described in Section 3 of the IM Audit Report, the SMNRA has an excellent starting point for developing and refining practices used for restoring and rehabilitating user-created routes and closed roads based on the work done at Mountain Springs.
• <u>Monitoring and Enforcement</u> – Programmatic recommendations are listed in Section 3 of the IM Audit Report regarding developing a cooperative law enforcement program associated with the motorized recreation management decisions reflected on the MVU Map.
• Wilderness motorized trespass is a significant issue that must be addressed in the SMNRA law enforcement program. Statutory violations associated with this use warrant more attention than the regulatory violations associated with the MVU Map. Focusing on this problem can serve as a foundation for a comprehensive motorized recreation enforcement program.

Table 3-7: Analysis and Evaluation of Monitoring Questions Related to Species Conservation (Cont.)

Monitoring Question 16 - How can the effects of existing recreation developments and uses be managed to minimize effects on CA species and their habitats? What are the effects of concentrated uses and their overlap with CA Species and their habitats?

Potential habitats for CA Species were mapped using information in the Species Reference Database and are displayed in Appendix B. Modeling of potential habitats will be improved once soil type issues between the Nye and Clark County soil surveys are resolved and species occurrence location data in NRM-NRIS are validated are made available for analysis. Recreation reconstruction projects and recreation management in concentrated use areas will be examined during the 2012 IM Audits.

- Intersecting potential habitat maps with existing recreation sites and areas of concentrated use footprints can be used to identify and determine the nature of use conflicts and set the stage for evaluating the effectiveness of management efforts and potential mitigation measures.

Monitoring Question 24 - Where are opportunities for restoration and/or creation of habitat for CA Species located?

These relationships cannot be determined at this time, insufficient data are available to construct accurate potential habitat maps

- Springs inventories are identifying restoration opportunities but have not been prioritized at this time.

Monitoring Question 28 - What is the average number of downed woody logs per acre?

FIA data include information on downed woody material that can address this Forest Plan monitoring requirement. However, GMP standard 0.37 requires a minimum of 50 linear feet/acre of downed trees with a minimum 12-inch diameter on sites being managed for the late seral stage of the Pinyon/Juniper and Mixed Conifer Land Type Associations to provide ground cover for small mammals, amphibians, reptiles, and invertebrates. GMP standard 0.91 addresses a similar requirement in fuel breaks and areas being managed for late seral stages of Pinyon/Juniper and Mixed Conifer Land Type Associations.

Appendix C-2.3 displays information for the SMNRA from the 2010-2011 data panels for down woody material by cover type.

- FIA data analysis was under preparation at the time this report was compiled and will be added when complete.
- This monitoring question should be revised to reflect the requirements of GMP standards 0.37 and 0.91.

Monitoring Question 26 - How many snags per acre are present in mixed conifer, riparian areas, and in P-J?

This Forest Plan monitoring requirement does not apply to NFS lands within the SMNRA because they have been "reserved for timber" production by Congress and are not considered "available productive (capable) Forest land" (GMP, Page 1 and Appendix C). GMP.

Appendix C-2.3 displays information for the SMNRA from the 2010-2011 data panels related to the number of snags by cover type.
Appendix D-3.2 contains information from the springs inventory program.

- FIA data analysis was under preparation at the time this report was compiled and will be added when complete.
- Only 19% of spring sites had live trees (greater than 5 cm in diameter) within the site, and each of those sites had just 1 to 11 individual trees.   The tree species that were most abundant in terms of cover were white fir (*Abies concolor*) with 5.2% cover, Rocky Mountain juniper (*Juniperus scopulorum*) with 4.3% cover, ponderosa pine (*Pinus ponderosa*) with 2.4% cover, quaking aspen (*Populus tremuloides*) with 1.5% cover, and Gambel oak (*Quercus gambelii*) with 1.2% cover.
- Standing dead trees were counted in 2011 (not 2010) and only two of those 28 sites (7%) had standing dead trees, and only one standing dead tree at each site.

Monitoring Question 27 - What percentage of mixed conifer is old growth habitat?

This Forest Plan monitoring requirement does not apply to NFS lands within the SMNRA because they have been "reserved for timber production" by Congress and are not considered "available productive (capable) Forest land" (GMP, Page 1 and Appendix C). GMP.

Appendix C-2.2 displays information for the SMNRA from the 2010-2011 data panels.
- FIA data analysis was under preparation at the time this report was compiled and will be added when complete.
- The definition of mixed conifer from the Multi-Species Habitat Conservation Plan (Clark County, 2008) and the 11 ecosystems used by Southern Nevada Agency Partnership (SNAP) consists of ponderosa pine, white fir and ponderosa pine/mountain shrub communities. On the Humbolt-Toiyabe NF, 150 or older is used as the definition of old growth stands.

Table 3-7: Analysis and Evaluation of Monitoring Questions Related to Species Conservation (Cont.)

Monitoring Question 18 - What are the direct and cumulative effects of woodcutting and gathering on CA Species and their habitats?
• Prohibitions and restrictions regarding woodcutting and gathering have been implemented as result of concerns regarding the effects of these activities on habitat for Palmer's chipmunk site disturbance and potential for erosion and disturbance of CA species habitats.
• Law enforcement records should provide an indicator of the effectiveness of the prohibitions and restrictions within the SMNRA. Specific monitoring related to this question should not be implemented unless law enforcement records indicate a need and only after additional law enforcement and public education measures are implemented.

Information developed by the I&M Program is providing the baseline to better understand species distribution, life history, and ecosystem response to management and drivers of ecosystem change. A perpetual issue facing parties to the CA has been the organization and access to current and best available data for supporting management decisions regarding species conservation.

These issues will be addressed as data from the I&M program is collected through the following steps:

1) Complete and maintain the species reference data base so all relevant information is compiled and readily available for analysis and evaluation;
2) Compile and standardize all available location data in the Forest Service's Natural Resource Information System. This step is underway for Tier 1 CA species;
3) Use of the GIS tools (Spatial Analyst) and the TEUI Geospatial Toolkit to produce potential habitat models and habitat characteristic models for all CA species; and
4) FIA data collected in 2011 will provide a statistically robust dataset of community distribution and CA species occurrence.

This information will then be used to update the Nevada Heritage/Nature Serve database for status reviews and provide the SMNRA with the information and tools needed to manage and conserve the biological diversity of the Spring Mountains.

c. Management Interactions

In addition to external factors, management interactions directly and indirectly affect the ecological context of CA Species and their habitats. In those cases where CA Species habitat is of limited extent, the cumulative effects of management activities and uses over time can cause significant effects.

Interactions between management activities and biological resources are often complicated and require a rigorous study design to determine cause-and-effect relationships. Structured systematic observations can also be used to evaluate these interactions and make adjustments in design and implementation. IM Audits investigate the linkages between planning and decision documents, implementing guidance and contracts, and on-the-ground results.

Monitoring Focus – Are the design measures and mitigation practices related to CA Species specified in the project or activity management NEPA decision implemented?

Design measures and mitigation practices are used to avoid or mitigate effects to CA Species. Implementation of design features and mitigation measures specified in NEPA decision documents may be compromised because contracts and instructions to crews are often subject to interpretation, there are changes in personnel between planning and implementing decisions, and there is too much time elapsing between a decision and its implementation.

The effectiveness of design measures or mitigation practices during implementation of projects or activities is also subject to interpretation in contract and project/activity administration. Processes for documenting changes are designed to record administration decisions. This documentation can provide a source of information for assessing the effectiveness of design measures or mitigation practices. Post treatment observations are another method of gathering this information.

Hazardous Fuel Treatment Monitoring

In partnership with the USGS, the SMNRA instituted a monitoring study designed to assess the effects of hazardous fuel treatments. Plots were established in different habitats at two scales (a) ecological sites and (b) micro-sites. Information was gathered prior to treatment. Post-treatment monitoring data have not been collected and currently there is no funding available to collect these data (James Hurja 2011).

Implementation and Monitoring Audits

IM Audits focus on implementation and effectiveness monitoring to develop observations and recommendations. IM Audits conducted in 2010 and 2011 addressed both focus areas associated with management interactions (METI, Inc. 2011 and 2012).

Activities and projects audited were identified based on priorities identified in the I&M Strategy. Priorities were determined using a combination of the risk and uncertainty associated with the effects of different management actions and the ability of management to influence the outcome. Wildland fire suppression and restoration and mechanical treatment of hazardous fuel were selected as priorities for the 2010 IM Audit. The management of OHV and recreation use near springs and riparian areas and spring/riparian protection measures were selected as priorities for the 2011 IM Audit.

Monitoring Question Analysis and Evaluation

Table 3-8 presents the analysis and findings developed based upon existing data, data collected in 2010 and 2011, and legacy data for those monitoring questions related to management interactions with CA species and their habitats (see Table 3-1). The order of presentation corresponds to the priorities established by in the SMNRA I&M Strategy (see Appendix A).

Table 3-8: Analysis and Evaluation of Monitoring Questions Related to Management Interactions

Monitoring Question 31 - How effective are design features and mitigation measures associated with mechanical fuels treatments in protecting/conserving CA Species habitats?

The 2010 IM Audit evaluated design features and mitigation measures used in the December 20, 2007 Spring Mountains Hazardous Fuels Reduction EA and decision documents. Review of the EA/DN and contract documents, in addition to on-site review of treatments in Kyle and Lee Canyons and along the Deer Creek Road, serve as the basis for the Audit's findings and recommendations.

- The relationship between desired conditions for ecological restoration and hazard reduction were not well coordinated.
  - Treatments in blackbrush were not necessary because existing conditions achieve desired conditions.
  - Hazard reduction treatment objectives were well defined and used interchangeably (e.g., fuel break vs. fire break).
  - Removal of surface fuels, especially large woody debris was not necessary to meet fire behavior objectives.
- Several design measures resulted in unintended consequences:
  - Pruning ladder fuels in P-J created vectors for insects and disease. Pruning in association with thinning and disrupting surface fuel continuity was not necessary to achieve fire behavior objectives.
  - Prescribed burning of piles within one year of treatment is not feasible and the consequences and effects of off-site disposal or chipping outweigh those of burning in a subsequent season.
  - Chipping and mastication of trees, shrubs and limbs created chip depths that may affect nutrient cycling, fire behavior, and other ecological functions.
- Design criteria used had varying degrees of effectiveness:
  - Measures for streambank protection, botany, and butterfly protection are well described and effective when properly applied.
  - Botany measures were effective where flagging occurred. However, it appears that there were inaccuracies in the GIS layers used (especially for milkvetch), so flagging did not protect all populations.
  - Visual design criteria (V 1 to V18) are out of sync with the complexity of the EA. Terms like "consider," "retain and enhance," and "natural appearing" are too subjective, ambiguous and difficult to translate to contract language for implementation. If visual resources are important to the SMNRA, which are expected with its high levels of recreation and public use, then they should be important enough to be reflected in project design.
  - Design criterion S2 gives a species preference for tree retention. Bristlecone pine should be designated as the most preferred tree species.
- Monitoring requirements are described and appear to be appropriate for this project.

Table 3-8: Analysis and Evaluation of Monitoring Questions Related to Management Interactions (Cont.)

Monitoring Question 33 - How effective are fuels treatments in restoring fire to its natural role in the environment?
The 2010 IM Audit evaluated the effectiveness of fuel treatments in restoring fire to its natural role in the environment by examining the desired conditions described in the December 20, 2007 Spring Mountains Hazardous Fuels Reduction EA and decision documents, the Cathedral Wildland Fire suppression actions, and a general evaluation of treatment locations with respect to the use of wildland fire for resource benefits. The audit team also reviewed the Clark County Community Wildland Fire Protection Plan (Resource Concepts Inc. 2005) and the recently completed Spring Mountains Multi-Jurisdictional 10-Year Hazardous Fuel and Fire Prevention Strategy (USFS, 2011c); both of these documents identify additional areas requiring treatment and values at risk.

- The ability to restore fire to its natural role in the SMNRA is dependent upon the reduction of risk to people, property and high value resources. Hazardous fuel treatment objectives described in the EA were defined based on altering fire behavior allowing direct attack by suppression crews within the areas treated (WUI).
- Desired conditions at times represent a compromise between fire and fuel objectives on one hand and ecological condition and function objectives on the other. For example, pinyon/juniper communities in the SMNRA have a skewed distribution of desired age classes with too much (approximately 95%) in the oldest age class instead of the 65% experienced historically. Retention of islands and clumps of these species instead of uniform thinning and retention of larger trees could have achieved fuel reduction objectives and begun to restore historic age class distribution.
- Current interpretation of Forest Plan direction (as amended by the General Management Plan) and the letter of delegation to the Incident Management Team for the Cathedral Wildland Fire do not allow for the use of wildland fire for resource benefits. This interpretation may not be correct based on the General Management Plan amendment to the Forest Plan.
- Additional treatments to provide protection of values at risk are needed based upon the recently completed Inter-Agency Hazardous Fuel Treatment Plan and Community Wildland Fire Protection Plans. Until these treatments can be accomplishe,d the ability to use wildland fire for resource benefits or prescribed fire to restore ecological conditions is generally infeasible because of the high degree of risk and uncertainty associated with the current fuel loading areas with values at risk.
- Maintenance of treatment areas recently accomplished and previously treated areas is critical to long-term restoration of wildland fire to the SMNRA.

Monitoring Question 38 - What wildland fire suppression strategies and techniques can be used to minimize impacts to CA Species?
The 2010 IM Audit evaluated the Letter of Delegation to the Incident Command Team and objectives established in the Wildland Fire Decision Support System for the Cathedral Wildland Fire regarding suppression strategies and techniques.

- The objectives in the Delegation of Authority letter to in-coming IMT's originate in Forest Plan direction that by its nature is general and broad in scope. Corresponding detailed direction has not been described for the SMNRA. There were some general objectives that did not specifically state what was important to protect or what some of the direction was to follow, i.e., "Follow the Humboldt National Forest Management Plan" ... and "minimize impacts to protect natural resources that occur in fire area."
- A single Resource Advisor was assigned and worked directly with the Type 3 IMT. This worked because the wildland fire was small (less than 20 acres) and of short duration and the Resource Advisor was knowledgeable regarding the area and its resources.
- Minimum Impact Suppression Tactics (MIST) were used on the Cathedral fire. Objectives in the Delegation of Authority letter specified use of MIST whenever practical in all wilderness areas, but were silent on the use of MIST outside designated wilderness.
- Although this fire was outside wilderness, MIST tactics used were effective. The amount of constructed fire line was minimized by using the road systems in the picnic area as fire lines and burning out from those roads. In addition, limited amounts of fire line were constructed on the east-side and top of the fire.

Table 3-8: Analysis and Evaluation of Monitoring Questions Related to Management Interactions (Cont.)

Monitoring Question 8 - How effective are efforts to reduce recreation effects to riparian and spring areas?

The 2011 IM audit evaluated the effectiveness of efforts to reduce recreation effects to riparian and spring areas by examining the desired conditions and standards in the Forest Plan and SMNRA General Management Plan, the SMNRA Conservation Agreement/Multi-Species Habitat Conservation Monitoring Plan, and the SMNRA Landscape Assessment/Inventory and Monitoring Strategy as well as environmental analysis and decision documents specific to each of the sites visited.

All five sites visited during the IM Audit provided information regarding efforts to reduce recreation effects to springs and riparian areas and their effectiveness. Willow Creek and Cold Creek illustrate sites with moderate to high use; both sites are easily accessible and are part of a larger use complex. West Mud Springs and Carpenter Canyon have limited accessibility via low standard roads where use is generally confined to a narrow corridor. Mountain Springs illustrates the management challenges associated with a combination of springs/riparian protection and motorized access to Wilderness adjacent to the roadway.

Key components of effective recreation management practices include:

- Visitor Education, Information and Signing – Establishing and maintaining visitor signing and information are difficult tasks requiring constant attention. The IM Audit identified concerns associated with recreation management, particularly with design image, travel management signing, use of the standard sign plan, partnerships and visitor education, and interpretive signing.

- Physical Barriers and Trail Management – The use of physical barriers to control access to and delimit use areas is an effective management practice. Coupled with route restoration practices used at Mountain Springs, practices employed at Cold Creek, Carpenter Canyon, and Willow Creek, the SMNRA has an excellent starting point for developing and refining practices used for managing use at springs/riparian areas and for restoring and rehabilitating user-created routes and closed roads.

- Monitoring and Maintenance – Similarly, the agreement between the SMNRA and Great Basin Institute provides a solid foundation for a monitoring and maintenance program for these areas.

Monitoring Question 39 - What wildland fire suppression techniques are most effective in setting the stage for post-fire restoration? (e.g., Fire retardant use restrictions)

The 2010 IM Audit evaluated the Letter of Delegation to the Incident Command Team and objectives established in the Wildland Fire Decision Support System for the Cathedral Wildland Fire regarding suppression strategies and techniques. This question will be reviewed in future IM Audits if suppression and restoration activities occur in the interim.

The Forest Service recently completed an Environmental Impact Statement and issued a Record of Decision regarding the aerial application of fire retardant. The EIS/ROD and guidelines for aerial application of fire retardant are available at: http://www.fs.fed.us/fire/retardant/index.html

- The Letter of Delegation specified mop-up and turn-back instructions which addressed restoration of firelines and areas disturbed during suppression efforts.

- An evaluation of the need for a Burned Area Evaluation and Restoration plan concluded that fire intensity and disturbance did not warrant restoration efforts beyond what would be accomplished by the Incident Management Team.

- A single Resource Advisor was assigned and worked directly with the Type 3 IMT. This worked because the wildland fire was small (less than 20 acres) and of short duration and the Resource Advisor was knowledgeable regarding the area and its resources.

- Minimum Impact Suppression Tactics (MIST) were used on the Cathedral fire. Objectives in the Delegation of Authority letter specified use of MIST whenever practical in all wilderness areas, but were silent on the use of MIST outside designated wilderness.

- Although this fire was outside wilderness, MIST tactics used were effective. The amount of hand fireline was minimized by using the road systems in the picnic area as fire lines and burning out from those roads. In addition, limited amounts of fireline were constructed on the east side and top of the fire.

Table 3-8: Analysis and Evaluation of Monitoring Questions Related to Management Interactions (Cont.)

Monitoring Question 5 - How effective are efforts to manage motorized recreation (OHV) and limit other uses (outfitters and guides) to the protection and conservation of CA Species and their habitats?
The focus of this year's IM Audit addressed only the component of this monitoring question associated with the management of motorized use, specifically off-highway vehicle use.

The Motorized Trail Designation Project (2004) and Motorized Vehicle Use Map (2009) established the framework for managing motorized recreation use within the SMNRA. These decisions reflect the standards and guidelines established in the Forest Plan/GMP, however the IM Audit has identified several areas where the implementation of these decisions have (1) not been fully implemented as designed, (2) not been maintained, or (3) program emphasis is not assuring compliance with established restrictions.

Key components of effective recreation management practices include:

- Understanding the Distribution and Ecological Significance of CA Species Habitats – Information on CA Species habitat and distribution are important factors in managing recreation use. This information needs to be considered in conjunction with the timing associated with key life history events. Information being developed as part of the I&M Strategy will address these needs by providing current life history information and potential habitat models.
- Visitor Education, Information and Signing – Establishing and maintaining visitor information for motorized recreation is a difficult task requiring constant attention. The IM Audit identified programmatic recommendations for revision of the MVU Map, Wilderness Portal management and signing, travel management signing, and partnerships and visitor education to address concerns identified.
- Route Closure and Restoration Practices – The SMNRA has an excellent starting point for developing and refining practices used for restoring and rehabilitating user-created routes and closed roads based on the work done at Mountain Springs.
- Monitoring and Enforcement – The IM Audit report recommends development of a cooperative law enforcement program associated with the motorized recreation management decisions reflected on the MVU Map.
- Wilderness motorized trespass is a significant issue that must be addressed in the SMNRA law enforcement program. Statutory violations associated with this use warrant more attention than the regulatory violations associated with the MVU Map. Focusing on this problem can serve as a foundation for a comprehensive motorized recreation enforcement program.

Monitoring Question 9 - How effective are management efforts in reducing negative effects to CA Species dependent on caves?
No management actions have been taken. Efforts to seek volunteer assistance from users to minimize effects and to monitor effects from caving are being pursued.

- Insufficient data are available to generate findings.

Table 3-8: Analysis and Evaluation of Monitoring Questions Related to Management Interactions (Cont.)

Monitoring Question 51 - How effective is riparian fencing in protecting springs and riparian areas? What thresholds warrant this level of mitigation?

The West Mud Springs exclosure and the Willow Creek exclosure fences illustrate differences in disturbance pressure, fence design and effectiveness of maintenance and monitoring. The Mountain Springs site illustrates a different situation – with no wild horse/burro use and low presence of elk. Factors affecting fencing design choices and effectiveness include:

- Ecological significance/CA Species habitat – A primary difference between these sites is their ecological significance and presences of CA Species habitat. Willow Spring has historically been considered the most ecologically significant site within the SMNRA, providing habitat for a variety of *Pyrgulopsis turbatrix* springsnails. West Mud Springs and springs near Mountain Springs have a lower ecological significance warranting less investment in protection of those sites.
- Use by wild horses/burros, elk, and recreation livestock – Both Willow Springs and West Mud Springs are used by wild horses/burros, recreation livestock, and elk. Willow Springs/Creek appears to have higher levels of use, which are likely a function of the volume of flow from the spring and presence of a perennial stream. Mountain Springs has little to no wild horse/burro use and elk have only recently started to inhabit this area.
- Recreation use and access – The Willow Creek site is accessed by a main road and numerous roads around the perimeter and as a result reduce material transportation and maintenance costs. However, this accessibility also increases recreation use and the amount of damage from vehicles to the fence. Spring sites within the vicinity of Mountain Springs have received low to moderate use by recreationists, with most use effects associated with OHVs. West Mud Springs does not have road access; increasing both transportation and maintenance costs, but lowers recreation use.

Exclosure design elements and their effectiveness are discussed below:
- Fence perimeters – At West Mud Springs and Willow Creek, fencing does not coincide with the full extent of the wetland area, exposing portions of the sites to continued use and impacts from horses/burros and recreation use.
- Fence type and maintenance – Two types of exclosure fences were observed and both illustrate certain advantages:

  - Metal t-posts and barbed wire are relatively low cost to install, but have high maintenance costs. Snow loading and pressure from horse and elk use reduce the serviceable life of these fences. Replacement cycles are approximately 10 years. Effectiveness of this design to exclude horse use is moderate to high. This design is not effective in prohibiting use by elk. This design is effective in reducing the effects of recreation use.
  - Post and wire rope fences have higher initial costs and lower overall maintenance costs. The exceptions are illustrated in locations like Willow Spring, where fence posts have been struck and broken by vehicles traveling along access roads. In absence of any damage from vehicles, the replacement cycles for these fences could approach 20-25 years. Sections of the fence were designed to facilitate access by elk. TWhen properly maintained, this design is highly effective in excluding horse use. When fences are not maintained, previous restration efforts can be affected when horses or burros access these sites, as in the case of the horse observed inside the Willow Springs exclosure during the 2011 IM Audit. Design features accommodate use by elk and therefore compromise the efficacy of spring protection, to the extent that elk are encouraged to enter the riparian area. This design is, however, highly effective in reducing the effects of recreation use.

  Other fence types being used include metal post/rail fences to manage recreation use at Cold Creek ponds and wooden rail/post fences. These fence types were not examined during the IM Audit.

- External water sources – These were not provided at West Mud Springs, creating continued pressure for wild horses/burros and elk to try to access the site for water and to a lesser extent forage and thermal relief. At Willow Creek, the lower portions of the creek provide water sources for recreation livestock and wild horses/burros. Access within the exclosure is provided for elk.
- Management of recreation use – This included the use of physical barriers (fencing, gates, and boulders) to control access points and routes. Willow Creek used a combination of all of these methods and interpretive signing. Sites at Mountain Springs employed a combination of boulders and route obliteration/restoration. Use at West Mud Springs is managed by re-routing trail use and the exclosure fence.
- Monitoring – Monitoring practices used and partnerships with Great Basin Institute are highly effective and provide a sound basis for making adaptive management decisions. The use of photo monitoring and frequency of monitoring are working well.

Table 3-8: Analysis and Evaluation of Monitoring Questions Related to Management Interactions (Cont.)

Monitoring Question 59 - Is recreation use or grazing by wild horses/burros or recreational livestock impacting bank stability?

Bank stability is not directly assessed in the protocol used at the spring/riparian sites. In addition, there are limited perennial streams, so there are limited stream banks to assess. Some information from the spring surveys that can be used to get a sense for the amount of disturbances to stream channels and stream banks are presented in Appendix D 4.3.

Disturbances noted as being present or absent during the 2010 and 2011 spring surveys by percentage of sites surveyed included:

- Animal Trails: 89% of sites.
- Channel Erosion: 55% of sites.
- Runout Channel Substantially Altered: 50% of sites.
- Flow Regulation Adversely Affects Site: 34% of sites.
- Herbivores Adversely Affects Site: 53% of sites.
- Recreation Uses Adversely Affects Site: 26% of sites

Monitoring Question 43 - Are P-J treatments being invaded by cheatgrass?

Will be audited in 2012. Invasive species inventories conducted in cooperation with the NPS also provide information to address this question.

- Insufficient data are available to generate findings.

Monitoring Question 56 - Are soil and water conservation practices being implemented and are they effective?

The 2010 IM Audit evaluated design features and mitigation measures used in the December 20, 2007 Spring Mountains Hazardous Fuels Reduction EA and decision documents. Review of the EA/DN and contract documents, in addition to on-site review of treatments in Kyle and Lee Canyons and along the Deer Creek Road, serve as the basis for the Audit's findings and recommendations.

The 2010 IM Audit evaluated the Letter of Delegation to the Incident Command Team and objectives established in the Wildland Fire Decision Support System for the Cathedral Wildland Fire regarding suppression strategies and techniques.

The 2011 IM Audit evaluated management activities to protect springs and riparian areas. The Audit evaluated decision and implementation documents for five projects, including fencing to limit access by elk, wild horses/burros, and recreationists; trail management; road/trail closures; and the use of signing.

Future IM Audits will also evaluate this question.

- Design measures for streambank protection in the 2007 Fuel Treatment EA were well described and effective.
- No soil erosion or sedimentation was observed during the 2010 Audit.
- Concerns regarding the movement of burn piles plugging drainage structures during high runoff events were experienced in the Mountain Springs area, but these situations were corrected and were not observed during the field portion of the Audit.
- Although the Cathedral wildland fire was outside of wilderness, MIST tactics used were effective. The amount of hand fireline was minimized by using the road systems in the picnic area as fire lines and burning out from those roads. In addition, limited amounts of fireline were constructed on the east side and top of the fire.
- Fencing and boulder protection is effective in limiting most access to springs and riparian areas. Monitoring and maintenance will be necessary to ensure continued effectiveness.
- Re-routing trails away from springs and providing off-site water for recreation stock is effective, and may also limit effects from elk and wild horses/burros.
- Visitor education, information, and signing are difficult to maintain and require constant attention.

Table 3-8: Analysis and Evaluation of Monitoring Questions Related to Management Interactions (Cont.)

Monitoring Question 57 - Are soil disturbing activities creating excessive sedimentation or soil loss?

The 2010 IM Audit evaluated design features and mitigation measures used in the December 20, 2007 Spring Mountains Hazardous Fuels Reduction EA and decision documents. Review of the EA/DN and contract documents, in addition to on-site review of treatments in Kyle and Lee Canyons and along the Deer Creek Road, serve as the basis for the Audit's findings and recommendations.

The 2010 IM Audit evaluated the Letter of Delegation to the Incident Command Team and objectives established in the Wildland Fire Decision Support System for the Cathedral Wildland Fire regarding suppression strategies and techniques.

The 2011 IM Audit evaluated management activities to protect springs and riparian areas. The Audit evaluated decision and implementation documents for five projects, including fencing to limit access by elk, wild horses/burros, and recreationists; trail management; road/trail closures; and the use of signing.

Future IM Audits will also evaluate this question.

Data from the spring surveys were used to evaluate sedimentation and soil loss (see Appendix D 4.2).

- The 2010 IM Audit concluded that the design measures for streambank protection were well described and effective.
- No soil erosion or sedimentation was observed during the field portion of the 2010 IM Audit.
- In the spring of 2010 burn piles in the Mountain Springs area were washed into and consequently plugged drainage structures (culverts) but the location of burn piles in future treatments were planned to avoid these kinds of problems. This adjustment was observed during the field portion of the 2010 IM Audit.
- The 2010 IM Audit noted that although the Cathedral fire was outside wilderness, MIST tactics used were effective. The amount of hand fireline was minimized by using the road systems in the picnic area as fire lines and burning out from those roads. In addition, limited amounts of fireline were constructed on the east side and top of the fire.
- The 2011 IM Audit noted that fencing and boulder protection are effective in limiting most access to springs and riparian areas and reducing soil erosion and sedimentation. Monitoring and maintenance will be necessary to ensure continued effectiveness.
- The 2011 IM Audit also observed that re-routing trails away from springs and providing off-site water for recreation stock is effective, and may also limit effects from elk and wild horses/burros and resulting soil erosion and sedimetnation.
- A number of "disturbances" related to soil alteration were noted at the spring sites, such as trampling, trails, excavation and other ground disturbance. Of the springs inventoried in 2010 and 2011 the following disturbances were noted as being present or absent, by percentage sites surveyed:
  - Trails & Tracks: 89% of sites.
  - Erosion: 55% of sites.
  - Soil Integrity Altered: 49% of sites.
  - Excavation or Other Ground Disturbance: 47% of sites
  - Landform Stability Altered: 38% of sites.
  - Recreational Uses Adversely Affecting Site: 26% of sites.
  - Construction and Roads Adversely Affecting Site: 15% of sites.
  - Deposition: 13% of sites.
  - Bare Ground (%): averaged 11% cover for all sites.

Monitoring Question 55 - How are management actions and human uses affecting water quality and quantity?

Data on water quality are presented in the table below and additional detail is presented in Appendix D 3.2. The relationship between management actions and water quality conditions of springs cannot be assessed without a more rigorous study design.

Attribute	Minimum	Median	Average	Maximum	Sites Measured
Temperature (centigrade)	3.0	11.2	11.36	19.5	n=43
pH	6.5	7.45	7.5	8.6	n=45
Specific Conductance (microsiemens/centimeter)	136	496	550	1011	n=43
Oxygen-reduction potential (mV)	-33.2	123.2	105.5	221.9	n=25
Dissolved oxygen (mg/L)	2.3	5 5	5.4	9.7	n=25

Analysis of these data will be provided in the 2012 Annual Report.

Table 3-8: Analysis and Evaluation of Monitoring Questions Related to Management Interactions (Cont.)

Monitoring Question 41 - What are the most effective methods of treatment of high priority invasive species? Are there specific thresholds of infestations at which treatments are no longer effective?
Will be audited in 2012.   • Insufficient data are available to generate findings.

IM Audits are conducted with the purpose of determining whether design measures and mitigation practices have been implemented and to evaluate their effectiveness. The 2010 IM Audit focused on the effects of wildland fire suppression and restoration and mechanical treatment of hazardous fuel. Many of the findings and recommendations generated during the IM Audit had direct application to future hazardous fuel treatments and wildland fire suppression and restoration actions. The 2011 IM Audit focused on management of recreation uses, including OHV and their effects on springs as well as spring/riparian protection measures. The results of this IM Audit were used to develop a management response framework that can be used to evaluate the need for and design of future proposals. Appendix E includes the management response frameworks developed as a result of these IM Audits.

Studies designed to assess pre- and post-treatment effects from hazardous fuel treatments were initiated. However, data on post treatment conditions are not currently funded or scheduled for collection.

4. Conclusions/Need for Change

Long-term conservation of species and their habitats within the SMNRA requires an adaptive approach based on a combination of quantitative data and qualitative information. Ecosystems and management interactions are composed of dynamic and complex interactions occurring at different temporal and spatial scales. Managers cannot accurately predict the interplay of all of these factors and must rely on continual monitoring and adaptive feedback to achieve conservation goals and outcomes.

Management adaptations originate from multiple information sources and often require adjustments to a variety of plans, programs and activities. Analysis and evaluation of the results described in the previous section serve as the basis for identifying potential changes. The following recommendations have been identified.

a. Need for Change in Forest Plan Direction

1. Monitoring Program Update

The GMP and Forest Plan contain monitoring items for species conservation and other management objectives. When these requirements were identified and incorporated into the GMP and Forest Plan, the focus of species conservation was linked to the concept of "biodiversity hotspots." This conceptual approach has major limitations. When the distribution of a species is unknown (a limitation for most SMNRA CA species), the design of the "biodiversity hotspot" model will not provide the data to fill this critical knowledge gap, and the data from hotspot sampling do not have the power to predict changes in the status of the species across the SMNRA. Preserving the genetic diversity of a species requires a larger area than is contained in most "hotspots" (Raphael and Molina 2007). In addition, some species included in the monitoring program no longer warrant monitoring based on their status as documented in the 5-year evaluation of the CA (US Forest Service (USFS), Intermountain Region, 2003). Other species' status has changed and the plan's monitoring program has not been updated or amended to reflect status changes.

The revised planning regulations (36 CFR 219) include provisions that require the plan monitoring program to be in place within 4 years of the effective date for the new rule or in April 2016.

> "Timing and process for developing the plan monitoring program and broader-scale strategies. (1) The responsible official shall develop the plan monitoring program as part of the planning process for a new plan development or plan revision. Where a plan's monitoring program has been developed under the provisions of a prior planning regulation and the unit has not initiated plan revision under this part, the responsible official shall modify the plan monitoring program within 4 years of the effective date of this part, or as soon as practicable, to meet the requirements of this section. " [36CFR219.12 (c)]

Unlike the 1982 planning rule, the language in 36 CFR 219.12 does not require an amendment of the Forest Plan/GMP to implement these changes [see 36 CFR 219.12 (a)(2)]. The final year of the I&M program will conclude in 2014, providing a basis for describing an updated monitoring program meeting the requirements of the new planning rule.

Recommendation: Update the SMNRA monitoring plan pursuant to revised 36 CFR 219.12 to eliminate species-specific requirements and replace monitoring items with a combination of continued implementation of successive rounds of the comprehensive program described in the SMNRA I&M Strategy for Conserving Biological Diversity (USDA Forest Service, 2008b) and the use of statistically valid species-specific survey designs based on projected species ranges in the potential habitat model or habitat characteristics models. Remove monitoring items that (1) repeat existing agency policy requirements, (2) are achieved by established agency reporting programs, and (3) are the responsibility of other agencies or entities.

2. Consolidated Forest Plan Direction

Direction and requirements established in The Toiyabe Forest Plan as amended by the General Management Plan (GMP) are not consistently understood or accurately interpreted by SMNRA and Forest Staff. Several NEPA documents reviewed during the IM Audits referenced direction in the GMP, but failed to incorporate or discuss direction in the Toiyabe Forest Plan applicable to the proposed action. In some instances, references were made to statements in programmatic agreements such as the Conservation Agreement or Landscape Assessment as constituting management direction or requirements. In summary, discussions with SMNRA and Forest staff during the 2010 and 2011 IM Audits identified a number of different aspects regarding inconsistent interpretations:

- **The relationship of the amendment (GMP) to the Toiyabe Forest Plan** - The SMNRA General Management Plan (Amendment # 4) and the Toiyabe Forest Plan set the management direction for the SMNRA. The GMP cannot be used as a stand-alone document and does not change some objectives, standards and guidelines, and monitoring requirements established at the Forest level.

- **The relationship of the GMP/Forest Plan and programmatic agreements and assessments** - The SMNRA landscape assessment and the Conservation Agreement are intended to coordinate priorities across program areas to achieve species conservation goals. They are not management direction but program coordination documents and expressions of management intent. In both cases, some direction from the GMP is repeated rather than using the GMP/Forest Plan as a reference. It also appears that, in developing these program agreements, some direction from the Toiyabe Forest Plan is not referenced or considered. Therefore, the foundation of these agreements may not fully consider applicable Forest Plan direction and, if interpreted as "direction," may diverge from the GMP/Forest Plan without an appropriate amendment or revision to the Forest Plan.

Recommendation: Develop a consolidated version of the Forest Plan direction that applies to the SMNRA that assembles the combined direction from the GMP and Toiyabe Forest Plan. Review the Landscape Assessment using the consolidated Forest Plan direction to determine if any management requirements were inadvertently omitted. Ensure all project proposals and NEPA documentation reference applicable direction in both the GMP and Toiyabe Forest Plan.

b. Need for Change in the Conservation Agreement

The Conservation Agreement (CA) is presently under revision. As a result, draft recommendations presented to SMNRA and Humboldt-Toiyabe Forest staff are not repeated here. These recommendations, which are being addressed as part of the revision process include:

- Ensuring consistenty with Forest Service policy and procedural changes resulting from recent revisions of the land management planning regulation (36 CFR 219.9 and 219.12)

- Eliminating repetition of and detail in the Conservation Strategy supporting the Conservation Agreement of statements in the Forest Plan and GMP. (see Section 4 b-2)

c. Changes in Management Activities or Programs

Monitoring and evaluation provides valuable information that can be used to modify ongoing and future activities and programs. The following recommendations were identified based on the findings in Section 3:

1. Develop and Apply Best Practices Specific to the SMNRA

Review of management actions during the 2010 and 2011 IM Audits identified three areas of concern:

- Inconsistent interpretation or incomplete references to the Forest Plan/GMP in framing the purpose and need for project proposals. Use of consolidated management direction (see Section 4a-2) will help streamline the development and analysis of future proposals.

- The analysis and assessment provided in the SMNRA Landscape Assessment as a starting point for framing programs and projects by was often discounted and, in some instances, ignored because it is not viewed as being "current", "binding" or "relevant" for a variety of reasons . The role of assessments under the revised planning rule is emphasized as a basis for both land management and project planning.

- Similar situations have, over time, resulted in a variety of management approaches and project design measures. The purpose of the IM Auidts is to assist with organizational learning and application of "lessons learned" from management action. Use of a consistent framework over time provides managers the ability to practice adaptive management and improve effectiveness by applying information gathered through monitoring programs and a critical evaluation of management design measures and their effectiveness in similar situations.

Recommendation: Once the Landscape Assessment has been reviewed and a determination made regarding consistency with Forest Plan and GMP management direction as described in Section 4 a-2, use the desired outcomes and program objectives resulting from this assessment to guide development of project proposals and resource management programs.

Recommendation: Adopt and apply a consistent management response framework for identifying and designing proposed management actions. Apply the management response frameworks described in Appendix E developed during the 2010 and 2011 IM Audits to ongoing projects and future project proposals. Improve these design features and mitigation practices and the management framework over time.

2. Adapt Program Priorities and Actions based on New Information or Changed Conditions

Adaptive management requires a response to new information and science developed in the Southern Nevada Area Partnership (SNAP), research, and inventory and monitoring programs. This adaptation includes the cessation of management actions and monitoring activities no longer warranted, based on best available science. This information also points to a change in spatial focus of conservation efforts, which has traditionally been limited to the developed east-side canyons based on using the "biodiversity hotspots" concept in the late 1990's, which has been demonstrated to have little utility in large area conservation efforts.

In some cases, the initiation of management actions based on improved understanding of CA Species and how they interact with habitats within the SMNRA is warranted. The "need" for action in a NEPA context is triggered by this new information or changed circumstances. Agency guidance and procedures for consideration of new information is described in FSH 1909.15. Two examples of the need for adaptation and response in management practices include:

- Information on the limited extent and species differentiation of Spring Mountains Dark Blue Butterfly (petitioned for listing under ESA) and host species in the West Mud Springs/Cold Creek/Willow Springs portion of the SMNRA indicates the potential need for action to avoid disruption of these species/sub-species during egg-laying periods.

- Information resulting from the genetic analysis of Palmer's chipmunk reveals the presence of a healthy and robust population. Direction in the Toyiabe Forest Plan and GMP, including standards and guidelines and monitoring requirements were established with assumptions regarding this species' status should be revisited.

Recommendation: Concerns regarding the effectiveness of OHV management practices and their enforcement in this same area were identified during the 2011 IM Audit and recommended actions that can be linked to Spring Mountains Dark Blue Butterfly and watershed and spring protection measures were described in the 2011 IM Audit report (see Appendix E-4).

Recommendation: Review standards and guidelines, as well as mitigation measures in the GMP developed for Palmer's chipmunk, to determine if they are needed given new information about the population status. Use information presented in this report to support project-specific amendments to Forest Plan direction related to Palmer's chipmunk (e.g. GMP Standard 0.91).

d. Changes in the Monitoring and Evaluation Program

As with other aspects of the management approach for species conservation in the SMNRA, monitoring and evaluation programs must also be evaluated to determine whether the monitoring components and focus need to be changed. Given the complexity of the SMNRA inventory and monitoring program, these changes are anticipated to originate from a combination of implementation experience, changed conditions and information, and management determination that monitoring is no longer warranted or that new monitoring questions need to be addressed.

The following recommendations for change in the monitoring and evaluation program were identified based on an evaluation of legacy data sets and data collected during 2010 and 2011. A detailed review of the Forest Plan and GMP has also identified that some monitoring requirements, previously thought to apply to the SMNRA, do not apply and should be eliminated from the monitoring questions included in the monitoring program.

1. Drop or Modify Monitoring Questions

Monitoring questions identified and priorities established in the SMNRA Inventory and Monitoring Strategy (USDA Forest Service 2008b) were recognized as being subject to modification or elimination over time. Following two years of monitoring and evaluation, it is apparent that several questions need to be dropped from the I&M program.

Recommendation: Several monitoring questions either no longer warrant consideration for monitoring or warrant modification based on a variety of rationales. Supporting rationales for dropping individual monitoring questions are summarized in Table 4-2. Table 4.3 describes modifications to monitoring questions and supporting rationale.

Table 4-2: Monitoring Questions to be Dropped and Supporting Rationale

MQ 18 – What are the direct and cumulative effects of woodcutting and gathering on CA Species and their habitats?
• This question originated from concerns with the effects of woodcutting and gathering on Palmer's chipmunk, which has now been determined to have a self-sustaining and healthy population within the SMNRA. • Prohibitions on woodcutting in the developed canyons, and restrictions within the SMNRA, have been implemented. Monitoring of the effectiveness of prohibitions and restrictions should rely on a review of law enforcement records in the LEMARS database to determine if monitoring is needed. • If it is determined that monitoring is warranted, it should focus on the site disturbance and soil erosion potential associated with woodcutting/gathering.
MQ 26 – How many snags per acre are present in mixed conifer, riparian areas, and in P-J?
• This Forest Plan monitoring requirement does not apply to NFS lands within the SMNRA because they have been "reserved for timber production" by Congress and are not considered "available productive (capable) Forest land" (GMP, Page 1 and Appendix C). GMP.
MQ 27 - What percentage of mixed conifer is old growth habitat?
• This Forest Plan monitoring requirement does not apply to NFS lands within the SMNRA because they have been "reserved for timber production" by Congress and are not considered "available productive (capable) Forest land" (GMP, Page 1 and Appendix C). GMP.
MQ 42 – What role should wildland fire play in areas with invasive plant species? What are the consequences and threats by invasive species that typically follow fire such as cheatgrass in lower elevations? **MQ 37 – What is the rate of wildfire recovery on burned species? Is there a difference in recovery time for high vs. low intensity?**
• Information relative to both monitoring questions is being developed as part of the Fire Surrogate Studies supported by the Joint Fire Sciences Program. Studies specific to the Humboldt-Toiyabe National Forest are being conducted with results published by Rocky Mountain Research Station scientists located at the Reno Laboratory. • The RMRS Fire Modeling Institute maintains the Fire Effects Information System, which is a database containing the best available information and science regarding fire effects to vegetation, soils, hydrology and other resources.
MQ 23 – What are the effects of air quality on vegetation?
• Information collected as part of the FIA inventory will provide a baseline for evaluating this question relative to ozone damage, but the question is best evaluated as part of a specific research project.
MQ 44 – What are the consequences of climate change and drought on CA Species and their habitats?
• Climate change models produce data that is best used to assess the direction of community change (Rehfelt, 2006). Due to the large number of variables used to compute climate models, the data is much less useful for predicting fine scale results, e.g. individual species response to climate change. There are some generalizations with regard to the life history features of species that relate to climate change and detailed individual species studies might provide some insight.

Table 4-3: Monitoring Questions to be Modified and Supporting Rationale

MQ 28 – What is the average number of downed woody logs per acre?
• GMP standard 0.37 requires a minimum of 50 linear feet/acre of downed trees with a minimum 12-inch diameter on sites being managed for late seral stage of the Pinyon/Juniper and Mixed Conifer Land Type Associations to provide ground cover for small mammals, amphibians, reptiles, and invertebrates. GMP standard 0.91 addresses this standard within areas being managed as shaded fuelbreaks. • This monitoring question should be revised to reflect the requirements of GMP standards 0.37 and 0.91. (See Appendix C -2.4)

2. Species-Specific Survey and Monitoring Design

The role of individual or multiple species surveys is crucial in addressing overarching questions on CA Species occurrence, trend, and status, as well as in practicing adaptive management designed to protect and conserve CA Species. Equally important is that these surveys be conducted within a framework that allows for the development of information of sufficient data quality to identify and support change in management. Rather than de-emphasizing individual species monitoring, in later phases of the program it may be necessary to increase the amount of effort devoted to these surveys.

Review of species-specific survey design and reports conducted within the SMNRA (Pendleton 2012b) has identified a number of concerns related to data quality and quality assurance associated with the data resulting from these surveys. Of primary concern is the ability to apply information derived from these studies to other potential habitats within the SMNRA as well as other locations.

Recommendation: Species-specific survey and monitoring design should be framed using maps of potential habitat to define survey boundaries and establish sampling intensity and location. Protocols for sampling within potential habitats should utilize standardized, published methodologies for collecting data and, when possible, use methodologies consistent with national Forest Service inventory and monitoring protocols. Quality control and assurance procedures should be described and information on data quality and QA/QC included in the metadata for specific survey reports and entries into NRM-NRIS or local data systems (e.g., ArcView files).

3. Improved Inventory and Monitoring Program Coordination

Numerous inventory and monitoring projects or activities by multiple entities are occurring within the SMNRA. All research projects should have a permit and study plan on file with the SMNRA. In some instances, activities may be occurring without proper authorization or approval (e.g., special use permit or cooperative agreement).

Activities within Wilderness must be authorized consistent with establishment legislation and Wilderness management plans. Similarly, activities within the Carpenter Creek Research Natural Area must be coordinated with and approved by the Director of the Rocky Mountain Research Station.

Research needs are coordinated and monitored through the Southern Nevada Agency Partnership (SNAP). There is no equivalent process to review proposals, coordinate efforts, and apply results of inventory and monitoring conducted outside the scope of the SMNRA I&M Strategy. The current system for issuing permits and tracking research activities within the SMNRA, including all research activities funded by federal, state and local agencies, is not adequate to ensure that information gathered by research projects enters the I&M data stream.

Recommendations: Although these recommendations were made in the 2010 Monitoring and Evaluation Report, they have not been implemented. The need to ensure capture of information on species inventory and monitoring in the SMNRA is becoming more critical as financial resources supporting these efforts become more restricted.

a) Investigate approaches to improve coordination of inventory and monitoring activities within the SMNRA, including data capture and application. Processes used by the USFWS and FS can be used as models for improving the research tracking abilities of the SMNRA.

b) Ensure appropriate authorizations or approvals are in place for inventory and monitoring activities. In particular, inventory and monitoring activities within Wilderness must be authorized as consistent with establishment legislation and employ minimum impact techniques (see FSM 2324.42). A national agreement between FIA and the NFS addresses requirements for conducting this inventory within Wilderness and the SMNRA intensified FIA program is consistent with these requirements.

c) Ensure activities within the Carpenter Creek Research Natural Area, but outside of wildernes, are reviewed and approved by the Director of the Rocky Mountain Research Station. For activities within the wilderness, approval by the Station Director is not mandatory, however notification should be made.

Literature Cited

Anderson, D.C. 1998. Distribution of Clokey's eggvetch (*Astragalus ooporus* var. *clokeyanus*) on the Nevada Test Site. Las Vegas: Bechtel Nevada, prepared for the U.S. Department of Energy under contract DE-AC08-96NV11718.

Boyd, B.M. 2005. *Speyeria carolae*: Study in the Spring Mountains, Clark County, Nevada 2004-2005. Unpublished report submitted to the U.S. Forest Service, Spring Mountains National Recreation Area, Clark and Nye Counties, Nevada. 10 p.

Boyd, B.M. and Austin, G.T. 1999. Final Report on butterfly investigations in the Spring Mountains, Nevada, 1998, and a proposed monitoring program for endemic species. Unpublished report submitted to U.S. Forest Service, Spring Mountains National Recreation Area, Las Vegas, Nevada. 94 p.

Boyd, B.M.; Austin, G.T. and Boyd, B.M. **2000**. Report on butterfly investigations in the Spring Mountains, Nevada, 1999. Unpublished report submitted to the U.S. Forest Service, Spring Mountains National Recreation Area, Las Vegas, Nevada. 36 p.

Boyd, B.M. and Murphy, D. **2008**. A Report on the Status of the Mount Charleston Blue Butterfly and its Essential Resources at and Adjacent to the Las Vegas Ski and Snowboard Resort—2008 Unpublished report submitted to the Las Vegas Ski and Snowboard Resort, Las Vegas, Nevada.

Breshears, D.D.; Cobb, N.S.; Rich, P.M.; Price, K.P.; Allen, C.D.; Balice, R.G.; Romme, W.H.; Kastens, J.H.; Floyd, M.L.; Belnap, J.; Anderson, J.J.; Myers, O.B.; Meyer, C.W. 2005. Regional vegetation die-off in response to global-change-type drought. Proceedings of the National Academy of Sciences. 102(42): 15144-15148. www.pnas.org/cgi/doi/10.1073/pnas.0505734102

Breshears, D.D.; Myers, B.M.; Meyer, C.W.; Barnes, F.J.; Zou, C.B.; Allen, C.D.; McDowell, N.G. and Pockman, W.T. 2009. Tree die-off in response to global change-type drought: mortality insights from a decade of plant water potential measurements. Frontiers in Ecology and Environment. 7: 185-189.

Bureau of Land Management (BLM). 2011. Bureau of Land Management National Wild Horse and Burro Program. http://www.blm.gov/wo/st/en/prog/wild_horse_and_burro.html

Chambers, J.C.; McArthur, E.D.; Monson, S.B.; Meyer, S.E.; Shaw, N.L.; Tausch, R.J.; Blank, R.R.; Bunting, S.; Miller, R.R.; Pellant, M.; Roundy, Bruce A.; Walker, Scott C.; Whittaker, Alison. 2005. Sagebrush steppe and pinyon-juniper ecosystems: effects of changing fire regimes, increased fuel loads, and invasive species. Joint Fire Sciences Report. Project #00-1-1-03. 66 p. http://www.treesearch.fs.fed.us/pubs/23523

Christensen, G.C. 1996. Chuckar (*Alectoris chucker*). The Birds of North America Online (A. Poole, Ed.) Ithica, N.Y.: Cornell Lab of ornithology. http://bna.birds.cornell.edu/bna/species/258/articles/introduction

Clark County, Nevada. 2008. Adaptive management report for the Clark County, Nevada multiple species habitat conservation plan. Department of Air Quality and Environmental Management, Desert Conservation Program, Las Vegas, Nevada. 132 p. plus appendices. http://www.clarkcountynv.gov/Depts/eco_county/Documents/HabitatSpeciesConservationPlan.pdf

Clokey, I.W. 1951. Flora of the Charleston Mountains, Clark County, Nevada. Berekley, CA: University of California Press: 274 p.

Cole, A.C. 1956. Studies of Nevada Ants. II. A New Species of *Lasius* (*Chthonolasius*) (*Hymenoptera: Formicidae*). Journal of the Tennessee Academy of Science. 31(1): 26-27.

Cummings, P. 2010. Units 261-268: Clark and Southern Nye Counties. In: Nevada Department of Wildlife: 2009-2010 Big game status. p 24. http://www.ndow.org/about/pubs/reports/10_bg_status.pdf

ENTRIX, Inc. 2008. Spring Mountains National Recreation Area Landscape Analysis. Unpublished report submitted to the U.S. Department of Agriculture, Forest Service, Humboldt-Toiyabe National Forest, Las Vegas, Nevada.

Esque, T.C.; Inman, R.; Prentice, K.L.; Lund, C.L.; Drake, K.K. and Thomas, K.A. 2009. Blackbrush and fire: Regional assessment of recent losses in Nevada and California. Eastern Nevada Landscape Coalition. Nevada. Unpublished poster presentation.

Federal Geographic Data Committee (FGDC). 2011. National Vegetation Classification Standard http://www.fgdc.gov/standards/projects/FGDC-standards-projects

Glenne, G. 2003. Humboldt-Toiyabe National Forest Spring Mountains National Recreation Area weeds guide. Unpublished document in U.S. Forest Service files.

Harvell, C.D.; Mitchell, C.E.; Ward, J.R.; Altizer, S.; Dobson, A.P.; Ostfeld, R.S. and Samuel, M.D. 2002. Climate warming and disease risks for terrestrial and marine biota. Science. 296: 2158-2162.

Howell, C. 2011. Humboldt-Toiyabe National Forest Climate Change Vulnerability Report: April 2011. Unpublished document in U.S. Forest Service files. 17 p.

Hurja, James. 2011. Personal communication.

Hurja, James. 2012. Personal communication.

International Organization for Standardization (ISO). 2007. Environmental Management. http://www.iso.org/iso/iso_14000_essentials

Loarie, S.R.; Duffy, P.B.; Hamilton, H.; Asner, G.P.; Field, D.B. and Ackerly, D.D. 2009. The velocity of climate change. Nature. 462: 1052-1055.

Manning, M.E. and Padgett, W.G. 1995. Riparian community type classification for Humboldt and Toiyabe National Forests, Nevada and eastern California. Ogden, UT: U.S. Department of Agriculture, Forest Service, Intermountain Region.

McKelvey, K.S.; Ramirez, J.E.; Schwartz, M.K.; Pilgrim, K. 2012. Genetic sampling of Palmer's chipmunks in the Spring Mountains, Nevada: report on sampling 2010-2011. Unpublished report, U.S. Department of Agriculture, Forest Service, Rocky Mountain Research Station. 14 p.

METI, Inc. 2011. Implementation and monitoring audit report: mechanical hazardous fuel treatments and wildland fire suppression and restoration. Management and Engineering Technologies International, Inc., El Paso, Texas. Unpublished report submitted to the Spring Mountains National Recreation Area. 26 p.

METI, Inc. 2012. Implementation and monitoring audit report: recreation (OHV) management and springs/riparian management. Management and Engineering Technologies International, Inc., El Paso, Texas. Unpublished report submitted to the Spring Mountains National Recreation Area. 31 p, plus appendices.

Nachlinger, J. 2000a. Biological monitoring plan for three high elevation plant communities on the Humboldt-Toiyabe National Forest, Spring Mountains National Recreation Area. The Nature Conservancy, Northern Nevada Office, Reno, NV. Unpublished report on file with the U.S. Fish and Wildlife Service, Las Vegas, Nevada and with the U.S. Department of Agriculture, Forest Service, Humboldt-Toiyabe National Forest, Spring Mountains National Recreation Area, Las Vegas, Nevada. 27 p.

Nachlinger, J. 2000b. Baseline 1998-1999 biological monitoring report for alpine herbaceous, bristlecone pine woodland, and riparian spring-fed high elevation plant communities. Humboldt-Toiyabe National Forest, Spring Mountains National Recreation Area. The Nature Conservancy, Northern Nevada Office, Reno, NV. Unpublished report on file with the U.S. Fish and Wildlife Service, Las Vegas, Nevada and with the U.S. Department of Agriculture, Forest Service, Spring Mountains National Recreation Area, Las Vegas, Nevada.

Nachlinger, J. and Combs, J. 1996a. Biological Monitoring Plan for *Angelica scabrida* (rough angelica) on the Toiyave National Forest, Spring Mountains National recreation Area. The Nature Conservancy, Northern Nevada Office, Reno, Nevada. 15 p plus appendices.

Nachlinger, J. and Combs, J. 1996b. Biological Monitoring Plan for *Astragalus oophorus* var. *clokeyanus* (Clokey eggvetch) on the Toiyabe National Forest, Spring Mountains National Recreation Area. The Nature Conservancy, Northern Nevada Office, Reno, Nevada.

Nachlinger, J. and Reese, G.A. 1996. Plant community classification of the Spring Mountains National Recreation Area, Clark and Nye Counties, Nevada. The Nature Conservancy, Northern Nevada Office, Reno, Nevada. Submitted to the U.S. Department of Agriculture, Forest Service, Humboldt-Toiyabe National Forest, Spring Mountains National Recreation Area, Las Vegas, Nevada.

NDOW 2011. Unit 262: Spring Mountains; Clark and Southern Nye Counties. In: Nevada Department of Wildlife: 2010-2011 Big game status. p 60-61. www.ndow.org/about/pubs/reports/2011_bg_status.pdf

Pendleton, B.K. 2010. Resolving the status of the Charleston ant (*Lasius nevadensis*);a report from the Charleston ant safari July–August 2009. Report submitted to the U.S. Department of Agriculture, Forest Service, Spring Mountains Recreation Area, Las Vegas, Nevada. January 2010.

Pendleton, B.K. 2012a. Resolving the status of the Charleston ant; a report from the first three years of the Charleston ant safari. An unpublished report submitted to the U.S. Department of Agriculture, Forest Service, Spring Mountains National Recreation Area, Las Vegas, Nevada.

Pendleton, B.K. 2012b. An Evaluation of the long-term studies, 1996-2006, Spring Mountains National Recreation Area. Unpublished report submitted to the U.S. Department of Agriculture, Forest Service, Spring Mountains National Recreation Area, Las Vegas, Nevada.

Provencher, L. 2008. Fire Regime Condition Class Mapping for the Spring Mountains Southern Nevada. Draft Report to the U.S. Forest Service, Spring Mountains National Recreation Area. Soliciation AG-9360-S-08-004.The Nature Conservancy of Nevada , Reno, Nevada. U.S. Department of Agriculture, Forest Service. 333 p.

Public Law 102-63. 1993. Organic Act for the SMNRA. Spring Mountains National Recreation Area Act. August 4, 1993. p. 697-700. http://www.gpo.gov/fdsys/pkg/USCODE-1996-title16/pdf/USCODE-1996-title16-chap1.pdf

Raphael, M.G.; Molina, R. 2007. Conservation of Rare or Little-Known Species: biological, social, and economic considerations. Island Press, Washington, DC. 375 p.

Rau, B.M.; Tausch, R.; Reiner, A.; Johnson, D.W.; Chambers, J.C.; Blank, R.R. 2012. Developing a model framework for predicting effects of woody expansion and fire on ecosystem carbon and nitrogen in a pinyon-juniper woodland. Journal of Arid Environments. 76: 97-104.

Rehfeldt, G.E.; Crookston, N.L.; Warwell, M.V. and Evans, J.S. 2006. Empirical analyses of plant-climate relationships for the western United States. International Journal of Plant Science. 167: 1123-1150.

Resource Concepts, Inc. 2005. Nevada Community Wildfire Risk/Hazard Assessment Project: Clark County. Prepared for: The Nevada Fire Safe Council, Carson City, Nevada. http://www.rci-nv.com/reports/clark/index.html

Smith, F.J. 2001. Current knowledge and conservation status of *Astragalus oophorus* var. *clokeyanus* Barneby (Fabaceae), the Clokey eggvetch. Report prepared for Nevada Natural Heritage Program, Carson City, Nevada, and U. S. Fish and Wildlife Service, Reno, Nevada. 33p plus appendices.

Smith, M.D.; Knapp, A.K. and Collins, S.L. 2009. A framework for assessing ecosystem dynamics in response to chronic resource alterations induced by global change. Ecology. 90(12): 3279-3289. http://www.esajournals.org/doi/pdf/10.1890/08-1815.1

Solem, S. J.; Pendleton, B. K.; Coles-Ritchie, M.; Ledbetter, J.; McKelvey, K.S.; Berg, J.; Nelson, K. and Menlove, J. 2011. 2010 Annual Report: Monitoring and evaluation for conserving biological resources of the Spring Mountains National Recreation Area. El Paso, TX: Management and Engineering Technologies International, Inc. (METI) and Albuquerque, NM: U.S. Department of Agriculture, Forest Service, Rocky Mountain Research Station. 117 p.

Thompson, D.; Garrett, P. and Stephen, H. 2011. Final Report. Butterfly Autecology Study–Spring Mountains National Recreation Area, Nevada. Unpublished report submitted to the U.S. Forest Service, Springs Mountains National Recreation Area, Las Vegas, Nevada. 73p.

Tousignant, M.-Ê.; Pellerin, S. and Brisson, J. 2010. The relative impact of human disturbances on the vegetation of a large wetland complex. Wetlands. 30: 333-344.

USDA Forest Service (USFS). 1986. Toiyabe National Forest land and resource management plan. Ogden, UT: U.S. Department of Agriculture, Forest Service, Intermountain Region.

USDA Forest Service (USFS). 1996. General management plan for the Spring Mountains National Recreation Area: An amendment to the land and resource management plan, Toiyabe National Forest. Ogden, UT: U.S. Department of Agriculture, Forest Service, Intermountain Region. 75 p.

USDA Forest Service (USFS). 1997. Properly Functioning Condition: Rapid Assessment Process (including the Properly Functioning Condition Assessment for the Utah High Plateaus and Mountain Section); September 8, 1997. Ogden, UT: Intermountain Region. 71 p.

USDA Forest Service (USFS). 1998. Conservation agreement for the Spring Mountains National Recreation Area, Clark and Nye Counties, Nevada. U.S. Forest Service, Intermountain Region; State of Nevada, Department of Conservation and Natural Resources; and U.S. Fish and Wildlife Service, Pacific Region.

USDA Forest Service (USFS). 2003. Conservation Agreement Report and Five-year Analyses for the Spring Mountains National Recreation Area, Clark and Nye Counties, Nevada. U.S. Forest Service, Intermountain Region; State of Nevada, Department of Conservation and Natural Resources; and U.S. Fish and Wildlife Service, Pacific Region.

USDA Forest Service (USFS). 2008a. Threatened, endangered and sensitive plants element occurrence field guide. Washington D.C.: U.S. Department of Agriculture, Forest Service, Rangeland Management Staff. 49 p.

USDA Forest Service (USFS). 2008b. Comprehensive inventory and monitoring strategy for conserving biological resources of the Spring Mountains National Recreation Area. El Paso, Texas: Management and Engineering Technologies International, Inc. (METI) and Albuquerque, New Mexico: U.S. Department of Agriculture, Forest Service, Rocky Mountain Research Station. 125 p.

USDA Forest Service (USFS). 2009. Humboldt-Toiyabe National Forest Motorized Vehicle Use Map. Spring Mountains National Recreation Area. U.S. Department of Agriculture, Forest Service. http://www.fs.usda.gov/detailfull/htnf/home/?cid=stelprdb5246242&width=full http://www.fs.usda.gov/Internet/FSE_DOCUMENTS/stelprdb5246285.pdf http://www.fs.usda.gov/Internet/FSE_DOCUMENTS/stelprdb5246284.pdf

USDA Forest Service (USFS). 2010. Forest inventory and analysis national core field guide, Volume 1: Field data collection procedures for phase 2 plots: Version 5.0. U.S. Department of Agriculture, Forest Service, Northern Research Station. On line at: http://www.fia.fs.fed.us/library/field-guides-methods-proc/docs/Complete%20FG%20Document/NRS%20FG%205.0-Oct%202010-Complete%20Document.pdf

USDA Forest Service (USFS). 2011a. Conservation Agreement and Strategy for the Spring Mountains National Recreation Area, Clark and Nye counties, Nevada (2/28/11 Draft). U.S. Department of Agriculture, Forest Service, Intermountain Region; State of Nevada, Department of Conservation and Natural Resources; and U.S. Fish and Wildlife Service, Pacific Region.

USDA Forest Service (USFS). 2011b Spring Mountains Multi-Jurisdictional Fuel Reduction and Wildfire Protection Strategy. U.S. Department of Agriculture, Forest Service; Bureau of Land Management; Nevada Division of Forestry; Nevada Division of State Lands; Nevada Fire Safe Council; Clark County Fire Department; Nye County Fire Department; and Pahrump Valley Fire Department.

USDA Forest Service (USFS). 2012 Groundwater-dependent ecosystems: Level II inventory field guide: Inventory methods for project design and analysis. General Technical Report WO-86b. Washington, DC: U.S. Department of Agriculture, Forest Service.
http://www.fs.fed.us/geology/GDE_Level_II_FG_final_March2012.pdf

Walker, K.C. 2005. 2005 Biological Monitoring Report for Angelica scabrida on the Humboldt-Toiyabe National Forest Spring Mountains National Recreation Area. Unpublished report for the Humboldt-Toiyabe National Forest, Spring Mountains National Recreation Area, Las Vegas, Nevada. 11 p. plus appendices.

Weiss, S.B.; Weiss, A.D.; Murphy, D.D. and Austin, G.T. 1997. Final Report on Endemic Butterflies of the Spring Mountains. Unpublished report submitted to the U.S. Fish and Wildlife Service, Nevada State Office, Reno, NV. 90 p.

Appendices - Monitoring Observation and Analysis Reports

Appendix A – Monitoring Questions and Priorities
Appendix B – CA Species Fact Sheets and Potential Habitat
Appendix C – Forest Inventory and Analysis Report Tables
Appendix D – Springs Inventory Data Reports
Appendix E – Management Response Frameworks

Question Number	Priority Group A – Resiliency to Wildland Fire
29	How does current wildland fire management affect CA Species[5] and habitats compared to historical fire patterns? What are the consequences of wildland fire on CA Species and their habitats?
31	How effective are design features and mitigation measures associated with mechanical fuels treatments in protecting/conserving CA Species habitats?
32	What are the effects (positive/negative) on CA Species habitats from mechanical fuel treatments?
35	What effects has wildland fire had on the conditions in key CA Species habitats and should these and other areas be protected from wildland fire?
36	What actions can be taken to reduce wildland fire occurrences (severity) resulting in unwanted type conversion or unacceptable environmental effects?
30	How do we restore fire dependent ecosystems where it has been excluded? What are the consequences of wildland fire suppression?
33	How effective are fuels treatments in restoring fire to its natural role in the environment?
34	How can we maintain the appropriate amounts of wildland fire to maintain healthy ecosystems?
38	What wildland fire suppression strategies and techniques can be used to minimize impacts to CA Species?

Question Number	Priority Group B – Resiliency to Wildland Fire/Recreation Management
4	Are recreational climbing activities affecting CA Species plants in cliff areas or disrupting roosting areas for CA Species bats and other nesting CA Species?
3	How do recreation activities affect CA Species and habitats? Which types and locations of recreation activities are having more substantial effects on CA Species and habitats?
8	How effective are efforts to reduce recreation effects to riparian and spring areas?
17	What are the consequences of distributing recreation use outside presently developed canyons and increasing disturbance in previously undisturbed areas? Are there CA Species habitats where recreation impacts to habitat should be avoided?
37	What is the rate of wildfire recovery on burned species? Is there a difference in recovery time for high vs. low intensity?
1	What are the effects and impacts of dispersed recreation uses, including OHVs to CA Species and their habitats?
39	What wildland fire suppression techniques are most effective in setting the stage for post-fire restoration? (e.g., Fire retardant use restrictions)
5	How effective are efforts to manage motorized recreation (OHV) and limit other uses (outfitters and guides) to the protection and conservation of CA Species and their habitats?
7	Are management actions to limit effects to CA Species from recreational climbing activities effective?
9	How effective are management efforts in reducing negative effects to CA Species dependent on caves?
16	How can the effects of existing recreation developments and uses be managed to minimize effects on SOC/SOI and their habitats? What are the effects of concentrated uses and their overlap with CA Species and their habitats?

---

[5] **Note:** References to Species of Concern and Species of Interest have been converted to Conservation Agreement Species (CA Species).

Appendix A – Monitoring Questions and Priorities (Continued)

Question Number	Priority Group C – Water Resources/Invasive Species Management
49	Where are springs, fen, and streams distributed and how are baseline conditions, including water quality and yield being affected?
50	What are the current riparian vegetation composition, structure and pattern associated with springs, fens, and streams?
51	How effective is riparian fencing in protecting springs and riparian areas? What thresholds warrant this level of mitigation?
53	What is the ecological status of riparian areas?
59	Is recreation use or grazing by wild horses/burros or recreational livestock impacting bank stability?
40	What is the current trend (distribution and abundance) of invasive species?
43	Are P-J treatments being invaded by cheatgrass?
42	What role should wildland fire play in areas with invasive plant species? What are the consequences and threats from invasive species that typically follow fire such as cheatgrass in lower elevations?
56	Are soil and water conservation practices being implemented and are they effective?
57	Are soil disturbing activities creating excessive sedimentation or soil loss?
55	How are management actions and human uses affecting water quality and quantity?

Question Number	Priority Group D – Invasive Spp./CA Species Habitat Mgmt./Other Disturbances & Uses
24	Where are opportunities for restoration and/or creation of habitat for CA Species located?
41	What are the most effective methods of treatment of high priority invasive species? Are there specific thresholds of infestations at which treatments are no longer effective?
45	Do wild horses adversely affect the habitats of some CA Species?
44	What are the consequences of climate change and drought on CA Spcies and their habitats?
28	What is the average number of downed woody logs per acre?
25	Are the landscapes being managed within a range of variability that promotes resiliency for CA Species and their habitats? Have ecological systems been altered – therefore, affecting CA Species and their habitats?
26	How many snags per acre are present in mixed conifer, riparian areas, and in P-J?
27	What percentage of mixed conifer is old growth habitat?
18	What are the direct and cumulative effects of woodcutting and gathering on CA Species and their habitats?
23	What are the effects of air quality on vegetation?

Appendix B – CA Species Fact Sheets and Potential Habitat Models

B-1: Acastus checkerspot (*Chlosyne acastus robusta*) – Potential Habitat

B-2: Spring Mountains dark blue butterfly *(Euphilotes ancilla purpurea)* - Potential Habitat [1]

B-3: Spring Mountains dark blue butterfly *(Euphilotes ancilla cryptica)* - Potential Habitat [1]

B-4: Morand's checkerspot (*Euphydryas chalcedona morandi*) - Potential Habitat

B-5: Mount Charleston blue butterfly (*Plebejus shasta charlestonensis*) - Potential Habitat [1]

B-6: Charleston ant (*Lasius nevadensis*) – Species Fact Sheet and Potential Habitat

B-7: Spring Mountains pyrg *(Pyrgulopsis deacon)* [2]

B-8: Southeast Nevada pyrg *(Pyrgulopsis turbatrix)* [2]

B-9: Clokey's milkvetch (*Astragalus aequalis*) - Potential Habitat

B-10: Egg milkvetch (*Astragalus oophorus var. clokeyanus*) – Species Fact Sheet and Potential Habitat

B-11: Spring Mountains milkvetch (*Astragalus remotus*) - Potential Habitat

B-12: Trianglelobe moonwort *(Botrychium ascendens)* [2]

B-13: Scalloped moonwort *(Botrychium crenulatum)* [2]

B-14: Narrowleaf moonwort *(Botrychium linare)* [2]

B-15: Moose moonwort *(Botrychium tunux)* [2]

B-16: Clokey's greasebush (*Glossopetalon clokeyi*) - Potential Habitat

B-17: Spring Mountains comma skipper (*Hesperia colorado mojavensis*) - Potential Habitat

B-18: Nevada admiral (*Limenitus weidemeyerii nevadae*) - Potential Habitat

B-19: Spring Mountains icarioides blue butterfly (*Plebejus icarioides austinorum*) - Potential Habitat

B-20: Carole's fritillary butterfly (*Speyeria carolae*) - Potential Habitat

B-21: Townsend's big eared bat (*Corynorhinus townsendii*) - Potential Habitat

B-22: Allen's big-eared bat (*Idionycteris phyllotis*) - Potential Habitat

B-23: Palmer's chipmunk (*Neotamias palmeri*) – Species Fact Sheet and Potential Habitat

B-24: Western redtail skink *(Eumeces gilbert rubricaudatus)* - Potential Habitat

B-25: Rough angelica (*Angelica scabrida*) – Species Fact Sheet and Potential Habitat

B-26: Charleston Mountain pussytoes (*Antennaria soliceps*) - Potential Habitat

B-27: King's rosy sandwort (*Arenaria kingii spp. rosea*) - Potential Habitat

B-28: Shortstyle draba (*Draba brachystylis*) - Potential Habitat

B-29: Spring Mountains rockcress *(Boechera nevadensis)* [2]

B-30: Jaeger's draba (*Draba jaegeri*) - Potential Habitat

B-31: Charleston Mountain draba (*Draba paucifructa*) - Potential Habitat

B-32: Nevada willowherb (*Epilobium nevadense*) - Potential Habitat

B-33: Clokey's buckwheat (*Eriogonum heermannii var. clokeyi*) - Potential Habitat

B-34: Dwarf greasebush (*Glossopetalon pungens*) - Potential Habitat

B-35: Charleston Peak mousetail (*Ivesia cryptocaulis*) - Potential Habitat

B-36: Jaeger's mousetail (*Ivesia jaegeri*) - Potential Habitat

B-37: Keck's beardtongue (*Penstemon leiophyllus* var. *keckii*) - Potential Habitat

B-38: Jaeger's beardtongue (*Penstemon thompsoniae spp. jaegeri*) - Potential Habitat

B-39: Clokey's catchfly (*Silene clokeyi*) - Potential Habitat

B-40: Compact chickensage (*Sphaeromeria compacta*) - Potential Habitat

B-41: Charleston Mountain kittentails (*Synthyris ranunculina*) - Potential Habitat

B-42: Jones' townsend daisy (*Townsendia jonesii var. tumulosa*) - Potential Habitat

B-43: Charleston Mountain violet (*Viola purpurea var. charlestonensis*) - Potential Habitat

[1] *Potential habitat models for these species will be developed once the 2011 butterfly autecology study has been published by UNLV.*
[2] *These species only occur at springs therefore a map of their actual distribution will be developed at a later time.*

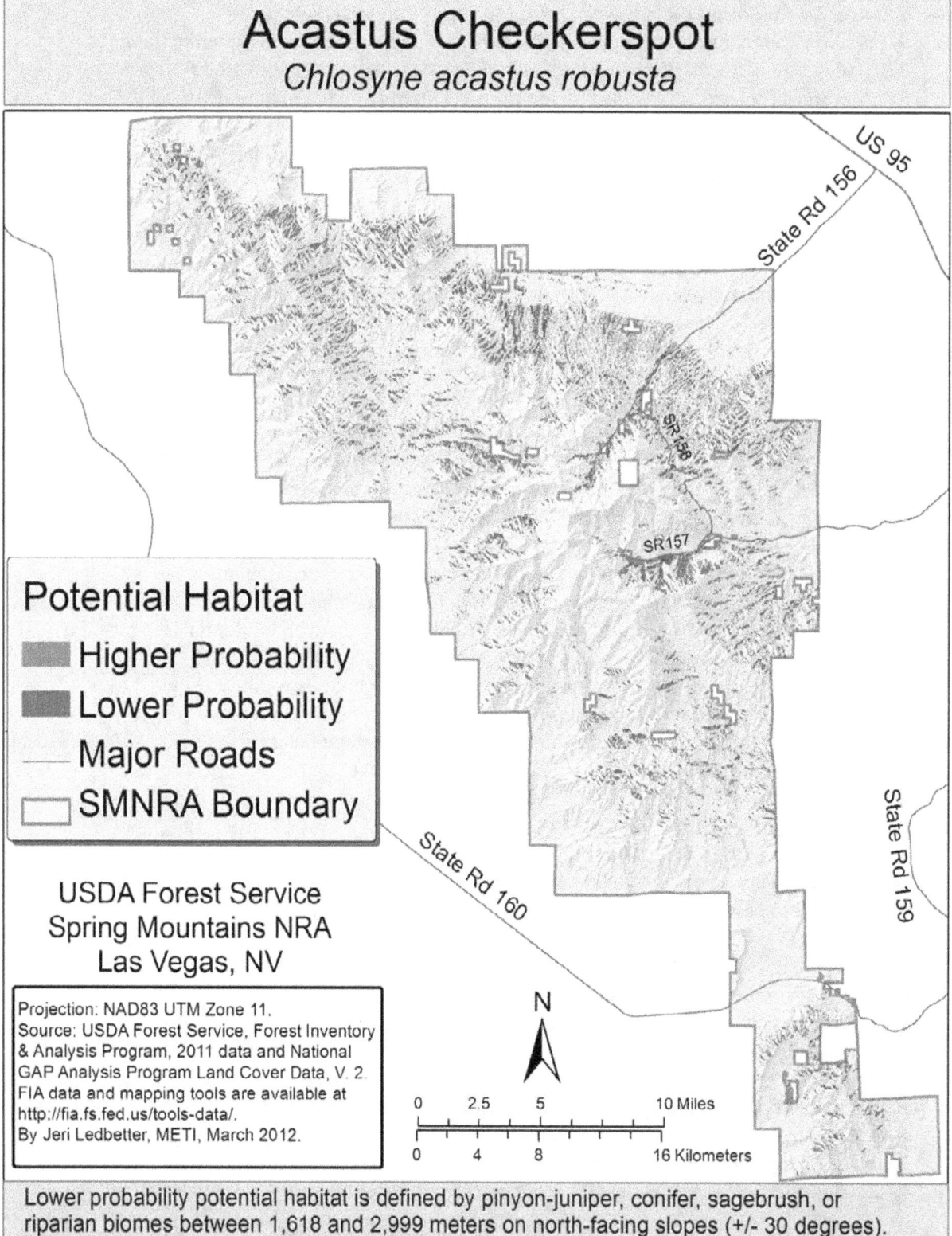

Acastus Checkerspot
Chlosyne acastus robusta

Potential Habitat

- Higher Probability
- Lower Probability
- Major Roads
- SMNRA Boundary

USDA Forest Service
Spring Mountains NRA
Las Vegas, NV

Projection: NAD83 UTM Zone 11.
Source: USDA Forest Service, Forest Inventory
& Analysis Program, 2011 data and National
GAP Analysis Program Land Cover Data, V. 2.
FIA data and mapping tools are available at
http://fia.fs.fed.us/tools-data/.
By Jeri Ledbetter, METI, March 2012.

| 0 | 2.5 | 5 | 10 Miles |
| 0 | 4 | 8 | 16 Kilometers |

Lower probability potential habitat is defined by pinyon-juniper, conifer, sagebrush, or
riparian biomes between 1,618 and 2,999 meters on north-facing slopes (+/- 30 degrees).
Higher probability potential habitat includes these areas that are in close proximity to streams,
roads, trails, washes, and springs.

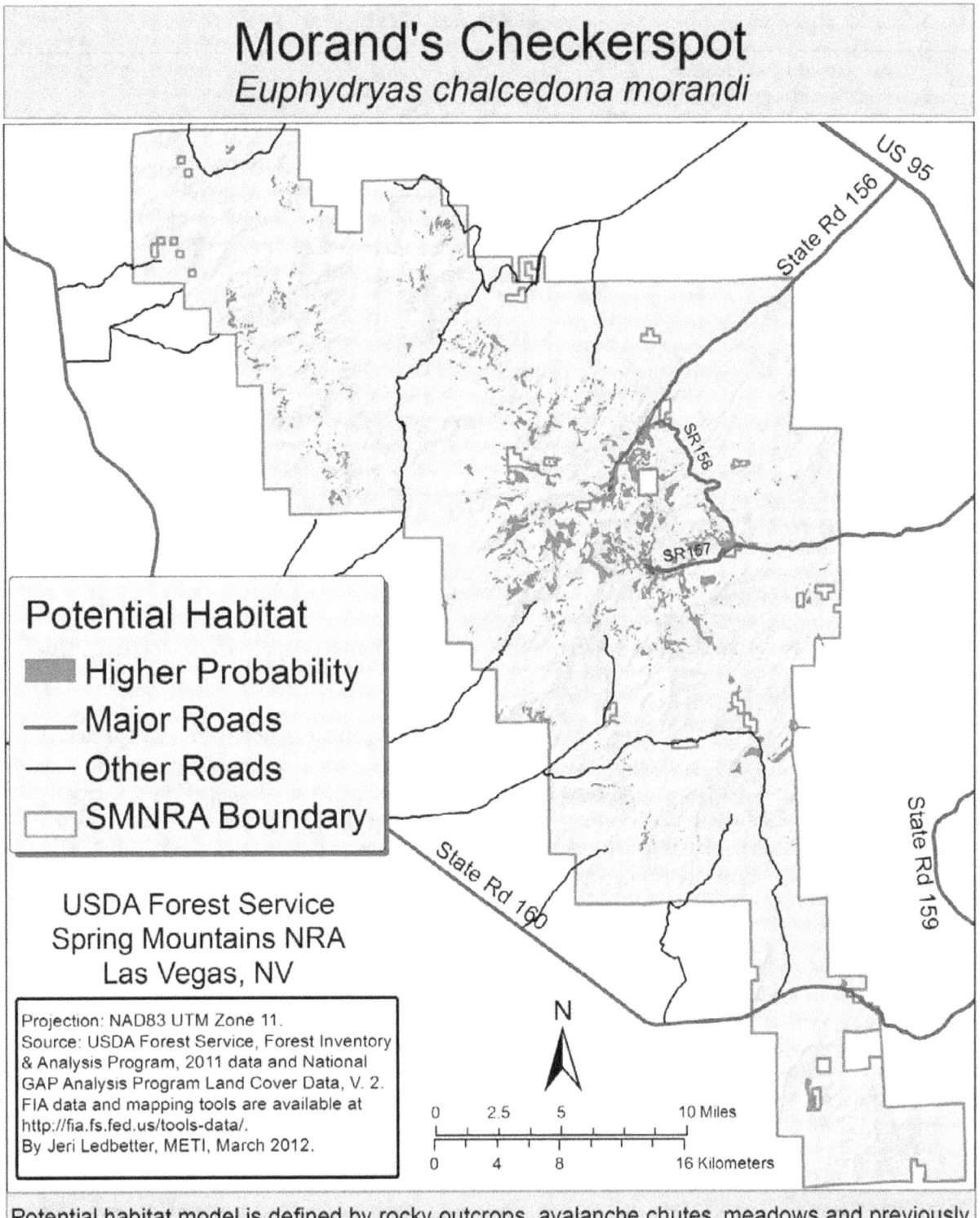

Morand's Checkerspot
Euphydryas chalcedona morandi

Potential Habitat

■ Higher Probability
— Major Roads
— Other Roads
☐ SMNRA Boundary

USDA Forest Service
Spring Mountains NRA
Las Vegas, NV

Projection: NAD83 UTM Zone 11.
Source: USDA Forest Service, Forest Inventory
& Analysis Program, 2011 data and National
GAP Analysis Program Land Cover Data, V. 2.
FIA data and mapping tools are available at
http://fia.fs.fed.us/tools-data/.
By Jeri Ledbetter, METI, March 2012.

0   2.5   5   10 Miles

0   4   8   16 Kilometers

Potential habitat model is defined by rocky outcrops, avalanche chutes, meadows and previously
burned areas between 1,733 and 3,497 meters that are within 200 meters of pinyon-juniper,
mixed conifer woodland, and inter-mountain basin subalpine limber and bristlecone biomes.

Appendix B-6: Charleston Ant (*Lasius nevadensis*) – Species Fact Sheet and Potential Habitat

<u>Species Fact Sheet</u>

Species: *Lasius nevadensis*
Common Names: Charleston ant

General SMNRA Habitat Characteristics: Higher probability habitat includes conifer or pinyon-juniper biomes between 2,225 and 2,743 meters. Lower probability habitat includes these biomes between 2,134 and 2,225 meters. Information is based on limited information, primarily regarding habitat characteristics of species in the same subgenus that are suspected to have parasitic relationships with this species.

Known Distribution: SMNRA endemic. This taxon has only been reported once: six populous colonies. (Cole 1956)

Known Distribution Within SMNRA: Only known location is in Kyle Canyon, Spring Mountains, Clark Co., Nevada. (Cole 1956)

Current FS-R4 Species Status: None

Genetic Information: No genetic work done for this species although work has been done on this wide spread genus.

Literature Review Synopsis: The genus *Lasius* has worldwide distribution and The Ants of Nevada (Wheeler and Wheeler 1986) report seven species of *Lasius* from the Spring Mountains. Cole (1956) is the only report of *Lasius nevadensis*. His paper details the original collection in 1954 and naming of the new *Lasius* species. There are no published reports of collection or collection efforts since 1954; therefore, we know that *L. nevadensis* is rarely collected (all specimens were collected during a 1-week period in 1954). The distribution, however, and rarity or commonness of this species is unknown. Members of the subgenus to which *L. nevadensis* has been assigned are exclusively subterranean, with the exception of summer mating flights. Cole collected the species during such a mating flight event. The subterranean habitat of the species makes it unlikely that human disturbance will impact nests and colonies.

Plans include consulting with ant biologists to refine the methodology for collecting ant specimens and developing a comprehensive plan for sampling appropriate areas of the SMNRA. The life history of the Charleston Ant, e.g. life underground except during the July-Aug mating flights, and the limited amount of research on ant biology conducted in southern Nevada during the last few decades provide a logical explanation for the single collection of *Lasius nevadensis*. Assumptions based on other *Lasius sp.* life histories and their elevational distributions in Nevada, along with the limited habitat information provided by Cole (1956), were used to construct a potential habitat map for *Lasius nevadensis*. Assumptions are detailed as follows: (1) it is extremely improbable that any *Lasius* species is restricted to only one location (in this case, the old ski tow site), because *Lasius sp.* are semi-parasitic on other members of the genus. (2) We assumed an elevational range similar to other species of *Lasius* found in the Spring Mountains. (3) Cole's collection was found in open coniferous forest and we therefore assumed that present-day *Lasius nevadensis* would also be found in this habitat. The degree of openness was based on an estimation of 1954 canopy cover. (4) Mating flights occurring during the season of summer monsoon thunderstorms dispersed across the entire EMNRA would seem probable. In fact, it would not be surprising if queens were blown onto nearby mountains during summer storms. *Lasius* life history (hemiparasitism) provides an explanation for the likelihood of colony establishment from these isolated events. The potential habitat map has a bias towards canyons, because the only known collection occurred within a canyon. A systematic search and collection plan for *Lasius nevadensis* will be included as an appendix to this report.

"Workers vary as follows: head length, 0.81-0.95 mm.; head width, 0.79·0.87 mm.; scape length, 0.73-0.79 mm.; scape index of the extremes, 90 and 92; eye length, 0.14-0.15 mm.; eye width, 0.11·0.14 mm.; pronotal width, 0.59·0.62 mm.; greatest width of hind tibia at its midlength, 0.10-0.14 mm.; extreme length of preapical hairs of first gastric tergite, 0.08·0.09 mm. Head width and associated scape index of a large series of females varied from 1.20 mm. (83) to 1.26 mm. (83). Head width of a large series of males varied from 0.65 mm. to 0.73 mm.; the scape index of the extremes being 71 and 74." (Cole 1956)

Worker. Small. Head and posterior portion of gaster yellowish brown, thorax and anterior portion of gaster yellow. Dull. (Wheeler and Wheeler 1986)

References:

Antbase.org is a collaborative effort between scientists from around the world, aiming at providing the best possible access to the wealth of information on ants. http://www.antbase.org/

Cole, A.C. 1956. Studies of Nevada ants. II. A new species of *Lasius* (*Chthonolasius*) (*Hymenoptera: Formicidae)*. Journal of the Tennessee Academy of Science. 31(1): 26-27.

Entrix. 2008. Landscape Analysis. Final Report. Prepared for USDA Forest Service, Spring Mountains National Recreation Area, Humboldt-Toiyabe National Forest. Las Vegas, NV. Chapter 4.

Fisher, B.L. and Cover, S.P. Ants of North America. London, England: University of California Press, Ltd. 2007.

NatureServe. 2011. NatureServe Explorer: An online encyclopedia of life [web application]. Version 7.1. NatureServe, Arlington, Virginia. Available http://www.natureserve.org/explorer.

To view pictures of Charleston ant specimens collected by A.C. Cole, go to http://www.antweb.org/ and search for *Lasius nevadensis.*

USDA Forest Service. 2011. Intermountain Region (R4) Threatened, Endangered, Proposed, and, Sensitive Species. Known/Suspected Distribution by Forest. July 27, 2011 update. 19 p. www.fs.fed.us/r4/resources/tes/r4_tes_lst.pdf

Wheeler, G.C. and Wheeler, J. 1986. The Ants of Nevada. Los Angeles: Natural History Museum of Los Angeles County. 138p.

Establishment and Maintenance Record

Version	Date	Author/Editor	Summary
1.0	5/7/12	Burton K. Pendleton, Research Ecologist, Rocky Mountain Research Station	Information compiled from the SMNRA Species Reference Database using information posted as of 5/7/12.

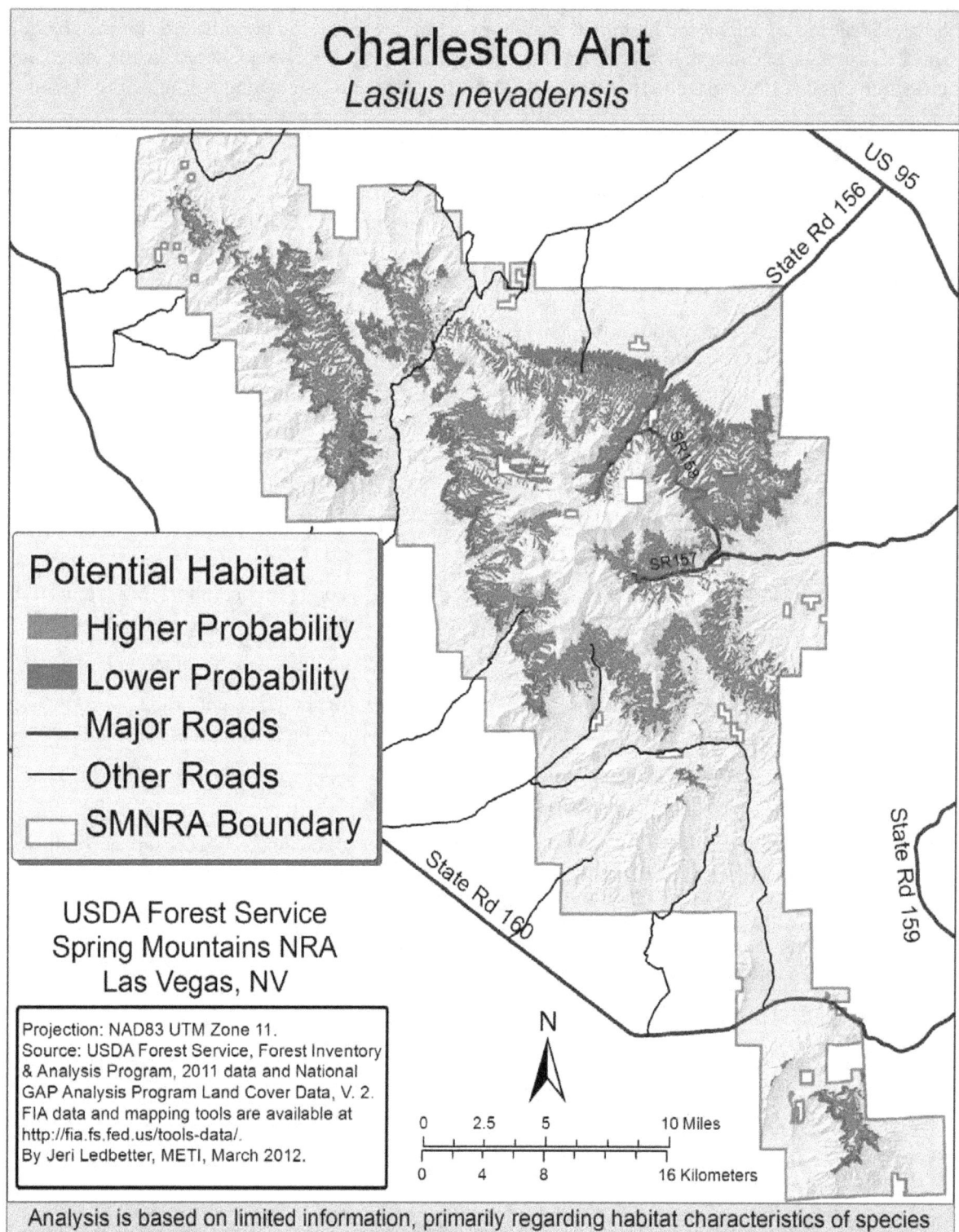

Charleston Ant
Lasius nevadensis

Potential Habitat

- **Higher Probability**
- **Lower Probability**
- —— Major Roads
- — Other Roads
- ☐ SMNRA Boundary

USDA Forest Service
Spring Mountains NRA
Las Vegas, NV

Projection: NAD83 UTM Zone 11.
Source: USDA Forest Service, Forest Inventory
& Analysis Program, 2011 data and National
GAP Analysis Program Land Cover Data, V. 2.
FIA data and mapping tools are available at
http://fia.fs.fed.us/tools-data/.
By Jeri Ledbetter, METI, March 2012.

US 95
State Rd 156
SR 158
SR 157
State Rd 160
State Rd 159

N

0   2.5   5   10 Miles
0   4   8   16 Kilometers

Analysis is based on limited information, primarily regarding habitat characteristics of species
in the same subgenus that are suspected to have parasitic relationships with this species.
Higher probability habitat includes conifer or pinyon-juniper biomes between 2225 and 2743
meters. Lower probability habitat includes these biomes between 2134 and 2225 meters.

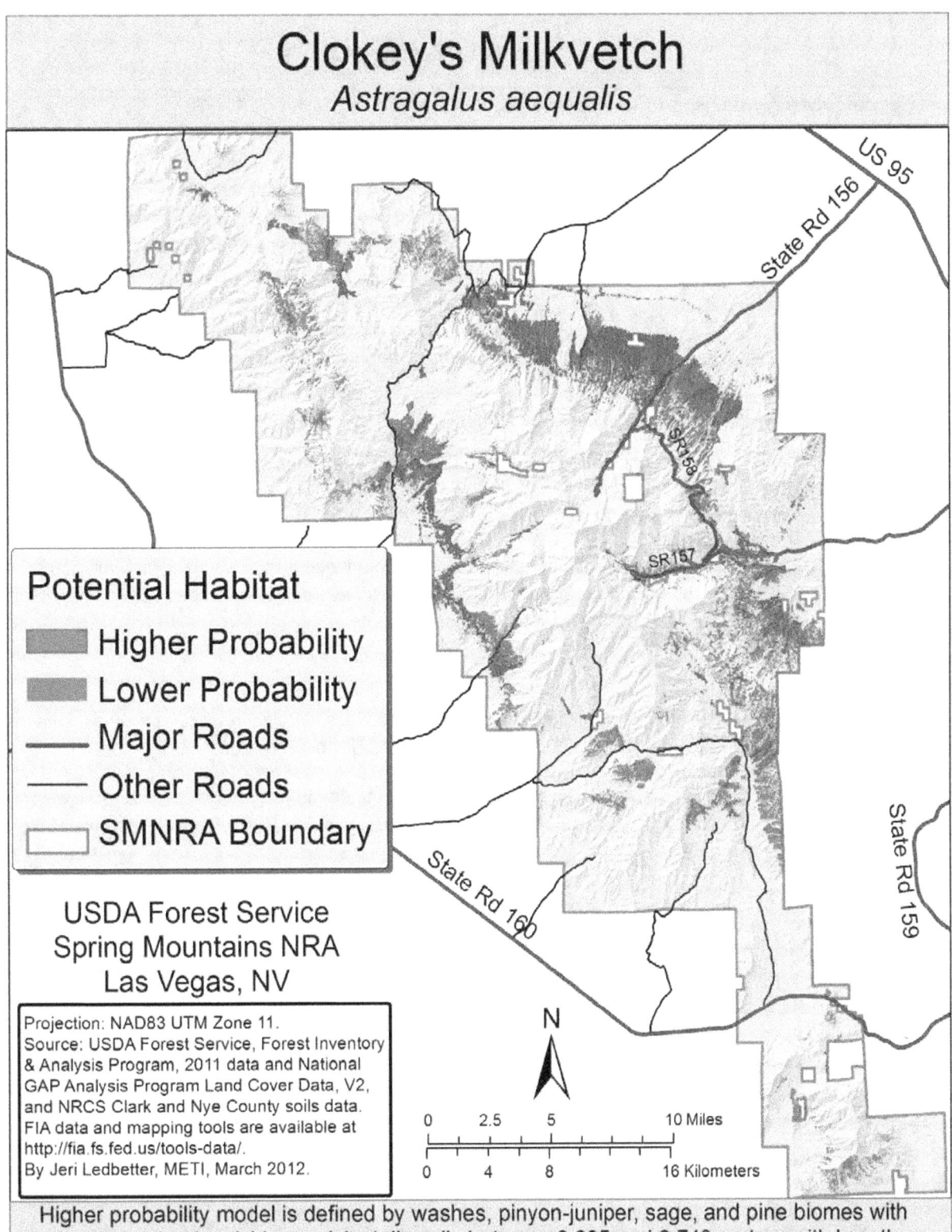

Clokey's Milkvetch
Astragalus aequalis

Potential Habitat

- Higher Probability
- Lower Probability
- —— Major Roads
- — Other Roads
- ☐ SMNRA Boundary

USDA Forest Service
Spring Mountains NRA
Las Vegas, NV

Projection: NAD83 UTM Zone 11.
Source: USDA Forest Service, Forest Inventory
& Analysis Program, 2011 data and National
GAP Analysis Program Land Cover Data, V2,
and NRCS Clark and Nye County soils data.
FIA data and mapping tools are available at
http://fia.fs.fed.us/tools-data/.
By Jeri Ledbetter, METI, March 2012.

N

0	2.5	5		10 Miles
0	4	8		16 Kilometers

Higher probability model is defined by washes, pinyon-juniper, sage, and pine biomes with
calcareous, haplocalcid, or calciustolls soils between 2,225 and 2,743 meters with less than
10 degree slopes on open ridges, gravelly flats, and moderate hillslopes. Lower probability
model includes areas with less than 30 degree slopes.

Species Fact Sheet (Provisional)[6]

Species: *Astragalus oophorus var. clokeyanus*
Common Names: Egg milkvetch

General SMNRA Habitat Characteristics: Potential habitat probability model is defined by openings in pinyon-juniper, mixed conifer, shrubland and woodland biomes between 1,913 and 2,738 meters and slopes less than 30 degrees. High probability areas have limestone soils with specific grain size criteria derived from the soils layer. Lower probability areas have limestone origins but less specific soils criteria.

Known Distribution: In 2001 recent and historical sites are now estimated to comprise at least 4428 individuals covering about 260 acres: NTS 23.3%, Nellis AFR 42%, SMNRA 33.5%, and private lands 1.2% It occurs at elevations between 5365 and 9005 feet (1635- 2745 meters). (Smith 2001, revised 2002).

Known Distribution Within SMNRA: Upper Lee Canyon, Upper Kyle Canyon, Wallace Canyon, Clark Canyon, Upper Deer Creek, and Upper Cold Creek. Occurrence data will be updated once geo-referencing issues with NRM-NRIS data are corrected and available for analysis.

Current FSR4 Species Status: Sensitive

Genetic Information: No studies of the genetic structure in *Astragalus oophorus* var. *clokeyanus* have been done. The varieties of this species are difficult to separate and often intergrade.

Literature Review Synopsis: A slender, perennial herb in the bean family. The leaves are 5-10 cm long, alternate, each divided into one terminal and 4-9 pair of lateral leaflets. The flowers are pea-like, bright reddish-purple with a whitish eyespot and wing tips, and in a loose group of 4-10. The longest petal, the banner, is 11-12 mm long; the calyx is hairless and forms a cup around the base of the flower. The fruit is a strongly inflated, opaque, papery pod with one chamber, 2-3 .7 cm long and 1-2 cm wide. The conspicuous pod is reddish mottled and detaches from the stalk when mature. The seeds, numbering about 23-28 per pod ,are 3-3.7 mm long, brown, dull, and finely dotted (Morefield 1993). A technical and more detailed description of *A. oophorus* var. *clokeyanus* is provided in Barneby (1964 and 1989). (Nachlinger and Combs 1996)

It is likely dependent on pollinating insects for reproduction although more definitive studies are needed. Its frequent occurrence in drainage bottoms, on roadsides, along foot trails, and occasionally on steep unstable slopes or recent burns, suggests that *Astragalus oophorus* var. *clokeyanus* is capable of opportunistically exploiting temporary disturbances, and may even be adapted to low levels of disturbance (Smith 2001, revised 2002).

---

[6] Provisional - Location information to be supplemented by data in NRM-NRIS from species and site-specific surveys.

Anderson, D.C. 1998. Distribution of Clokey's eggvetch (*Astragalus ooporus* var. *clokeyanus*) on the Nevada Test Site. Las Vegas: Bechtel Nevada, prepared for the U.S. Department of Energy under contract DE-AC08-96NV11718.

Beyer, C. and Sikula, N. 2002. 2002 Summary Report Draft of Biological Monitoring for *Astragalus oophorus* var. *clokeyanus* (Clokey eggvetch) on the Humboldt-Toiyabe National Forest, Spring Mountains National Recreation Area. U.S. Department of Agriculture, Forest Service. Unpublished document in U.S. Forest Service files.

Nachlinger, J and Combs, J. 1996. Biological Monitoring Plan for *Astragalus oophorus* var. *clokeyanus* (Clokey eggvetch) on the Toiyabe National Forest, Spring Mountains National Recreation Area. The Nature Conservancy, Northern Nevada Office, Reno, Nevada.

Nachlinger, J. and Sheldon, S. 1995. Status report for *Astragalus oophorus* var. *clokeyanus*. The Nature Conservancy, Reno, Nevada. Prepared for the U.S. Department of the Interior, Fish and Wildlife Service, Reno, Nevada. 20 p.

Photo copyright Gary A. Monroe. United States, NV, Clark Co., Lee Canyon. June 5, 2005. Obtained from USDA PLANTS website: http://plants.usda.gov

Smith, F.J. 2001. Current knowledge and conservation status of *Astragalus oophorus* var. *clokeyanus* Barneby (Fabaceae), the Clokey eggvetch. Report prepared for Nevada Natural Heritage Program, Carson City, Nevada, and U. S. Fish and Wildlife Service, Reno, Nevada. 33p plus appendices.

USDA Forest Service (USFS). 2003. Conservation Agreement Report and Five-year Analyses for the Spring Mountains National Recreation Area, Clark and Nye Counties, Nevada. U.S. Forest Service, Intermountain Region; State of Nevada, Department of Conservation and Natural Resources; and U.S. Fish and Wildlife Service, Pacific Region.

USDA Forest Service (USFS). 2011. Intermountain Region (R4) threatened, endangered, proposed, and, sensitive species: Known/suspected distribution by forest. July 27, 2011 update. 19 p. www.fs.fed.us/r4/resources/tes/r4_tes_lst.pdf

Walker, K.C. 2006. 2005 Biological Monitoring Report for *Astragalus oophorus* var. *clokeyanus* (Clokey eggvetch) on the Humboldt-Toiyabe National Forest Spring Mountains National Recreation Area. Unpublished report for the Humboldt-Toiyabe National Forest, Spring Mountains National Recreation Area, Las Vegas, Nevada. 15 p. plus appendices.

Establishment and Maintenance Record

Version	Date	Author/Editor	Summary
1.0	5/7/12	Burton K. Pendleton, Research Ecologist, Rocky Mountain Research Station	Information compiled from the SMNRA Species Reference Database using information posted as of 5/7/12. **Provisional Fact Sheet -** Location information to be supplemented by data in NRM-NRIS from species and site-specific surveys.

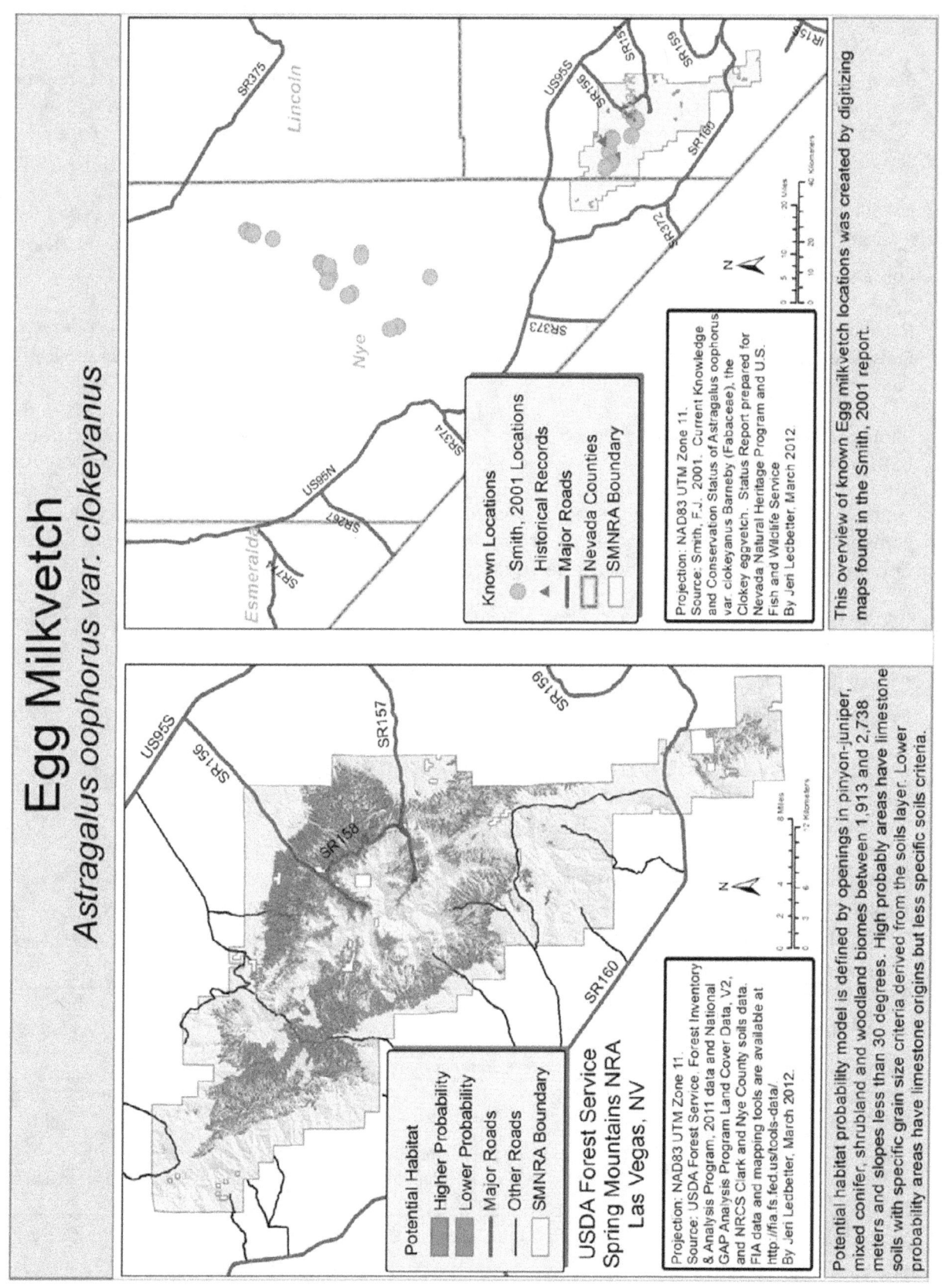

Egg Milkvetch
Astragalus oophorus var. clokeyanus

Known Locations
- Smith, 2001 Locations
- ▲ Historical Records
- —— Major Roads
- Nevada Counties
- SMNRA Boundary

Projection: NAD83 UTM Zone 11.
Source: Smith, F.J. 2001. Current Knowledge and Conservation Status of *Astragalus oophorus var. clokeyanus* Barneby (Fabaceae), the Clokey eggvetch. Status Report prepared for Nevada Natural Heritage Program and U.S. Fish and Wildlife Service
By Jeri Ledbetter, March 2012

This overview of known Egg milkvetch locations was created by digitizing maps found in the Smith, 2001 report.

Potential Habitat
- Higher Probability
- Lower Probability
- —— Major Roads
- Other Roads
- SMNRA Boundary

USDA Forest Service
Spring Mountains NRA
Las Vegas, NV

Projection: NAD83 UTM Zone 11.
Source: USDA Forest Service. Forest Inventory & Analysis Program, 2011 data and National GAP Analysis Program Land Cover Data, V2, and NRCS Clark and Nye County soils data. FIA data and mapping tools are available at http://fia.fs.fed.us/tools-data/.
By Jeri Ledbetter, March 2012.

Potential habitat probability model is defined by openings in pinyon-juniper, mixed conifer, shrubland and woodland biomes between 1,913 and 2,738 meters and slopes less than 30 degrees. High probably areas have limestone soils with specific grain size criteria derived from the soils layer. Lower probability areas have limestone origins but less specific soils criteria.

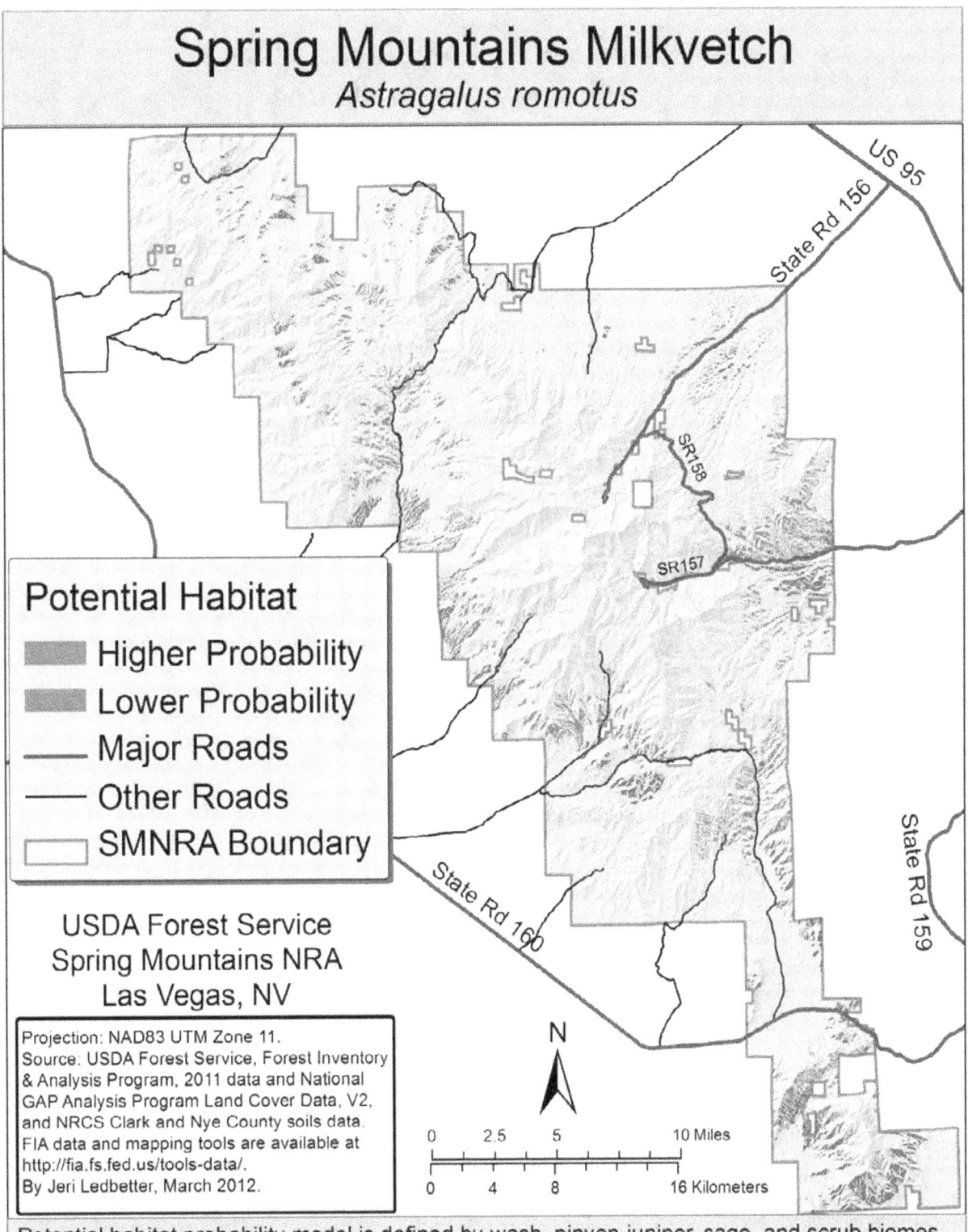

Spring Mountains Milkvetch
Astragalus romotus

Potential Habitat

- Higher Probability
- Lower Probability
- Major Roads
- Other Roads
- SMNRA Boundary

USDA Forest Service
Spring Mountains NRA
Las Vegas, NV

Projection: NAD83 UTM Zone 11.
Source: USDA Forest Service, Forest Inventory
& Analysis Program, 2011 data and National
GAP Analysis Program Land Cover Data, V2,
and NRCS Clark and Nye County soils data.
FIA data and mapping tools are available at
http://fia.fs.fed.us/tools-data/.
By Jeri Ledbetter, March 2012.

N

| 0 | 2.5 | 5 | | 10 Miles |
| 0 | 4 | 8 | | 16 Kilometers |

Potential habitat probability model is defined by wash, pinyon-juniper, sage, and scrub biomes
on south to SSE-facing slopes between 1,644 and 2,218 meters. High probability areas
have limestone soils with specific grain size criteria derived from the soils layer. Lower
probability areas have limestone origins but less specific soils criteria.

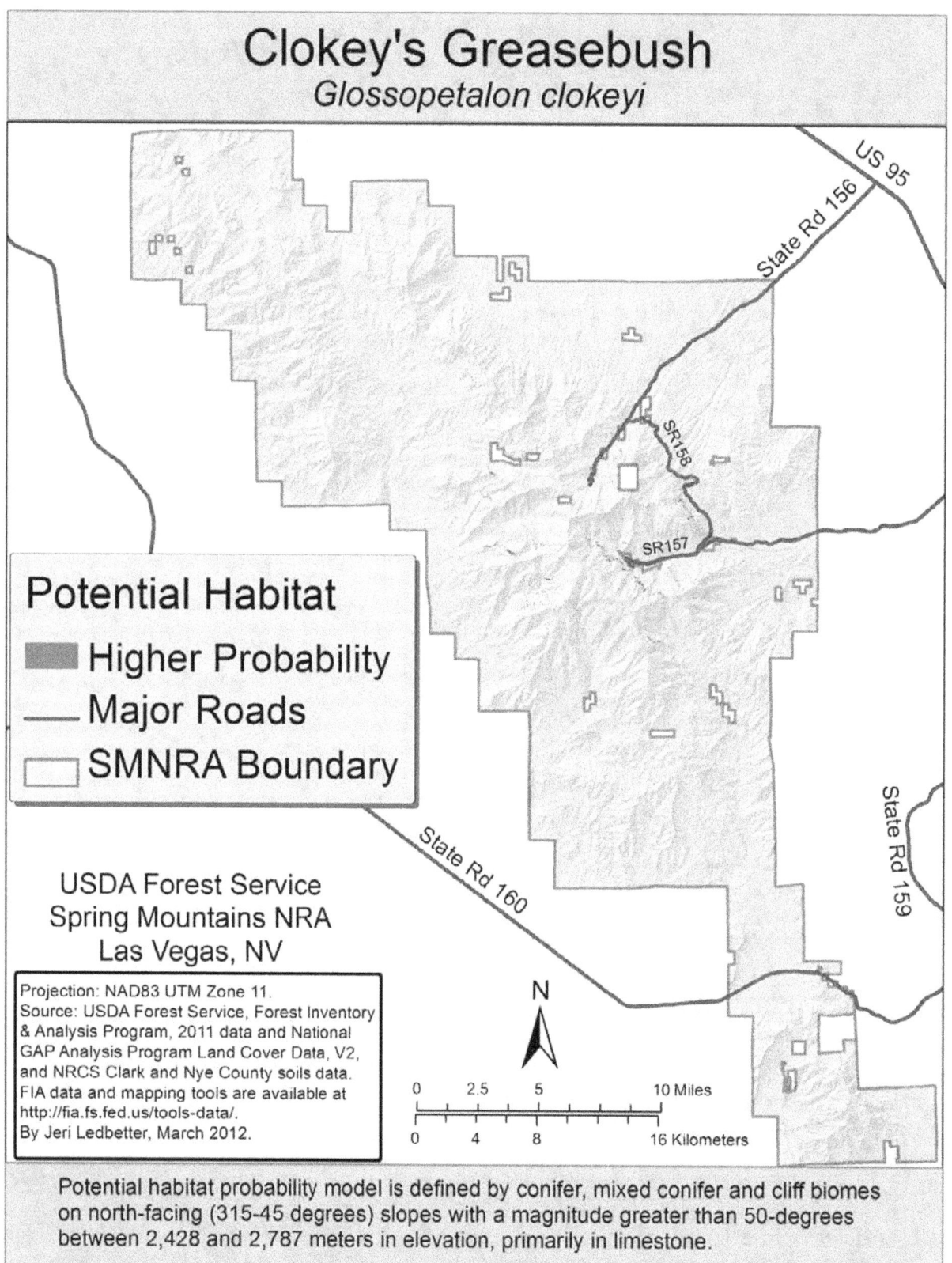

Clokey's Greasebush
Glossopetalon clokeyi

Potential Habitat

■ Higher Probability

— Major Roads

□ SMNRA Boundary

USDA Forest Service
Spring Mountains NRA
Las Vegas, NV

Projection: NAD83 UTM Zone 11.
Source: USDA Forest Service, Forest Inventory
& Analysis Program, 2011 data and National
GAP Analysis Program Land Cover Data, V2,
and NRCS Clark and Nye County soils data.
FIA data and mapping tools are available at
http://fia.fs.fed.us/tools-data/.
By Jeri Ledbetter, March 2012.

US 95
State Rd 156
SR158
SR157
State Rd 160
State Rd 159

N

0   2.5   5   10 Miles
0   4   8   16 Kilometers

Potential habitat probability model is defined by conifer, mixed conifer and cliff biomes
on north-facing (315-45 degrees) slopes with a magnitude greater than 50-degrees
between 2,428 and 2,787 meters in elevation, primarily in limestone.

Appendix B-17: Potential Habitat for Spring Mountains Comma Skipper *(Hesperia Colorado mojavensis)*

Spring Mountains Comma Skipper

Hesperia colorado mojavensis

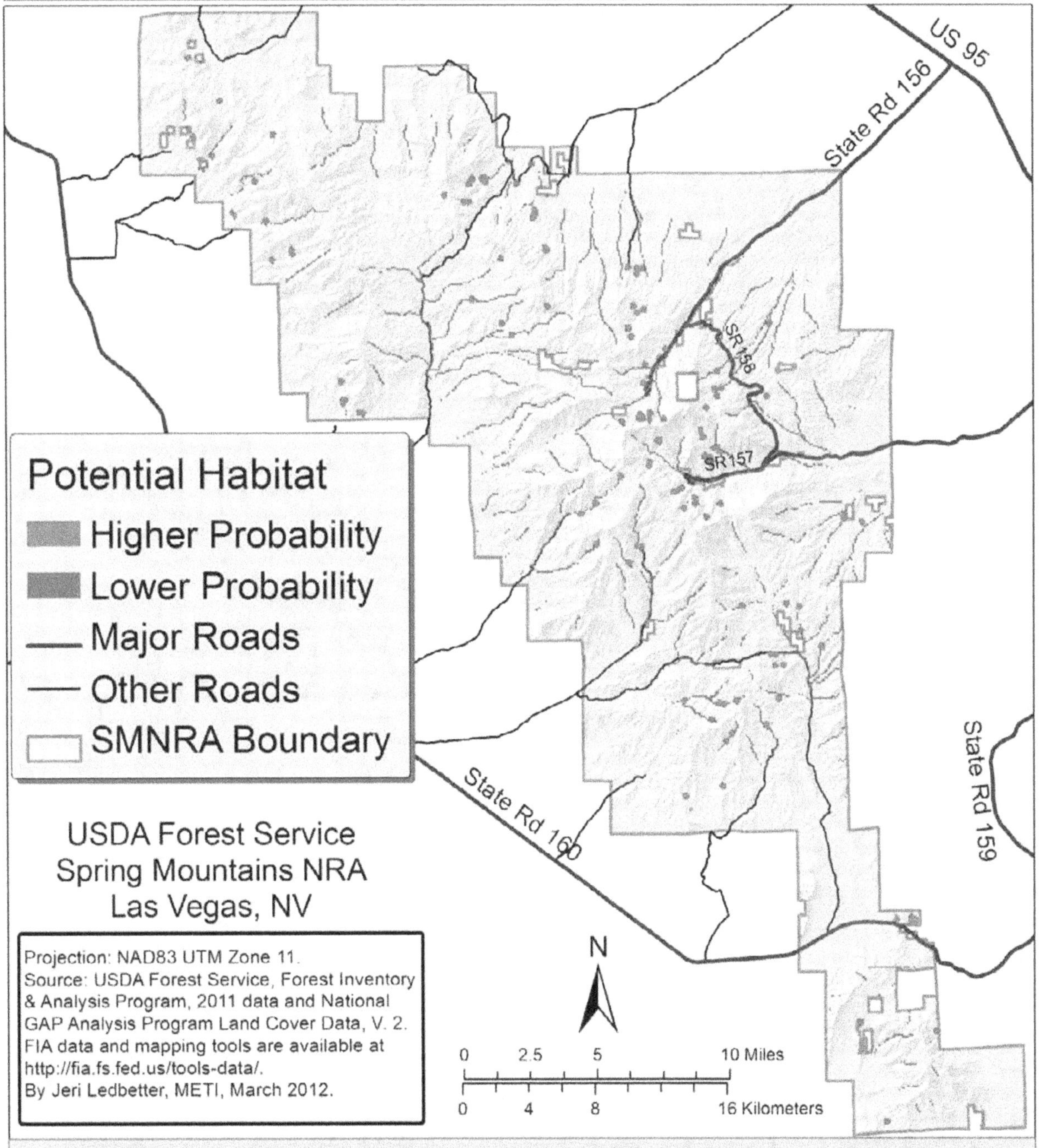
US 95
State Rd 156
SR 158
SR 157
State Rd 160
State Rd 159
Potential Habitat
Higher Probability
Lower Probability
Major Roads
Other Roads
SMNRA Boundary
USDA Forest Service
Spring Mountains NRA
Las Vegas, NV
Projection: NAD83 UTM Zone 11.
Source: USDA Forest Service, Forest Inventory & Analysis Program, 2011 data and National GAP Analysis Program Land Cover Data, V. 2.
FIA data and mapping tools are available at http://fia.fs.fed.us/tools-data/.
By Jeri Ledbetter, METI, March 2012.
N
0 2.5 5 10 Miles
0 4 8 16 Kilometers

Potential habitat is defined by elevations between 1,586 and 3,470 meters in mixed conifer forests and pinyon-juniper biomes near riparian areas with surface water. Higher probability habitat includes springs and perennial streams.

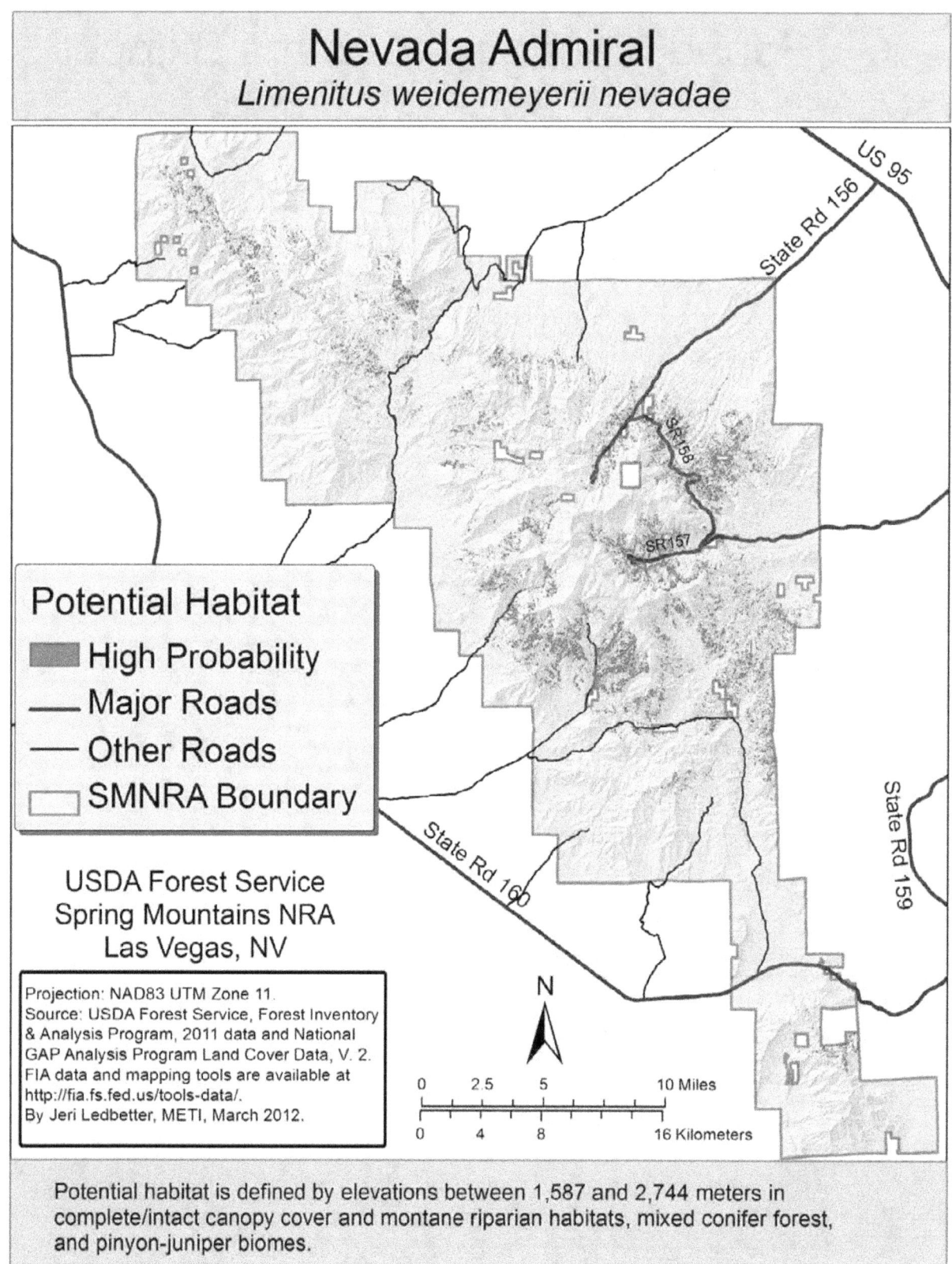

Nevada Admiral
Limenitus weidemeyerii nevadae

Potential Habitat
▓ High Probability
— Major Roads
— Other Roads
☐ SMNRA Boundary

USDA Forest Service
Spring Mountains NRA
Las Vegas, NV

Projection: NAD83 UTM Zone 11.
Source: USDA Forest Service, Forest Inventory
& Analysis Program, 2011 data and National
GAP Analysis Program Land Cover Data, V. 2.
FIA data and mapping tools are available at
http://fia.fs.fed.us/tools-data/.
By Jeri Ledbetter, METI, March 2012.

N

0	2.5	5		10 Miles
0	4	8		16 Kilometers

Potential habitat is defined by elevations between 1,587 and 2,744 meters in
complete/intact canopy cover and montane riparian habitats, mixed conifer forest,
and pinyon-juniper biomes.

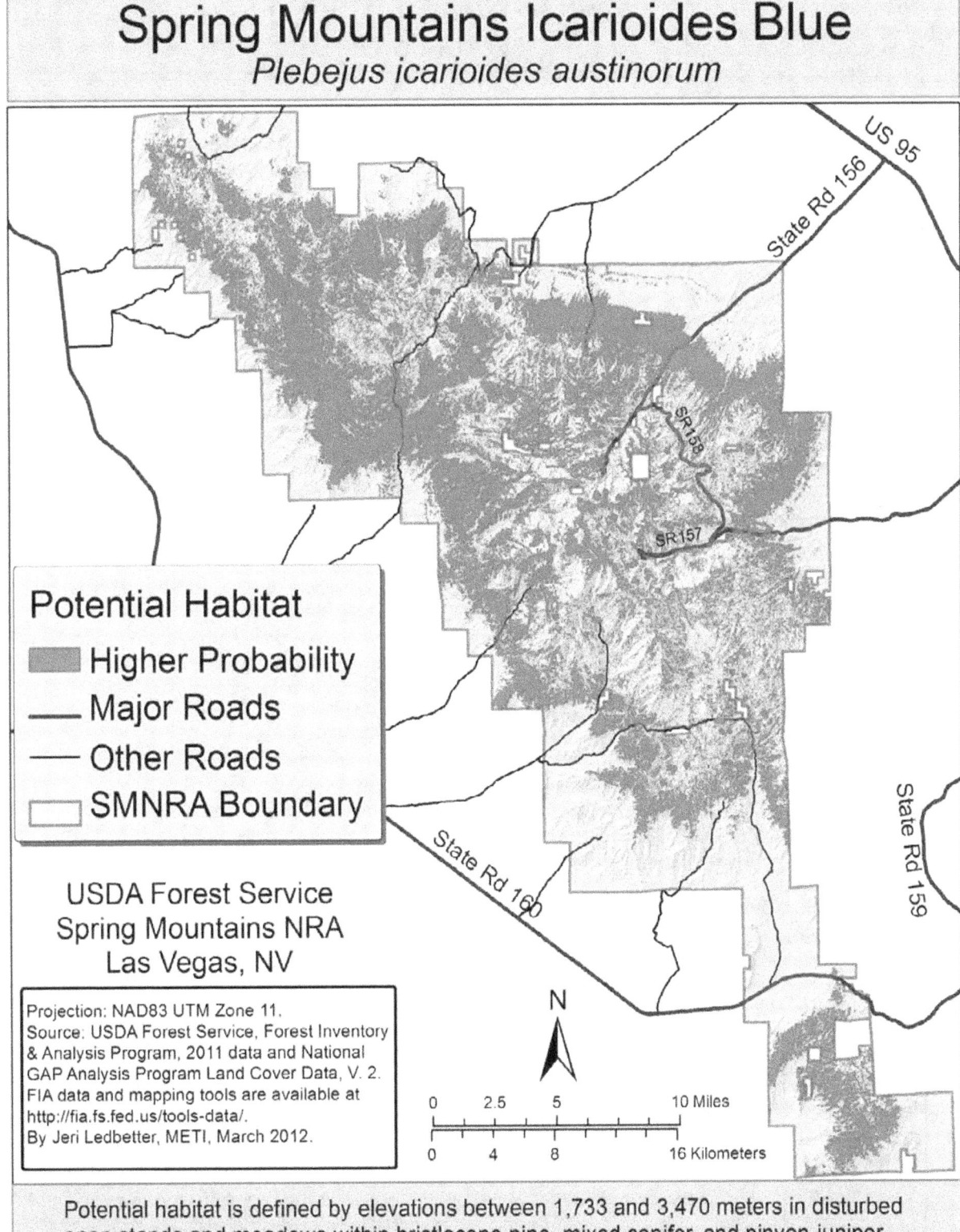

Spring Mountains Icarioides Blue
Plebejus icarioides austinorum

Potential Habitat
- Higher Probability
- Major Roads
- Other Roads
- SMNRA Boundary

USDA Forest Service
Spring Mountains NRA
Las Vegas, NV

Projection: NAD83 UTM Zone 11.
Source: USDA Forest Service, Forest Inventory
& Analysis Program, 2011 data and National
GAP Analysis Program Land Cover Data, V. 2.
FIA data and mapping tools are available at
http://fia.fs.fed.us/tools-data/.
By Jeri Ledbetter, METI, March 2012.

Potential habitat is defined by elevations between 1,733 and 3,470 meters in disturbed
open stands and meadows within bristlecone pine, mixed conifer, and pinyon-juniper
sagebrush communities, and wet areas near springs.

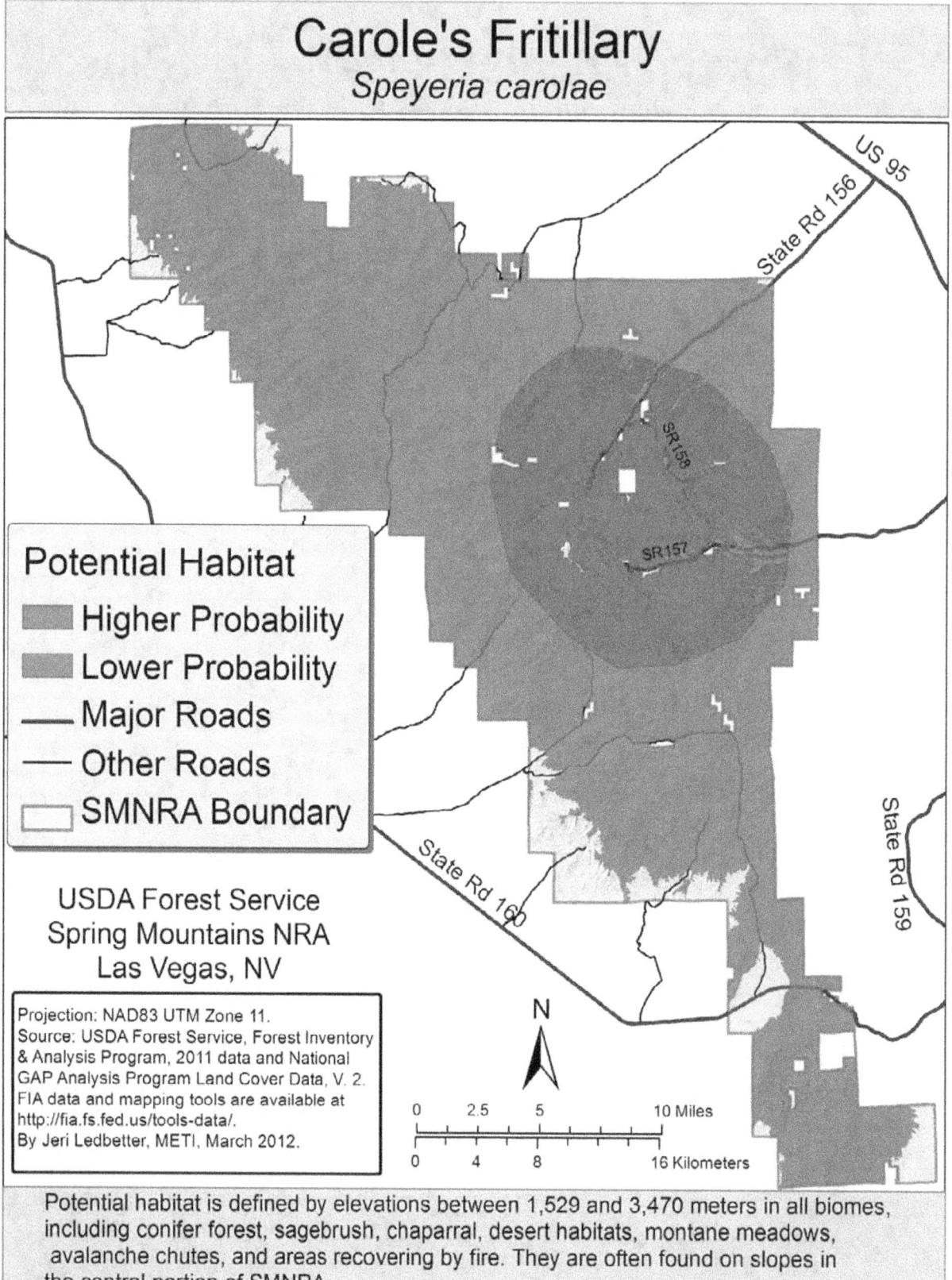

Carole's Fritillary
Speyeria carolae

Potential Habitat

- Higher Probability
- Lower Probability
— Major Roads
— Other Roads
☐ SMNRA Boundary

USDA Forest Service
Spring Mountains NRA
Las Vegas, NV

Projection: NAD83 UTM Zone 11.
Source: USDA Forest Service, Forest Inventory
& Analysis Program, 2011 data and National
GAP Analysis Program Land Cover Data, V. 2.
FIA data and mapping tools are available at
http://fia.fs.fed.us/tools-data/.
By Jeri Ledbetter, METI, March 2012.

0   2.5   5   10 Miles
0   4   8   16 Kilometers

Potential habitat is defined by elevations between 1,529 and 3,470 meters in all biomes,
including conifer forest, sagebrush, chaparral, desert habitats, montane meadows,
avalanche chutes, and areas recovering by fire. They are often found on slopes in
the central portion of SMNRA.

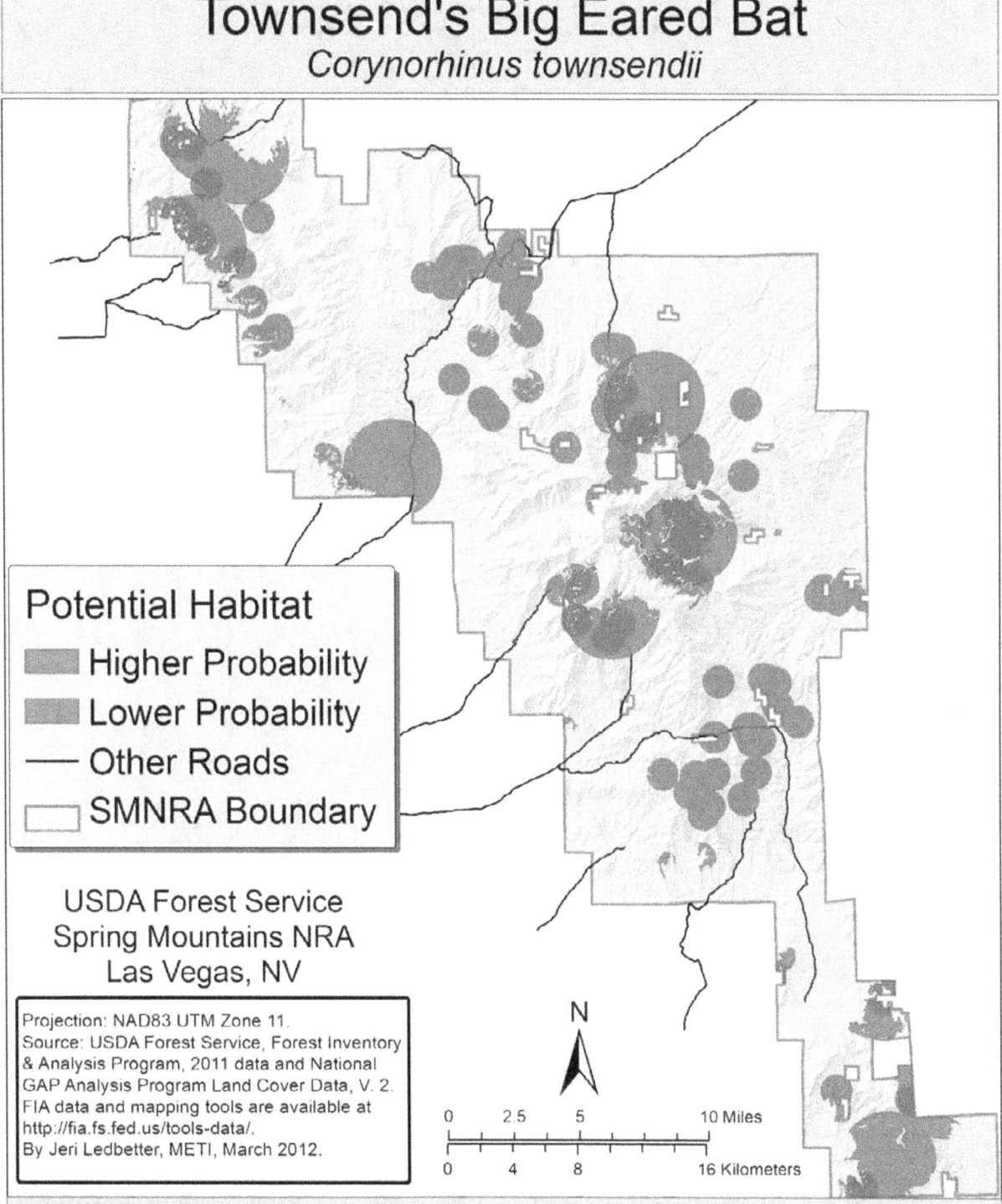

Townsend's Big Eared Bat
Corynorhinus townsendii

Potential Habitat
- Higher Probability
- Lower Probability
- Other Roads
- SMNRA Boundary

USDA Forest Service
Spring Mountains NRA
Las Vegas, NV

Projection: NAD83 UTM Zone 11.
Source: USDA Forest Service, Forest Inventory
& Analysis Program, 2011 data and National
GAP Analysis Program Land Cover Data, V. 2.
FIA data and mapping tools are available at
http://fia.fs.fed.us/tools-data/.
By Jeri Ledbetter, METI, March 2012.

N

| 0 | 2.5 | 5 | 10 Miles |
| 0 | 4 | 8 | 16 Kilometers |

Potential habitat is defined by elevations between 1,689 and 2,956 meters in forest, scrub,
sagebrush, and riparian biomes. High probability habitat is in mine tunnels and caves within 3 km
of springs or perennial streams. Lower probability habitat is within 1 km of springs or perennial
streams where they may roost in cliffs, cracks, crevices, and trees with cave-like spaces.

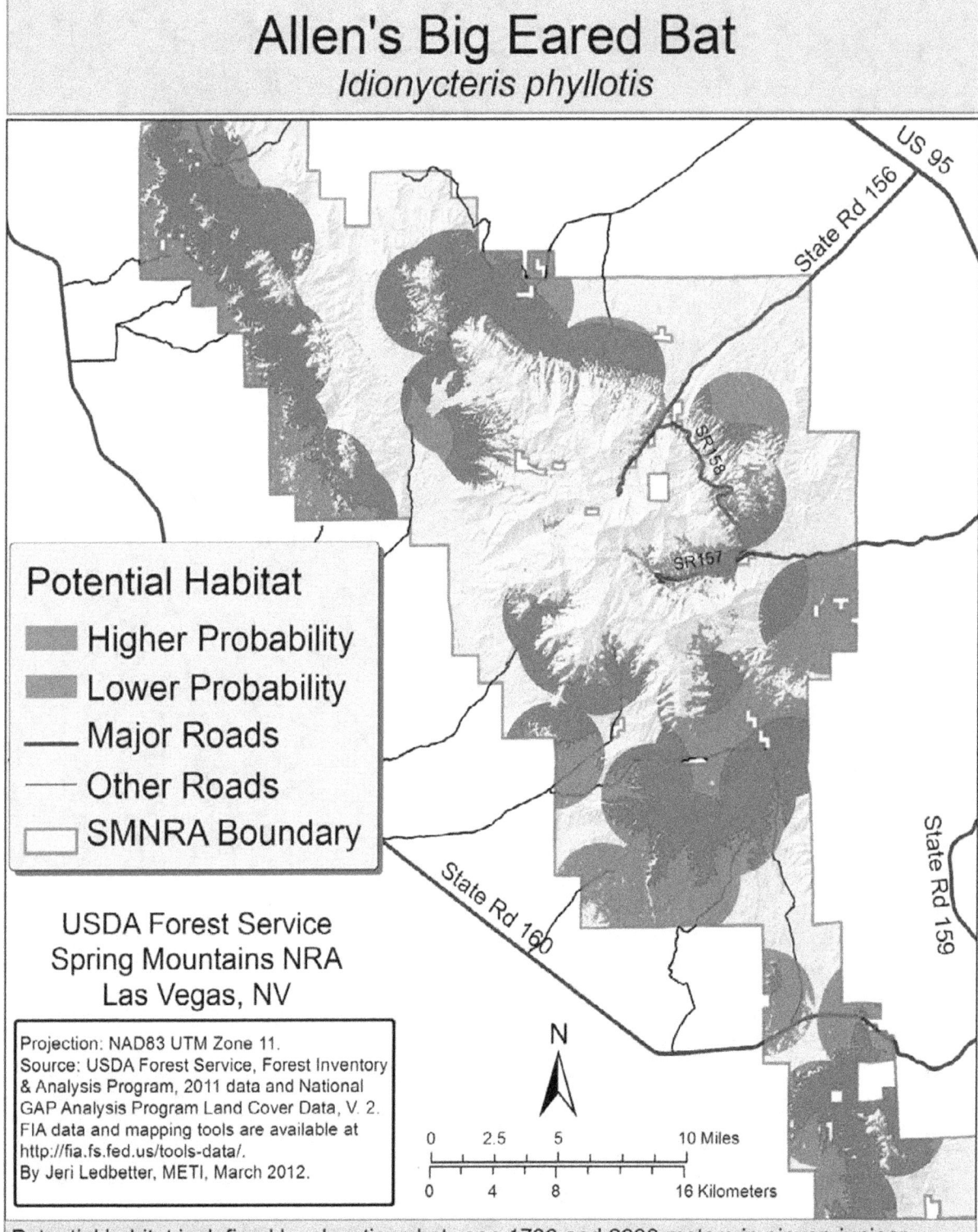

Allen's Big Eared Bat
Idionycteris phyllotis

Potential Habitat

- Higher Probability
- Lower Probability
- Major Roads
- Other Roads
- SMNRA Boundary

USDA Forest Service
Spring Mountains NRA
Las Vegas, NV

Projection: NAD83 UTM Zone 11.
Source: USDA Forest Service, Forest Inventory
& Analysis Program, 2011 data and National
GAP Analysis Program Land Cover Data, V. 2.
FIA data and mapping tools are available at
http://fia.fs.fed.us/tools-data/.
By Jeri Ledbetter, METI, March 2012.

0   2.5   5   10 Miles
0   4   8   16 Kilometers

Potential habitat is defined by elevations between 1736 and 2300 meters in pinyon-juniper,
chaparral, sagebrush and blackbrush biomes. High probability habitat is within 3 km of mines,
tunnels, and exposed rock features near springs. Lower probability habitat is in riparian forests
of all elevations as well as prime habitat near springs where they may roost in snags.

Species Fact Sheet

Species: *Neotamias palmeri*
Common Names: Palmer's chipmunk, Mount Charleston chipmunk

General SMNRA Habitat Characteristics: Potential habitat is likely between 2,400-2,550 meters of elevation and moderate between 2,100-3,600 meters of elevation in coniferous forests.

Known Distribution: SMNRA endemic

Known Distribution Within SMNRA: Can be locally abundant. Found more commonly on the east side of the Spring Mountain Range. Specifically, the species has been found at the following locations: Clark Canyon, Foxtail Canyon, Kyle Canyon campground, McWilliams campground, Mary Jane Falls trailhead, Deer Creek, Camp Stimpson (at the north fork of Deer Creek), and the Old Mill picnic area.

Current FS-R4 Species Status: None

Genetic Information: *Neotamias palmeri's* closest relative appears to be *Tamias umbrinus* (Uinta chipmunk). The two species are separated by an expanse of desert and developed areas, which prevent their interaction.

Literature Review Synopsis: Species description: Palmer's chipmunks are reddish-brown in color, ranging to more gray towards the shoulders, with black and white stripes down the back and a white underbelly (Figure 1). Adults average 220 mm in length, weigh 50-70 grams, and their average life span is 1-4 years. (Klinger 2005) They are diurnal and nest in burrows or they may use holes in trees or downed logs. (Klinger 2005) Palmer's chipmunk molts twice a year, shedding its winter coat in May, June, or July and its summer coat in August, September, or October. (Smithsonian 1999). Mating occurs probably in April and early May; births occur in late May or June; gestation lasts at least 33 days; litter size usually 3-6; young first emerge in June, continue to appear through August (Best 1993). *E. palmeri* is a tree-nesting chipmunk. It is during the period of weaning and exploration, just before the young disperse, that tree nests are used by a mother and her family. Chipmunks appear to be the only sciurids, and possibly the only rodents, in which the mother and her family use both underground and arboreal nests in a given year. (Broadbrooks 1974) Palmer's chipmunk activity is very limited during the cold winter months, with winter activity limited to sunny winter days (Hirshfield 1975)

Diet: Palmer's chipmunk eats seeds, particularly conifer seeds, fruits, fleshy fungi, green vegetation, and insects (Smithsonian 1999, Klinger 2005). Seeds, fruits, greens, and flowers occurred in all stomachs examined from March through September, with seeds and fruits generally greater in volume and equal in frequency to greens and flowers. Arthropods often were found, except in spring months. Small amounts of lichens, bark, and carrion also are consumed (Hirshfeld, 1975).

Habitat/Distribution: Palmer's chipmunk is endemic to the coniferous forests of the Spring Mountains. It is found in bristlecone pine, white fir, ponderosa pine, aspen, and the upper elevation pinyon-juniper communities. Studies have reported Palmer's chipmunk at a range of elevations from 2100m to timberline at 3700m (Deacon et al. 1964, Hirshfield and Bradley 1977,Best 1993, Lowery and Riddle 2004, McKelvey et al. 2012). According to most of these authors, Palmer's chipmunk is more common at higher elevations (above 2250m). Mckelvey et al.(2012) and Lowery and Longshore (2005) report that Palmer's chipmunk is relatively common in the high elevation forests across the SMNRA.

Genetics: McKelvey et.al. (2012) conducted trapping and genetic material collections during the 2010-12 field seasons. The objectives of the 2010 and 2011 studies were "1) to develop an effective approach to trap Palmer's chipmunks, 2) develop genetic markers that allow analysis of population structure in Palmer's, and 3) develop nuclear DNA markers that discriminate Palmer's from Panamint chipmunks and thereby allow reliable species identification without the need for extra genetic tests. In the second, full season (2011), our goals were to sample across the extent of the Spring Mountains to determine the range and population structure of Palmer's chipmunks. With this broader sample we also could evaluate the degree to which the 2 species overlapped, and look for signs of hybridization." The results of their studies produced data that address all of the objectives. Genetic makers were developed for both Palmer's and Panamint chipmunks, which allowed reliable differentiation between the species. Furthermore, they confirmed that the species are genetically well separated and do not produce hybrid individuals. Palmer's chipmunk exists in populations that are genetically well mixed, i.e. the species doesn't have subpopulations, has not undergone recent genetic bottlenecks and, that with the expected heterozygosities of approximately 0.5, indicates a fairly large population.

Future research: The ecotone between Palmer's chipmunk and Panamint chipmunk is very narrow with limited overlap. Most climate models predict an upward elevation shift of vegetation communities and narrow ecotones are ideal for the study of climate change response in vegetation communities and their associated fauna.

KcKelvey et al. (2012) outlines additional research that will further delineate the ecotone between Palmer's and Panamint through the placement of additional trapping grids along elevation gradients extending from ~2250-2350 m to test the robustness of a 2300 m elevational cutoff to delineate ranges of Palmer's and Panamint chipmunks. They further suggest "it might be worthwhile to sample in areas near to the summit of Mt. Stirling to be sure that Palmer's does not occur in high elevation piñyon-juniper forests. Lastly, it would be extremely useful to obtain chipmunks from high elevation areas within the Sheep Range to determine the degree of relatedness between Hidden Forest chipmunk (*Tamias umbrinus nevadensis)* and Palmer's."

References:

Ambos, Aaron M.; Tomlinson, Cris R. 1996. Distribution, abundance and habitat components of the Palmer's chipmunk (*Tamias palmeri*) in the Spring Mountains of southern Nevada. Cox, Mike K.; Herron, Gary B., eds. Nevada Division of Wildlife, Reno, NV. Job Performance Report. Federal Aid in Wildlife Restoration. Endangered Species Act—Section 6. Project EW-2-5. 1994 and 1995 survey seasons 21 p.

Request from the report: Persons are free to use material in these reports for educational purposes. However, since most reports treat only part of continuing studies, persons intending to use this material in scientific publications should obtain prior permission from the Division of Wildlife. In all cases, tentative conclusions should be identified as such in quotation, and due credit would be appreciated.

Best, Troy L. 1993. *Tamias palmeri: Tamias palmeri* (Merriam, 1897) Palmer's Chipmunk. Mammalian Species. No 443. p 1-6. Published by the American Society of Mammalogists.

Broadbrooks, H. E. 1974. Tree nests of chipmunks with comments on associated behavior and ecology Journal of Mammalogy, 55:630-649. http://www.jstor.org/stable/pdfplus/1379551.pdf

Gannon, William L.; Stanley, William T. 1991. Chip vocalization of Palmer's chipmunk (*Tamias palmeri*) Southwestern Naturalist, Sept. 1991; 36(3): 315-317

IUCN 2011. IUCN Red List of Threatened Species. Version 2011.1. <www.iucnredlist.org>. Downloaded on 28 July 2011.

Klinger, C.M. 2005. Species Investigations: Palmer's Chipmunk Survey and Inventory. Nevada Department of Wildlife. 13 p.

Lowrey, Chris; Riddle, Brett R. 2004. A protocol for monitoring relative changes in abundance of Palmers Chipmunk (*Tamias palmeri*). Prepared for the US Forest Service, Spring Mountains National Recreation Area under FWS agreement # 14320-9-J102

Lowrey, Christopher. 2002. Ecology and Growth of *Tamias Palmeri* and Testing of a Protocol to Monitor Habitat Relationships. M.S. Thesis, Unpublished document from UNLV Dept. of Biological Sciences University of Nevada, Las Vegas.

Lowrey, Christopher; Longshore, Kathleen. 2005 Draft. Long-term Conservation Strategy for the Palmers Chipmunk (*Tamias palmeri*) within the Spring Mountains, Nevada. US Geological Survey. Western Ecological Research Center, Las Vegas Field Station, Henderson, NV. Prepared for Clark County Multiple Species Habitat Conservation Plan. 43 p.

Merriam, C.H. 1897. Notes on the chipmunks of the genus *Eutamias* occurring west of the east base of the Cascade-Sierra system, with descriptions of new forms Proceedings of the Biological Society of Washington, 11:189-212.

McKelvey, K.S.; Ramirez, J.E.; Schwartz, M.K.; Pilgrim, K. 2012. Genetic sampling of Palmer's chipmunks in the Spring Mountains, Nevada: report on sampling 2010-2011. Unpublished report, U.S. Department of Agriculture, Forest Service, Rocky Mountain Research Station. 14 p.

NatureServe. 2011. Palmers Chipmunk (*Tamias Palmeri*). NatureServe Explorer: An online encyclopedia of life [web application]. Version 7.1. NatureServe, Arlington, Virginia. Available http://www.natureserve.org/explorer. (Accessed: July 22, 2011).

Photo from: Lowrey, Christopher; Longshore, Kathleen. 2005 Draft. Long-term Conservation Strategy for the Palmers Chipmunk (*Tamias palmeri*) within the Spring Mountains, Nevada. US Geological Survey. Western Ecological Research Center, Las Vegas Field Station, Henderson, NV. Prepared for Clark County Multiple Species Habitat Conservation Plan. 43 p.

Smithsonian. 1999. Palmer's chipmunk, *Tamias palmeri* In: D.E. Wilson, S. Ruff, eds. The Smithsonian Book of North American Mammals. Washington: The Smithsonian Institution Press in Association with the American Society of Mammalogists, p. 372-373

Tomlinson, C. R. 2001. 1999-2000 Palmer's Chipmunk Report. Distribution and abundance of the Palmer's chipmunk (*Tamias palmeri*) in the Spring Mountains of southern Nevada. Nevada Division of Wildlife, Reno, Nevada. 5p.

Request from the report: (Persons are free to use material in these reports for educational purposes. However, since most reports treat only part of continuing studies, persons intending to use this material in scientific publications should obtain prior permission from the Division of Wildlife. In all cases, tentative conclusions should be identified as such in quotation, and due credit would be appreciated.)

Establishment and Maintenance Record

Version	Date	Author/Editor	Summary
1.0	5/9/12	Burton K. Pendleton, Research Ecologist, Rocky Mountain Research Station	Information compiled from the SMNRA Species Reference Database using information posted as of 5/9/12.

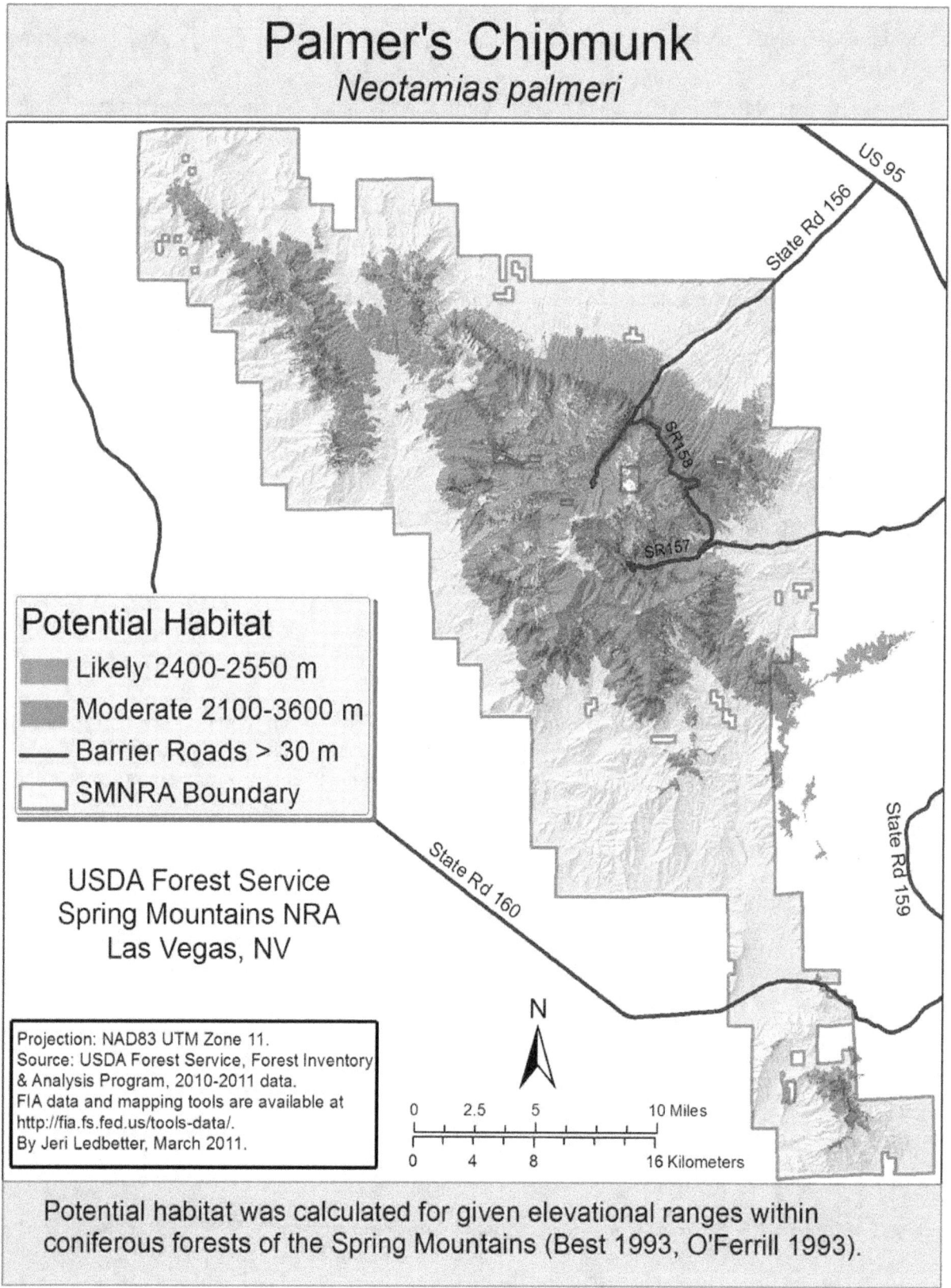

Palmer's Chipmunk
Neotamias palmeri

Potential Habitat

■ Likely 2400-2550 m

■ Moderate 2100-3600 m

— Barrier Roads > 30 m

☐ SMNRA Boundary

USDA Forest Service
Spring Mountains NRA
Las Vegas, NV

Projection: NAD83 UTM Zone 11.
Source: USDA Forest Service, Forest Inventory
& Analysis Program, 2010-2011 data.
FIA data and mapping tools are available at
http://fia.fs.fed.us/tools-data/.
By Jeri Ledbetter, March 2011.

N

| 0 | 2.5 | 5 | 10 Miles |

| 0 | 4 | 8 | 16 Kilometers |

Potential habitat was calculated for given elevational ranges within coniferous forests of the Spring Mountains (Best 1993, O'Ferrill 1993).

Appendix B-25: Rough angelica (*Angelica scabrida*) – Species Fact Sheet and Potential Habitat Map

Species Fact Sheet (Provisional)[7]

Species: *Angelica scabrida*
Common Names: Rough angelica, Charleston Mountain angelica

General SMNRA Habitat Characteristics: Potential habitat is defined by elevations between 1128 and 3500 meters in mixed conifer and riparian biomes on calcareous-based soils. High probability habitat is within 50 m of springs and streams. Lower probability habitat is on steep mountain slopes.

Known Distribution: Found on public (USFS and BLM) and private land. Occurs at 18 sites in the Spring Mountains National Recreation Area, and the Red Rock Canyon National Conservation Area. (Hermi and Boone 2003). "Maximum range dimension 27.7 km (17.2 mi)" (Morefield 2001)

Known Distribution Within SMNRA: Kyle Canyon area, Stanley B Spring, Fletcher Spring. (Beyer 2003;Hermi and Boone 2003), La Madre Spring, possibly around springs above the Narrows in Lovell Canyon (Lund 2003, Walker 2005)

Current FSR4 Species Status: Sensitive

Genetic Information: Unknown

Literature Review Synopsis: Rough angelica is a perennial plant growing to 1.5 m (60 in.) tall. The stems are rough and pubescent. Leaves are large with basal leaves to 1 m (39 in.) in diameter and stem leaves to 40 cm (15.7 in.) All leaves are pinnate with 9 leaflets arranged in groups of three; leaflets 8 - 16 cm (3 - 6 in.) long. Inflorescences are in umbels (umbrella-like), with up to 40 flowers on stalks 2 - 12 mm (to 0.5 in.) long. Flowers have sepals 5, petals 5, and are white. The fruit is a capsule, flattened, 8 - 14 mm (to 0.6 in.) long and has narrow wings, which are either rough or smooth at maturity. Phenology : flowering July to August. The pedicels and major stalks are rough to the touch, hence the specific name *scabrida*. (Hermi and Boone 2003).

References:

Beyer, C. 2003. Rough angelica monitoring in the Kyle Canyon summer homes fuels reduction area. 4p

ENTRIX, Inc. 2008. Spring Mountains National Recreation Area Landscape Analysis. Unpublished report submitted to the U.S. Department of Agriculture, Forest Service, Humboldt-Toiyabe National Forest, Las Vegas, Nevada. Chapter 4.

---

[7] Provisional - Location information to be supplemented by data in NRM-NRIS from species and site-specific surveys.

Hiatt, H. and Boone, J.,eds. 2003. Clark County, Nevada, Species Account Manual. Department of Comprehensive Planning. 218 p.

Lund, Bruce. 2003. Nevada Native Species Site Survey Report. Survey conducted 30 September 2003. Report on file (electronic) at the U.S. Department of Agriculture, Forest Service, Rocky Mountain Research Station, Albuquerque Lab, NM.

Morefield, J.D., ed. 2001. Rare Plant Fact Sheet. *Angelica scabrida*. Nevada Rare Plant Atlas. Nevada Natural Heritage Program. Nevada Department of Conservation and Natural Resources, Carson City, Nevada. Produced for the U.S. Department of the Interior Fish and Wildlife Service, Portland, Oregon and Reno, Nevada. http://heritage.nv.gov/atlas/atlasndx.htm

Nachlinger, J.L., and Combs, J. 1996. Biological Monitoring Plan for *Angelica scabrida* (rough angelica) on the Toiyave National Forest, Spring Mountains National recreation Area. The Nature Conservancy, Northern Nevada Office, Reno, Nevada. 15 p plus appendices.

Photo by Joanne Baggs. U.S. Department of Agriculture, Forest Service. Humboldt-Toiyabe National Forest website. http://www.fs.usda.gov/detail/htnf/learning/nature-science/?cid=fsm9_026885

USDA Forest Service (USFS). 1998. Conservation agreement for the Spring Mountains National Recreation Area, Clark and Nye Counties, Nevada. U.S. Forest Service, Intermountain Region; State of Nevada, Department of Conservation and Natural Resources; and U.S. Fish and Wildlife Service, Pacific Region.

USDA Forest Service (USFS). 2003. Conservation Agreement Report and Five-year Analyses for the Spring Mountains National Recreation Area, Clark and Nye Counties, Nevada. U.S. Forest Service, Intermountain Region; State of Nevada, Department of Conservation and Natural Resources; and U.S. Fish and Wildlife Service, Pacific Region.

USDA Forest Service (USFS). 2011. Intermountain Region (R4) threatened, endangered, proposed, and, sensitive species: Known/suspected distribution by forest. July 27, 2011 update. 19 p. www.fs.fed.us/r4/resources/tes/r4_tes_lst.pdf

Walker, K.C. 2005. 2005 Biological Monitoring Report for *Angelica scabrida* on the Humboldt-Toiyabe National Forest Spring Mountains National Recreation Area. Unpublished report for the Humboldt-Toiyabe National Forest, Spring Mountains National Recreation Area, Las Vegas, Nevada. 11 p. plus appendices.

Establishment and Maintenance Record

Version	Date	Author/Editor	Summary
1.0	5/7/12	Burton Pendleton, Research Ecologist, Rocky Mountain Research Station	Information compiled from the SMNRA Species Reference Database using information posted as of 5/7/12. **Provisional Fact Sheet** - Location information to be supplemented by data in NRM-NRIS from species and site-specific surveys.

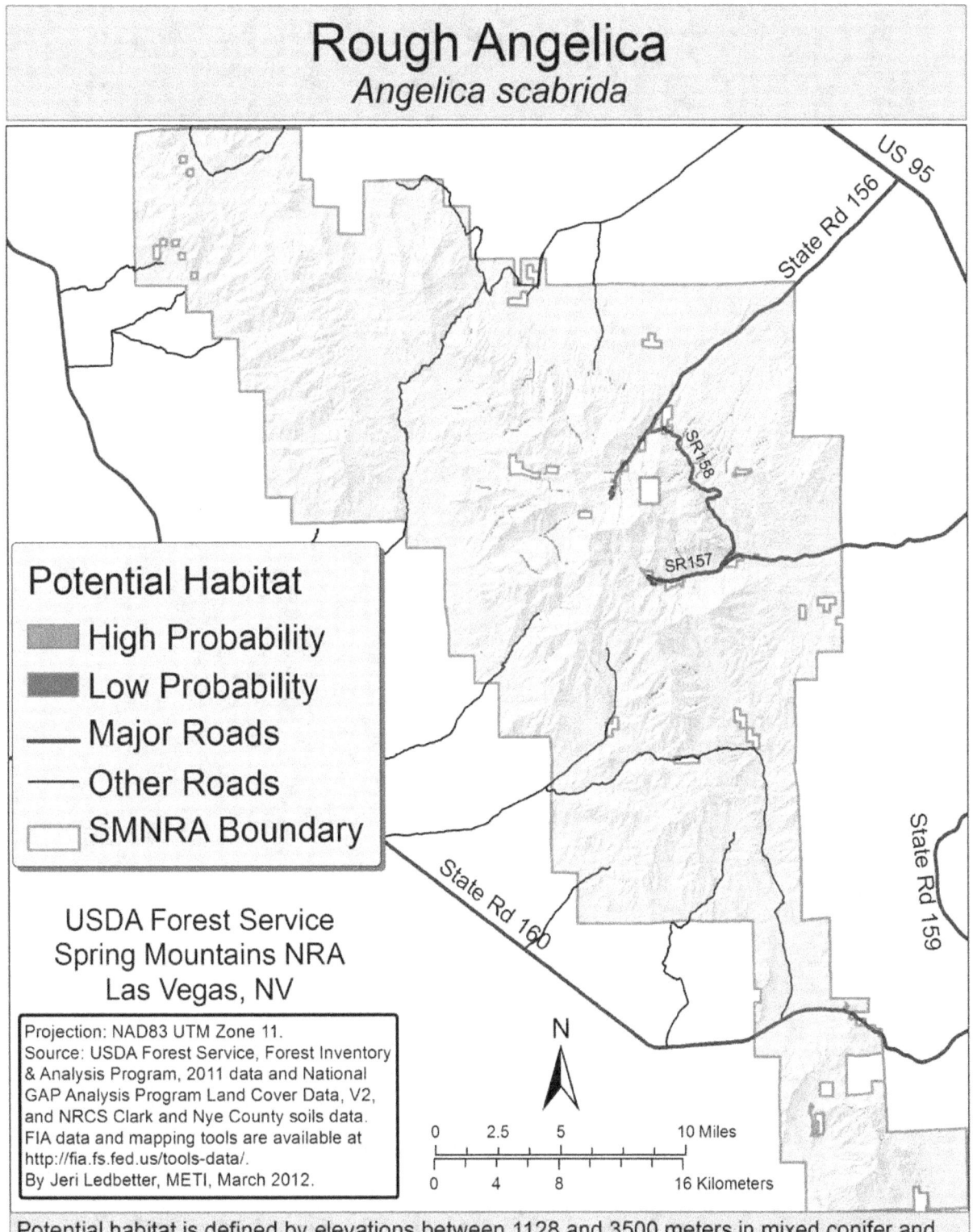

Rough Angelica
Angelica scabrida

Potential Habitat

- High Probability
- Low Probability
- Major Roads
- Other Roads
- SMNRA Boundary

USDA Forest Service
Spring Mountains NRA
Las Vegas, NV

Projection: NAD83 UTM Zone 11.
Source: USDA Forest Service, Forest Inventory
& Analysis Program, 2011 data and National
GAP Analysis Program Land Cover Data, V2,
and NRCS Clark and Nye County soils data.
FIA data and mapping tools are available at
http://fia.fs.fed.us/tools-data/.
By Jeri Ledbetter, METI, March 2012.

0   2.5   5   10 Miles

0   4   8   16 Kilometers

Potential habitat is defined by elevations between 1128 and 3500 meters in mixed conifer and riparian biomes on calcareous-based soils. High probability habitat is within 50 m of springs and streams. Lower probability habitat is on steep mountain slopes.

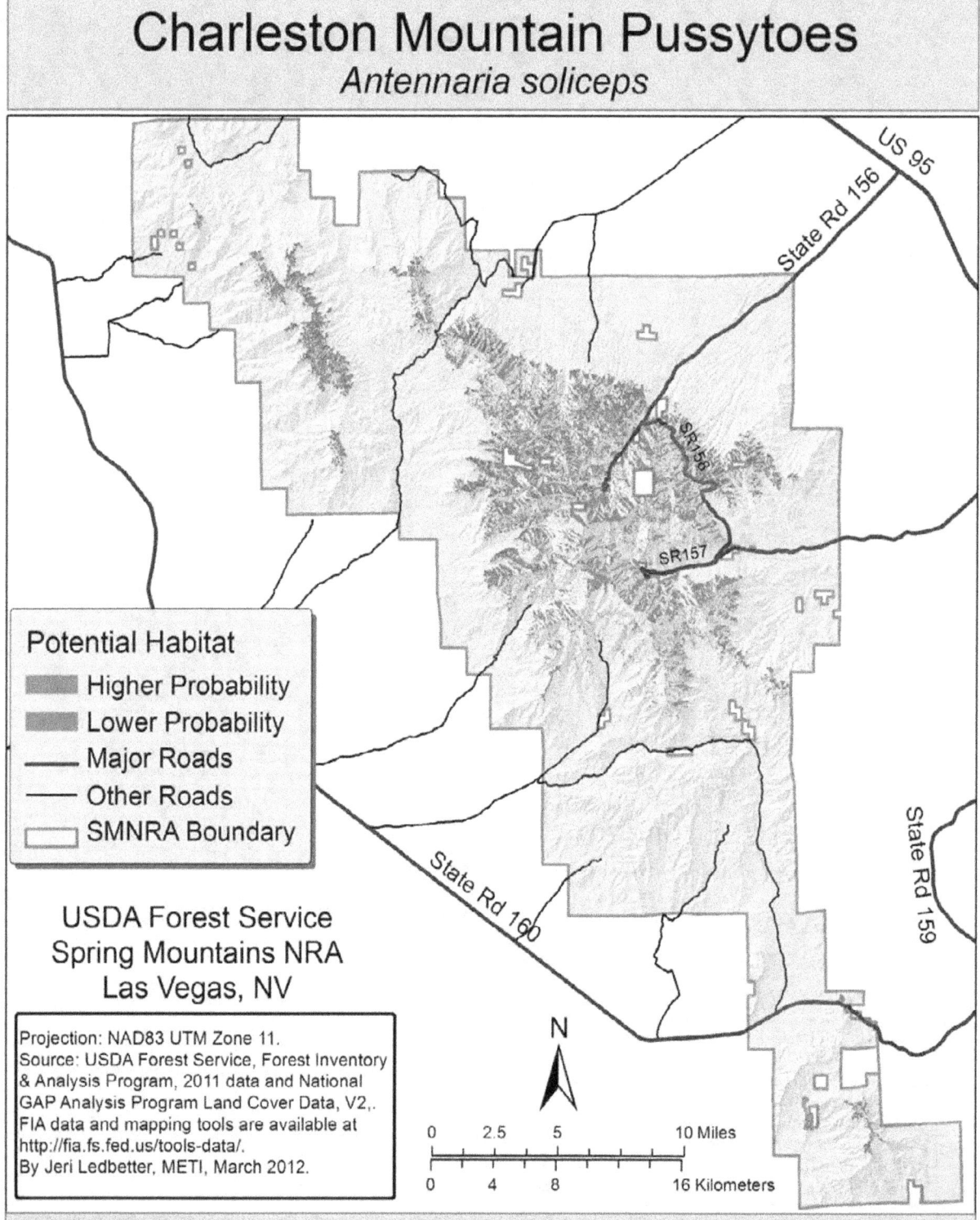

Charleston Mountain Pussytoes
Antennaria soliceps

Potential Habitat

- Higher Probability
- Lower Probability
- Major Roads
- Other Roads
- SMNRA Boundary

**USDA Forest Service
Spring Mountains NRA
Las Vegas, NV**

Projection: NAD83 UTM Zone 11.
Source: USDA Forest Service, Forest Inventory
& Analysis Program, 2011 data and National
GAP Analysis Program Land Cover Data, V2,.
FIA data and mapping tools are available at
http://fia.fs.fed.us/tools-data/.
By Jeri Ledbetter, METI, March 2012.

0   2.5   5   10 Miles

0   4   8   16 Kilometers

N

US 95
State Rd 156
SR156
SR157
State Rd 160
State Rd 159

Potential habitat is defined by elevations between 2359 and 3510 meters in mixed conifer and mountain meadow biomes. High probability habitat is on open talus or scree slopes. Lower probability habitat is on north-facing slopes (within 45 degrees of 0) in the same biome and elevation range.

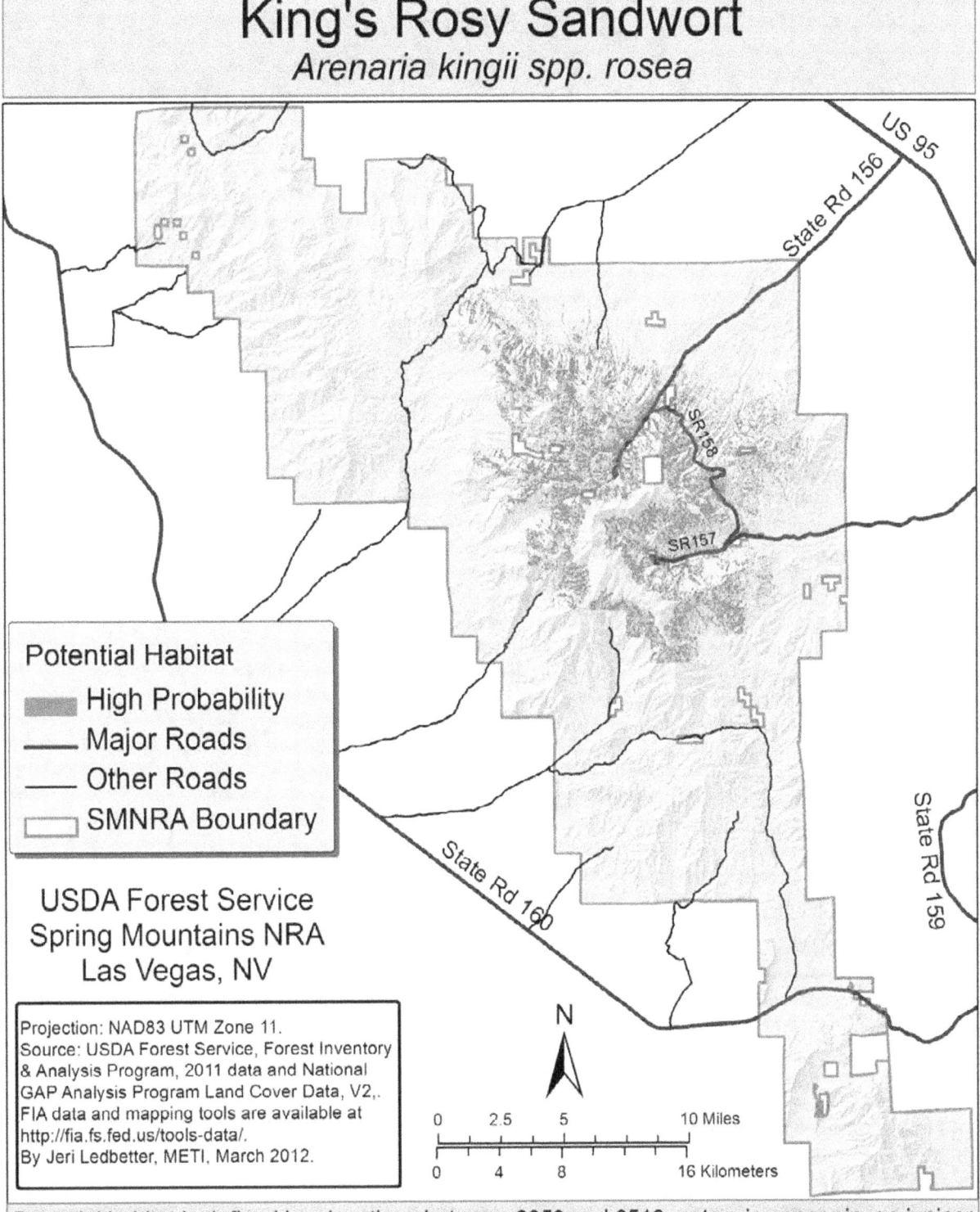

King's Rosy Sandwort
Arenaria kingii spp. rosea

Potential Habitat

- ▬ High Probability
- ── Major Roads
- ── Other Roads
- ▢ SMNRA Boundary

**USDA Forest Service
Spring Mountains NRA
Las Vegas, NV**

Projection: NAD83 UTM Zone 11.
Source: USDA Forest Service, Forest Inventory
& Analysis Program, 2011 data and National
GAP Analysis Program Land Cover Data, V2,.
FIA data and mapping tools are available at
http://fia.fs.fed.us/tools-data/.
By Jeri Ledbetter, METI, March 2012.

0 2.5 5 10 Miles
0 4 8 16 Kilometers

Potential habitat is defined by elevations between 2359 and 3510 meters in upper pinyon-juniper and mixed conifer biomes with a relatively open (30-60%) cover in the eastern portion of the Spring Mountains NRA.

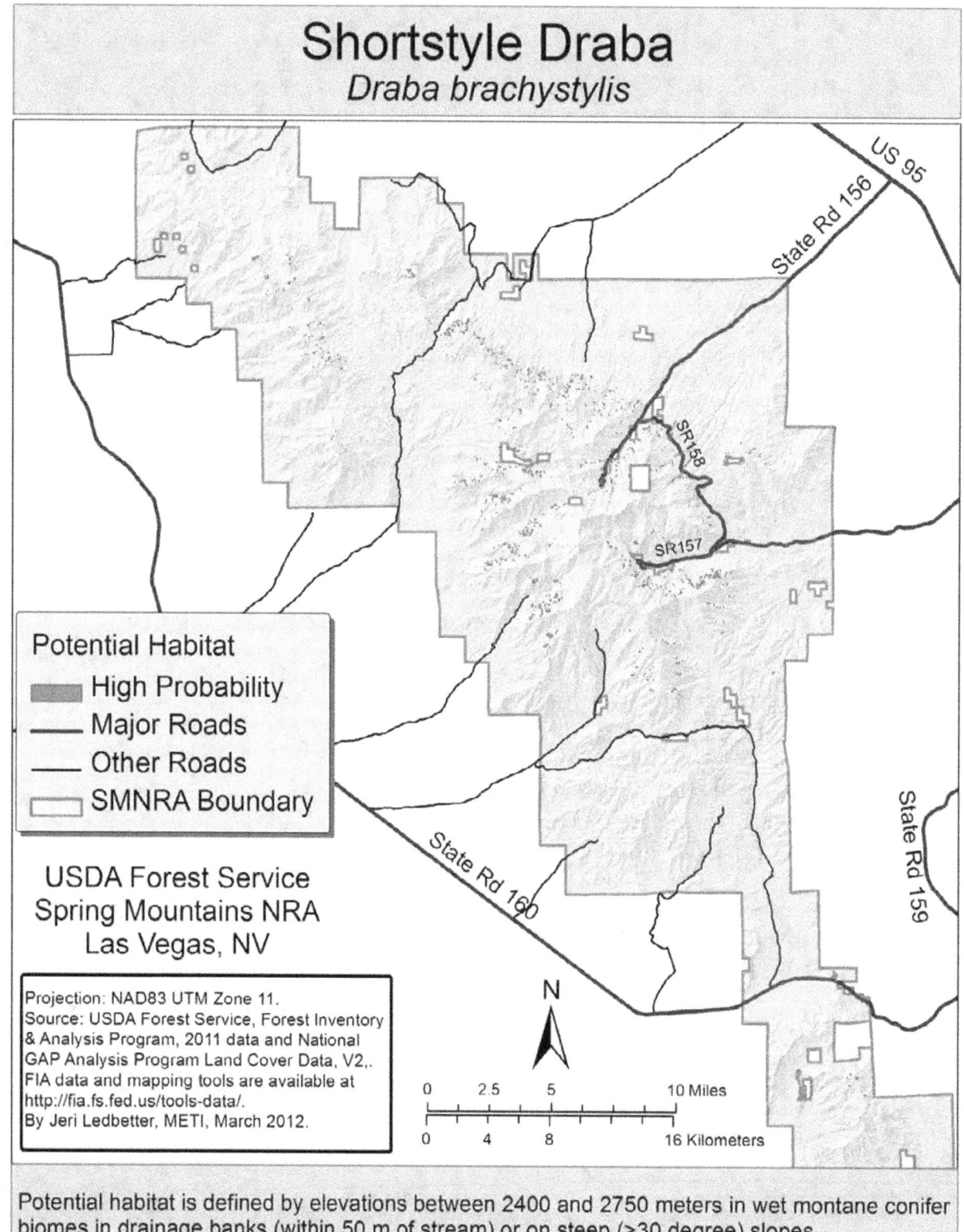

Shortstyle Draba
Draba brachystylis

Potential Habitat
- High Probability
- Major Roads
- Other Roads
- SMNRA Boundary

USDA Forest Service
Spring Mountains NRA
Las Vegas, NV

Projection: NAD83 UTM Zone 11.
Source: USDA Forest Service, Forest Inventory
& Analysis Program, 2011 data and National
GAP Analysis Program Land Cover Data, V2,.
FIA data and mapping tools are available at
http://fia.fs.fed.us/tools-data/.
By Jeri Ledbetter, METI, March 2012.

| 0 | 2.5 | 5 | 10 Miles |
| 0 | 4 | 8 | 16 Kilometers |

Potential habitat is defined by elevations between 2400 and 2750 meters in wet montane conifer biomes in drainage banks (within 50 m of stream) or on steep (>30 degree) slopes.

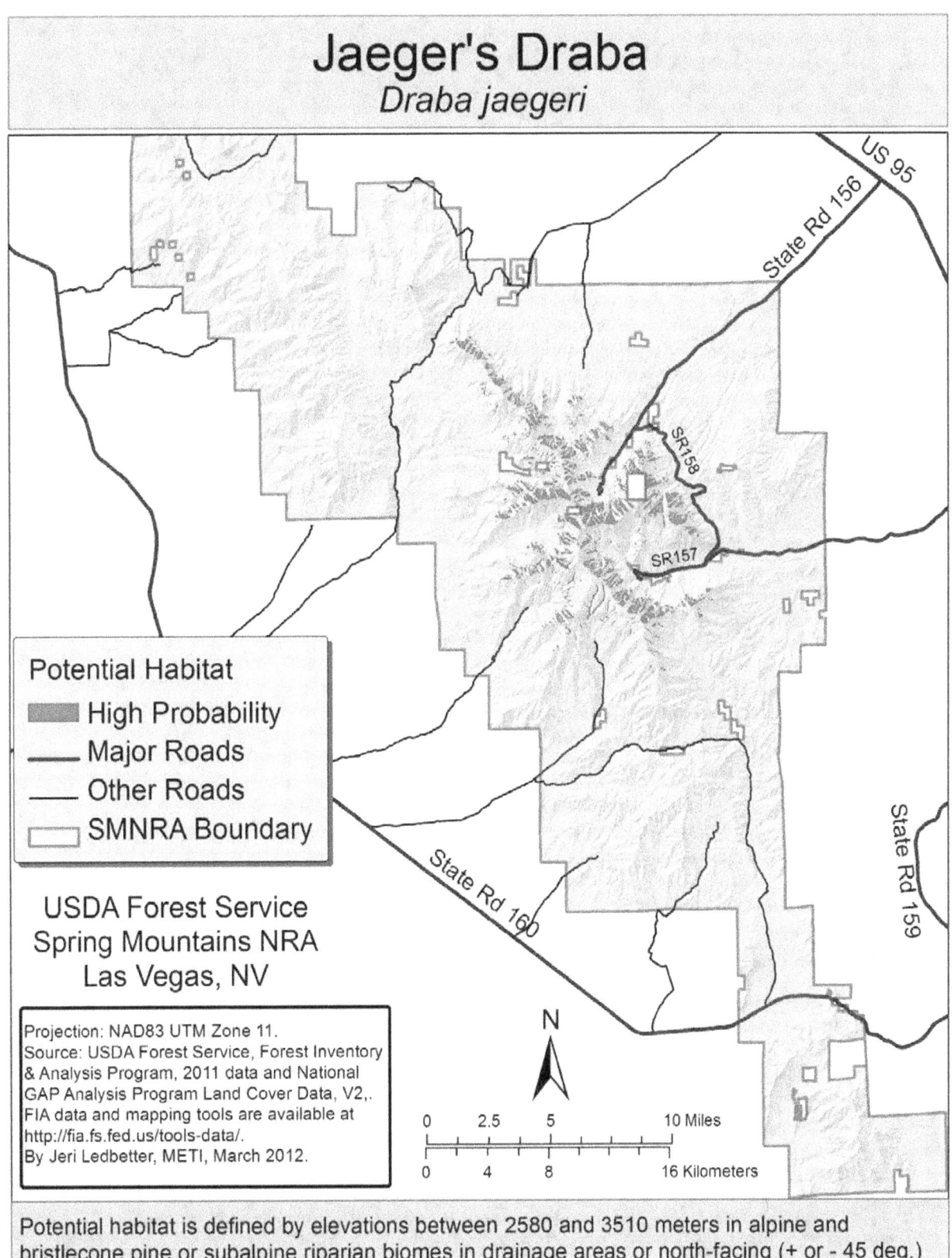

Jaeger's Draba
Draba jaegeri

Potential Habitat

■ High Probability
— Major Roads
— Other Roads
☐ SMNRA Boundary

USDA Forest Service
Spring Mountains NRA
Las Vegas, NV

Projection: NAD83 UTM Zone 11.
Source: USDA Forest Service, Forest Inventory
& Analysis Program, 2011 data and National
GAP Analysis Program Land Cover Data, V2,.
FIA data and mapping tools are available at
http://fia.fs.fed.us/tools-data/.
By Jeri Ledbetter, METI, March 2012.

N

| 0 | 2.5 | 5 | | 10 Miles |
| 0 | 4 | 8 | | 16 Kilometers |

Potential habitat is defined by elevations between 2580 and 3510 meters in alpine and
bristlecone pine or subalpine riparian biomes in drainage areas or north-facing (+ or - 45 deg.)
slopes where snowdrifts would lie until late summer.

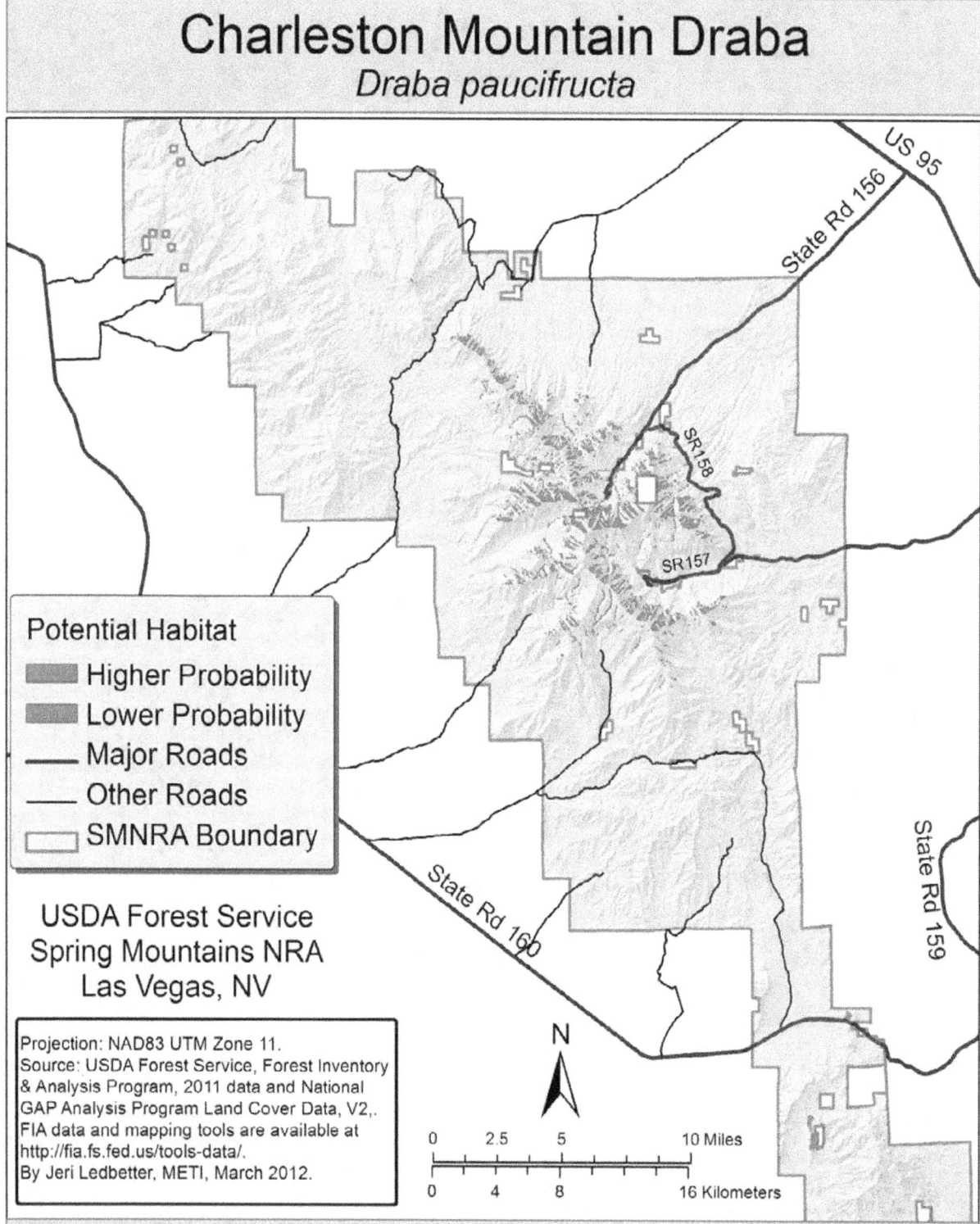

Charleston Mountain Draba
Draba paucifructa

Potential Habitat

▨ Higher Probability
▨ Lower Probability
— Major Roads
— Other Roads
▢ SMNRA Boundary

**USDA Forest Service
Spring Mountains NRA
Las Vegas, NV**

Projection: NAD83 UTM Zone 11.
Source: USDA Forest Service, Forest Inventory
& Analysis Program, 2011 data and National
GAP Analysis Program Land Cover Data, V2,.
FIA data and mapping tools are available at
http://fia.fs.fed.us/tools-data/.
By Jeri Ledbetter, METI, March 2012.

N

| 0 | 2.5 | 5 | 10 Miles |
| 0 | 4 | 8 | 16 Kilometers |

Higher probability habitat is defined by elevations between 2500 and 3484 meters in bristlecone
pine biomes in drainage areas or north-facing (+ or - 45 deg.) slopes where snowdrifts would lie
until late summer. Lower probability habitat is defined by the same elevation parameters in
mixed conifer forests on wetland margin areas (within 50 m of a spring or stream).

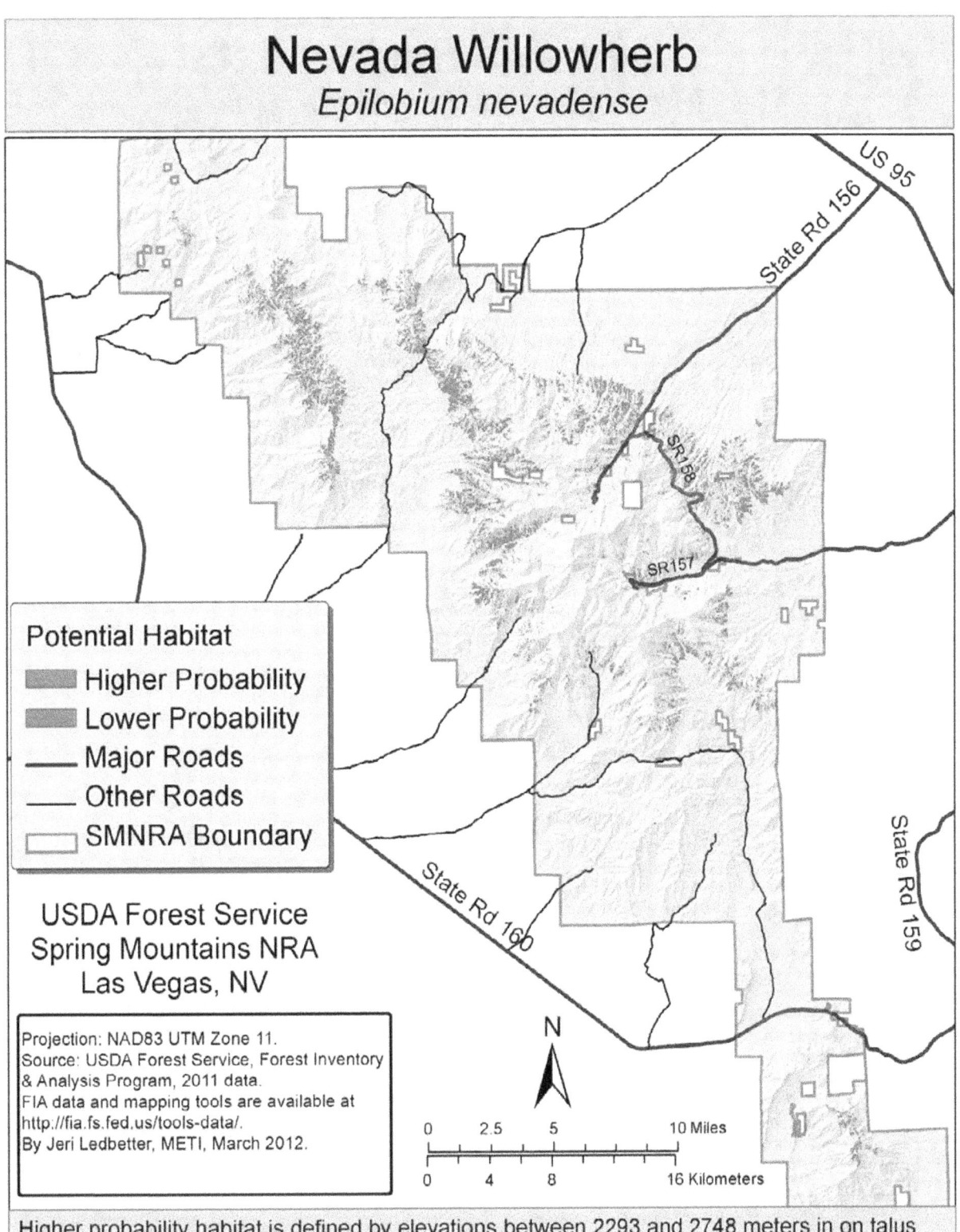

Nevada Willowherb
Epilobium nevadense

Potential Habitat

▬ Higher Probability
▬ Lower Probability
— Major Roads
— Other Roads
☐ SMNRA Boundary

USDA Forest Service
Spring Mountains NRA
Las Vegas, NV

Projection: NAD83 UTM Zone 11.
Source: USDA Forest Service, Forest Inventory
& Analysis Program, 2011 data.
FIA data and mapping tools are available at
http://fia.fs.fed.us/tools-data/.
By Jeri Ledbetter, METI, March 2012.

Higher probability habitat is defined by elevations between 2293 and 2748 meters in on talus slopes with topographic position from slope to upper slope in Clark County. Lower probability habitat is defined by the same elevation, soil, and topographic parameters in Nye County.

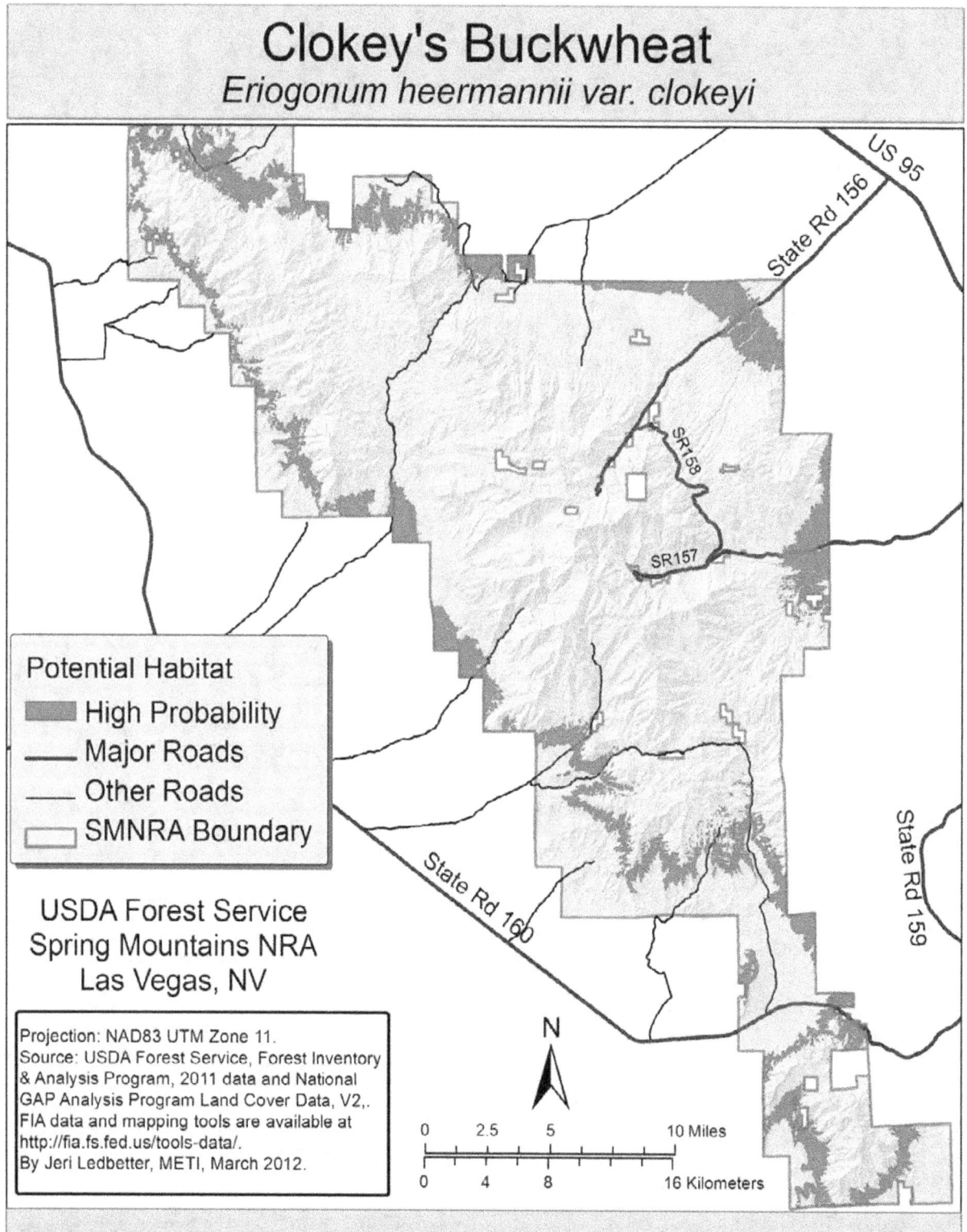

Clokey's Buckwheat
Eriogonum heermannii var. clokeyi

Potential Habitat
High Probability
Major Roads
Other Roads
SMNRA Boundary

USDA Forest Service
Spring Mountains NRA
Las Vegas, NV

Projection: NAD83 UTM Zone 11.
Source: USDA Forest Service, Forest Inventory
& Analysis Program, 2011 data and National
GAP Analysis Program Land Cover Data, V2,.
FIA data and mapping tools are available at
http://fia.fs.fed.us/tools-data/.
By Jeri Ledbetter, METI, March 2012.

0   2.5   5   10 Miles
0   4   8   16 Kilometers

Habitat is defined by elevations between 1642 and 1827 meters in creosote-bursage, shadscale, and blackbrush communities with total canopy cover of less than 10 percent.

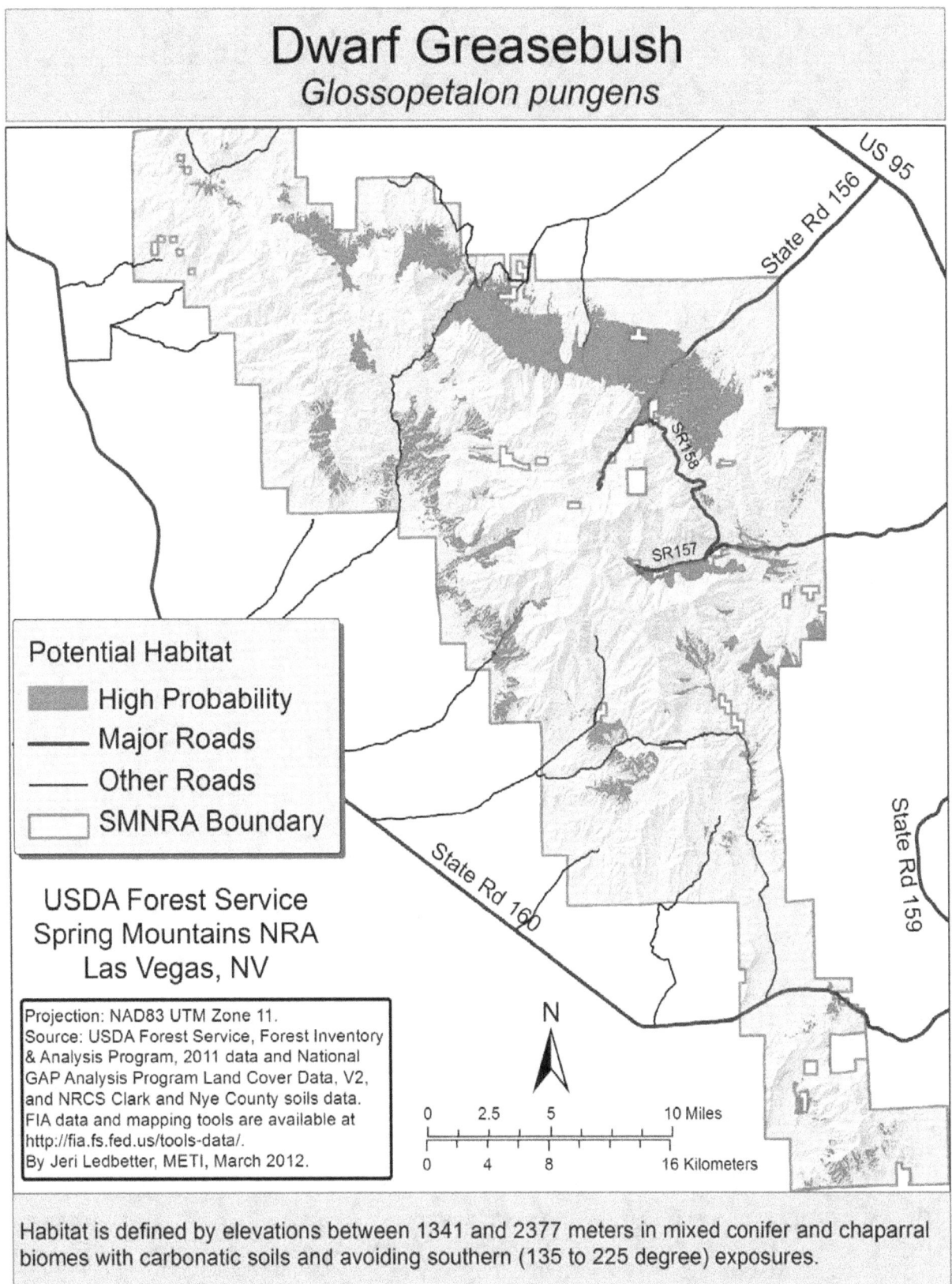

Dwarf Greasebush
Glossopetalon pungens

Potential Habitat

High Probability
Major Roads
Other Roads
SMNRA Boundary

USDA Forest Service
Spring Mountains NRA
Las Vegas, NV

Projection: NAD83 UTM Zone 11.
Source: USDA Forest Service, Forest Inventory
& Analysis Program, 2011 data and National
GAP Analysis Program Land Cover Data, V2,
and NRCS Clark and Nye County soils data.
FIA data and mapping tools are available at
http://fia.fs.fed.us/tools-data/.
By Jeri Ledbetter, METI, March 2012.

0   2.5   5   10 Miles

0   4   8   16 Kilometers

Habitat is defined by elevations between 1341 and 2377 meters in mixed conifer and chaparral biomes with carbonatic soils and avoiding southern (135 to 225 degree) exposures.

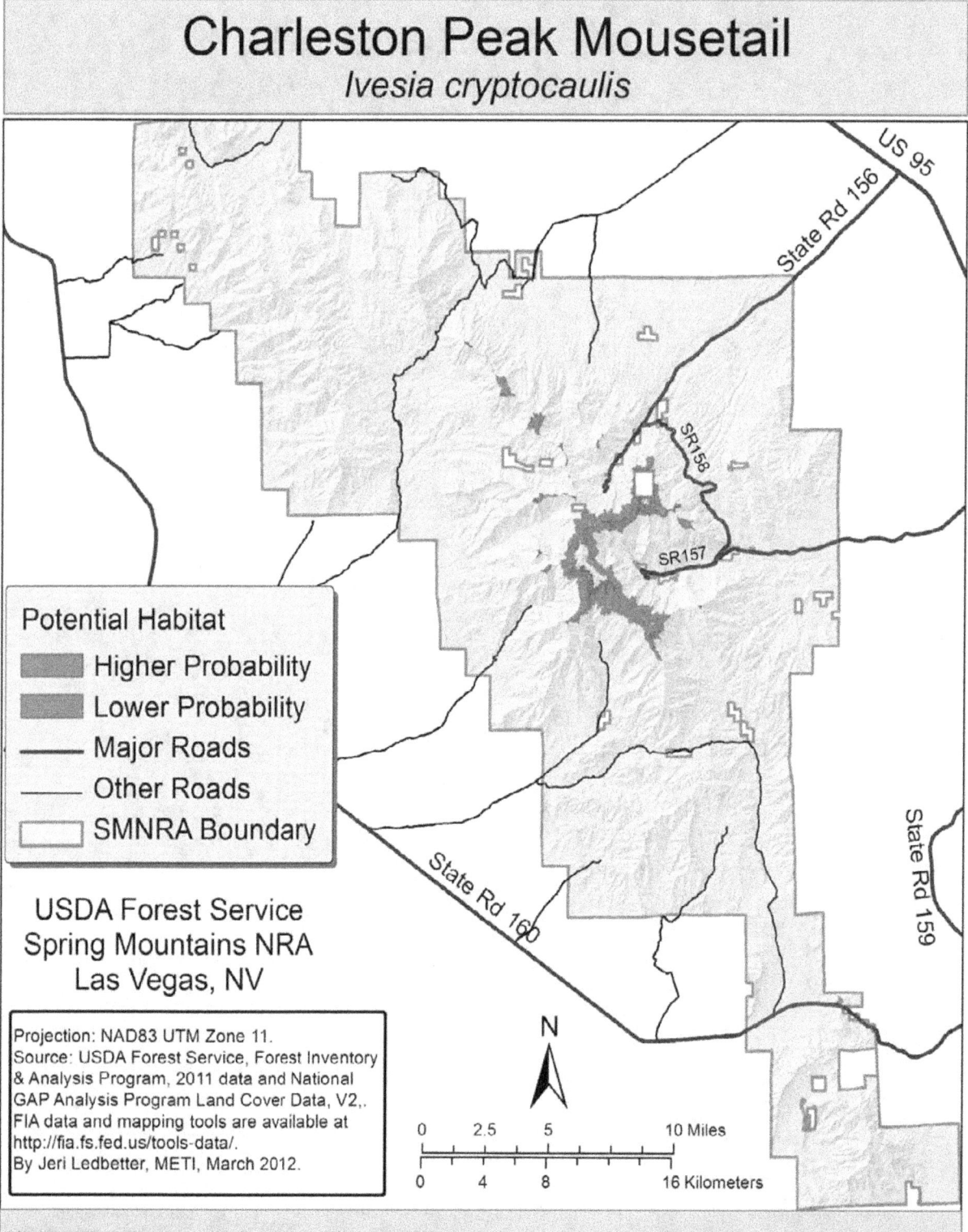

Charleston Peak Mousetail
Ivesia cryptocaulis

Potential Habitat

- **Higher Probability**
- **Lower Probability**
- —— Major Roads
- — Other Roads
- ☐ SMNRA Boundary

USDA Forest Service
Spring Mountains NRA
Las Vegas, NV

Projection: NAD83 UTM Zone 11.
Source: USDA Forest Service, Forest Inventory
& Analysis Program, 2011 data and National
GAP Analysis Program Land Cover Data, V2,.
FIA data and mapping tools are available at
http://fia.fs.fed.us/tools-data/.
By Jeri Ledbetter, METI, March 2012.

0   2.5   5   10 Miles

0   4   8   16 Kilometers

High probability habitat is defined by elevations above 3006 meters in mixed conifer biomes in open talus and scree areas. Lower probability habitat is with similar elevation and vegetation parameters where it may be found in local outcrops or gravelly soils.

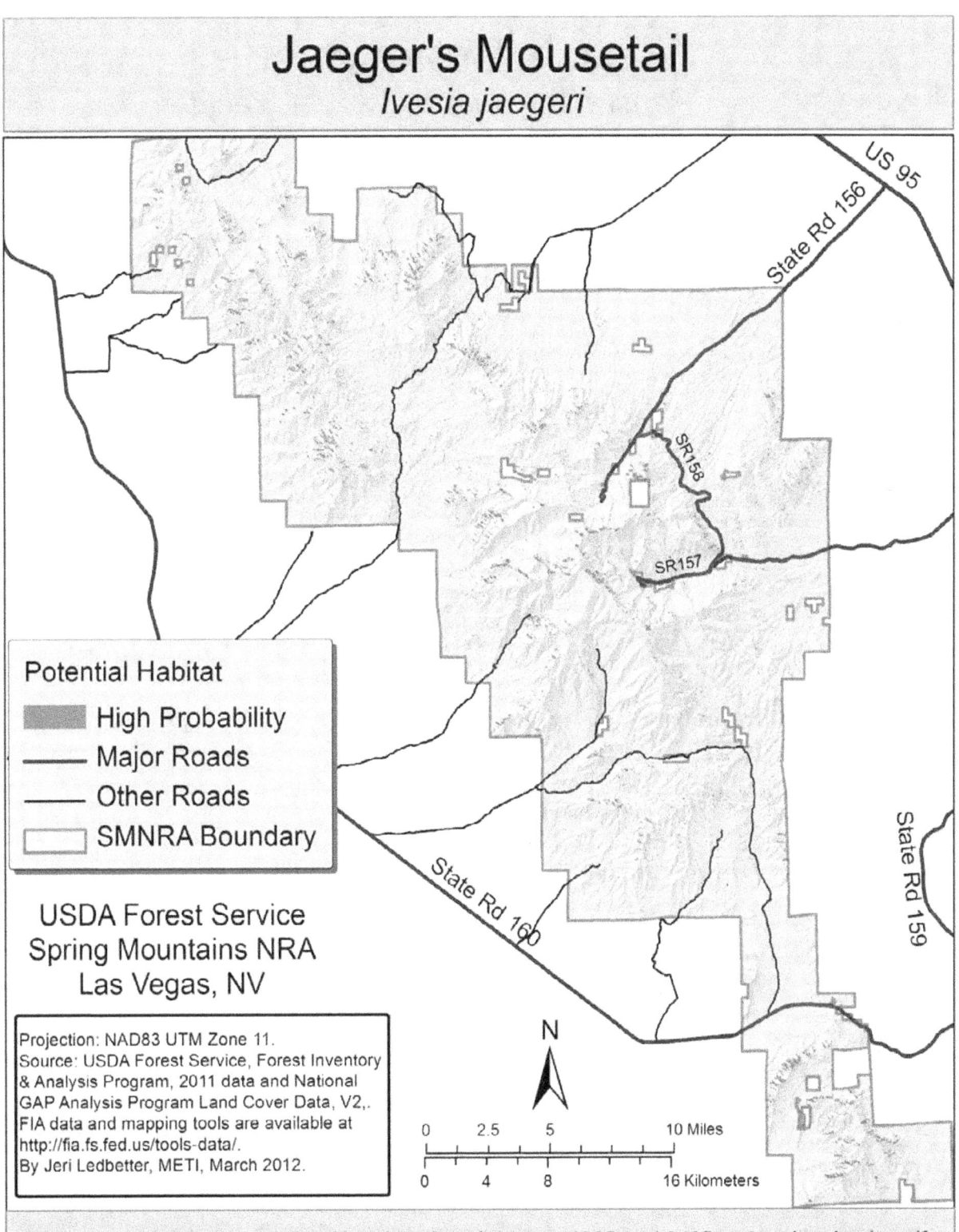

Jaeger's Mousetail
Ivesia jaegeri

Potential Habitat

- High Probability
- Major Roads
- Other Roads
- SMNRA Boundary

**USDA Forest Service
Spring Mountains NRA
Las Vegas, NV**

Projection: NAD83 UTM Zone 11.
Source: USDA Forest Service, Forest Inventory
& Analysis Program, 2011 data and National
GAP Analysis Program Land Cover Data, V2,.
FIA data and mapping tools are available at
http://fia.fs.fed.us/tools-data/.
By Jeri Ledbetter, METI, March 2012.

0   2.5   5   10 Miles

0   4   8   16 Kilometers

High probability habitat is defined by elevations between 1825 and 3435 meters in mixed conifer
biomes with a canopy cover <= 10% on steep (>30 degree), north-facing (+/- 45 degrees from 0)
slopes.

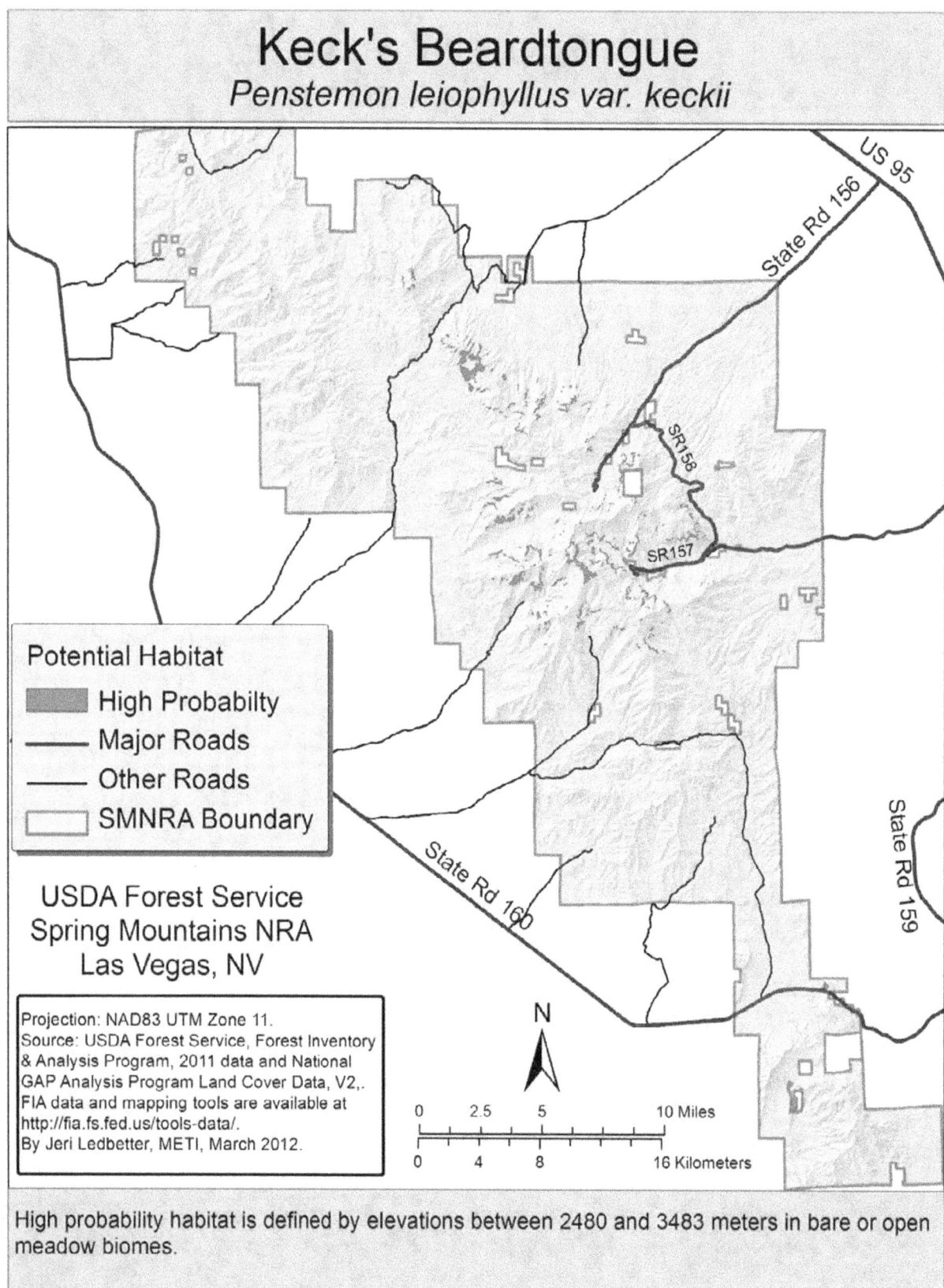

Keck's Beardtongue
Penstemon leiophyllus var. keckii

Potential Habitat
- High Probabilty
- Major Roads
- Other Roads
- SMNRA Boundary

USDA Forest Service
Spring Mountains NRA
Las Vegas, NV

Projection: NAD83 UTM Zone 11.
Source: USDA Forest Service, Forest Inventory
& Analysis Program, 2011 data and National
GAP Analysis Program Land Cover Data, V2,.
FIA data and mapping tools are available at
http://fia.fs.fed.us/tools-data/.
By Jeri Ledbetter, METI, March 2012.

N

| 0 | 2.5 | 5 | 10 Miles |
| 0 | 4 | 8 | 16 Kilometers |

High probability habitat is defined by elevations between 2480 and 3483 meters in bare or open meadow biomes.

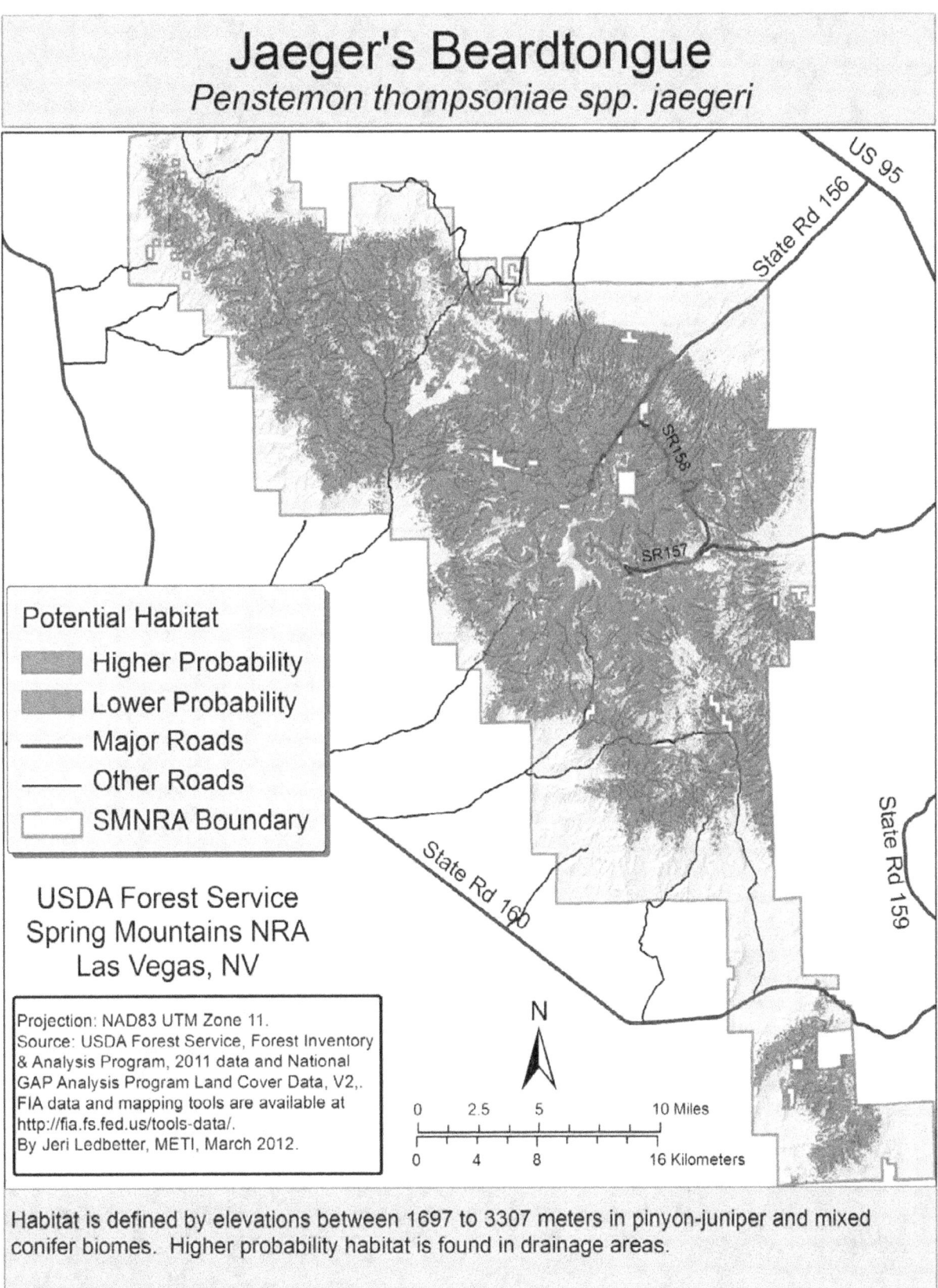

Jaeger's Beardtongue
Penstemon thompsoniae spp. jaegeri

Potential Habitat

- Higher Probability
- Lower Probability
- —— Major Roads
- —— Other Roads
- SMNRA Boundary

USDA Forest Service
Spring Mountains NRA
Las Vegas, NV

Projection: NAD83 UTM Zone 11.
Source: USDA Forest Service, Forest Inventory
& Analysis Program, 2011 data and National
GAP Analysis Program Land Cover Data, V2,.
FIA data and mapping tools are available at
http://fia.fs.fed.us/tools-data/.
By Jeri Ledbetter, METI, March 2012.

N

0   2.5   5   10 Miles

0   4   8   16 Kilometers

Habitat is defined by elevations between 1697 to 3307 meters in pinyon-juniper and mixed conifer biomes. Higher probability habitat is found in drainage areas.

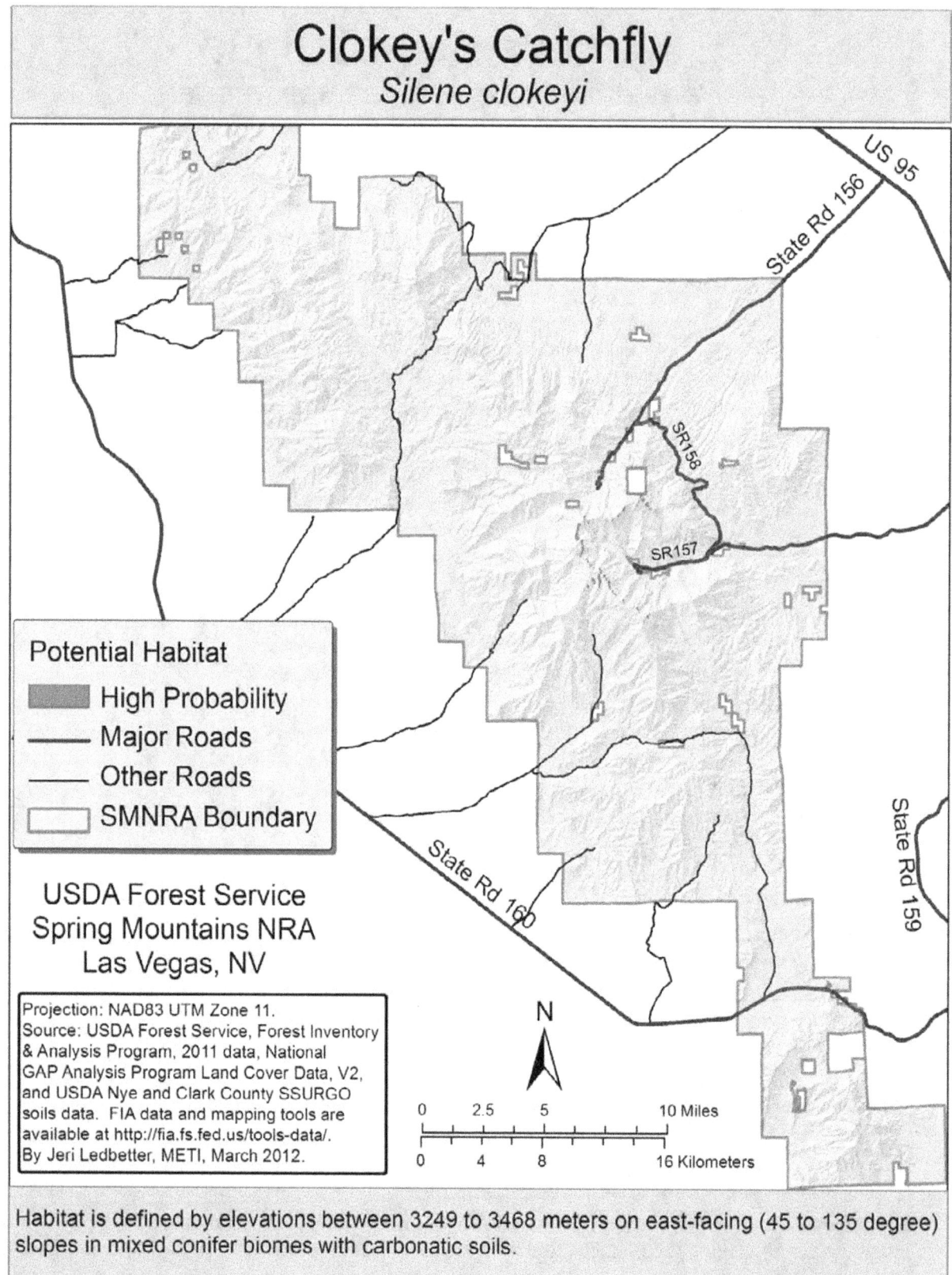

Clokey's Catchfly
Silene clokeyi

Potential Habitat

- High Probability
- Major Roads
- Other Roads
- SMNRA Boundary

**USDA Forest Service
Spring Mountains NRA
Las Vegas, NV**

Projection: NAD83 UTM Zone 11.
Source: USDA Forest Service, Forest Inventory
& Analysis Program, 2011 data, National
GAP Analysis Program Land Cover Data, V2,
and USDA Nye and Clark County SSURGO
soils data. FIA data and mapping tools are
available at http://fia.fs.fed.us/tools-data/.
By Jeri Ledbetter, METI, March 2012.

0   2.5   5   10 Miles
0   4   8   16 Kilometers

Habitat is defined by elevations between 3249 to 3468 meters on east-facing (45 to 135 degree) slopes in mixed conifer biomes with carbonatic soils.

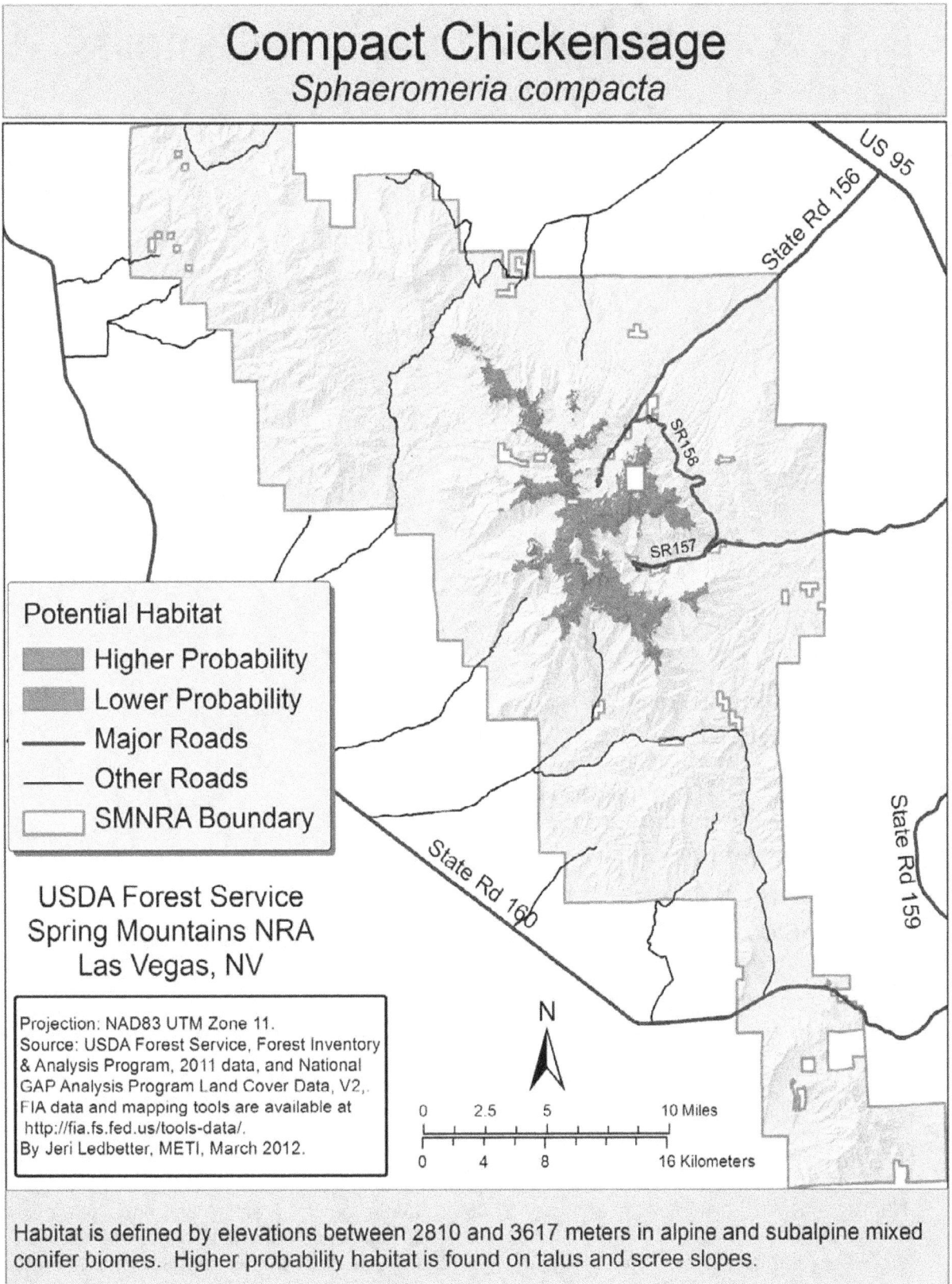

Compact Chickensage
Sphaeromeria compacta

Potential Habitat
- Higher Probability
- Lower Probability
- Major Roads
- Other Roads
- SMNRA Boundary

USDA Forest Service
Spring Mountains NRA
Las Vegas, NV

Projection: NAD83 UTM Zone 11.
Source: USDA Forest Service, Forest Inventory
& Analysis Program, 2011 data, and National
GAP Analysis Program Land Cover Data, V2,.
FIA data and mapping tools are available at
http://fia.fs.fed.us/tools-data/.
By Jeri Ledbetter, METI, March 2012.

US 95
State Rd 156
SR158
SR157
State Rd 160
State Rd 159

N

0   2.5   5   10 Miles
0   4   8   16 Kilometers

Habitat is defined by elevations between 2810 and 3617 meters in alpine and subalpine mixed
conifer biomes. Higher probability habitat is found on talus and scree slopes.

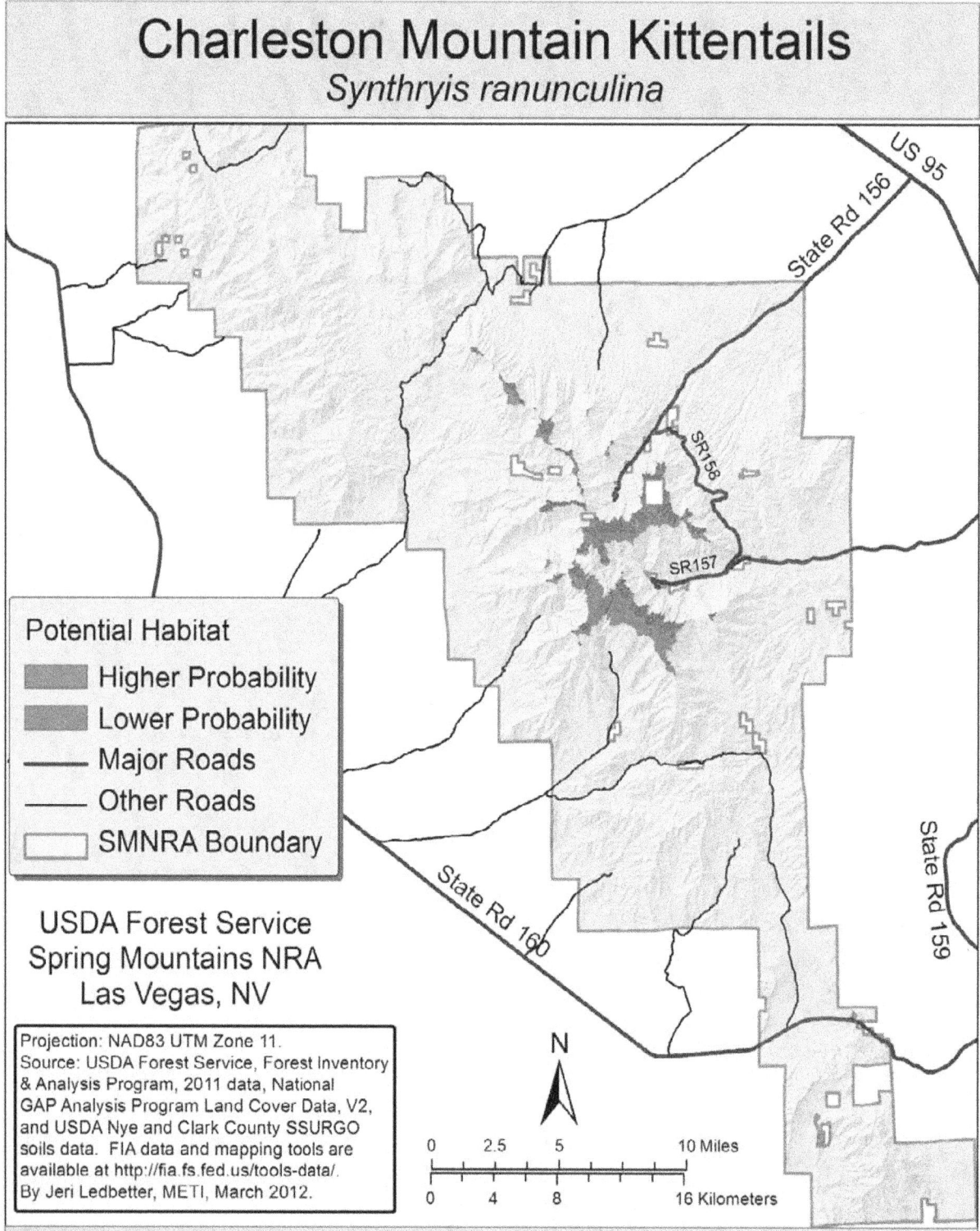

Charleston Mountain Kittentails
Synthryis ranunculina

Potential Habitat

- ▨ Higher Probability
- ▨ Lower Probability
- —— Major Roads
- — Other Roads
- ☐ SMNRA Boundary

USDA Forest Service
Spring Mountains NRA
Las Vegas, NV

Projection: NAD83 UTM Zone 11.
Source: USDA Forest Service, Forest Inventory
& Analysis Program, 2011 data, National
GAP Analysis Program Land Cover Data, V2,
and USDA Nye and Clark County SSURGO
soils data. FIA data and mapping tools are
available at http://fia.fs.fed.us/tools-data/.
By Jeri Ledbetter, METI, March 2012.

N

0	2.5	5		10 Miles
0	4	8		16 Kilometers

Habitat is defined by elevations between 2966 and 3594 meters in alpine and subalpine mixed
conifer, mountain meadow, and riparian biomes with organic soil content >30%. Higher
probability habitat is found on north-facing (+/- 45 degrees of 0) slopes and/or within 50 meters of
a spring or stream.

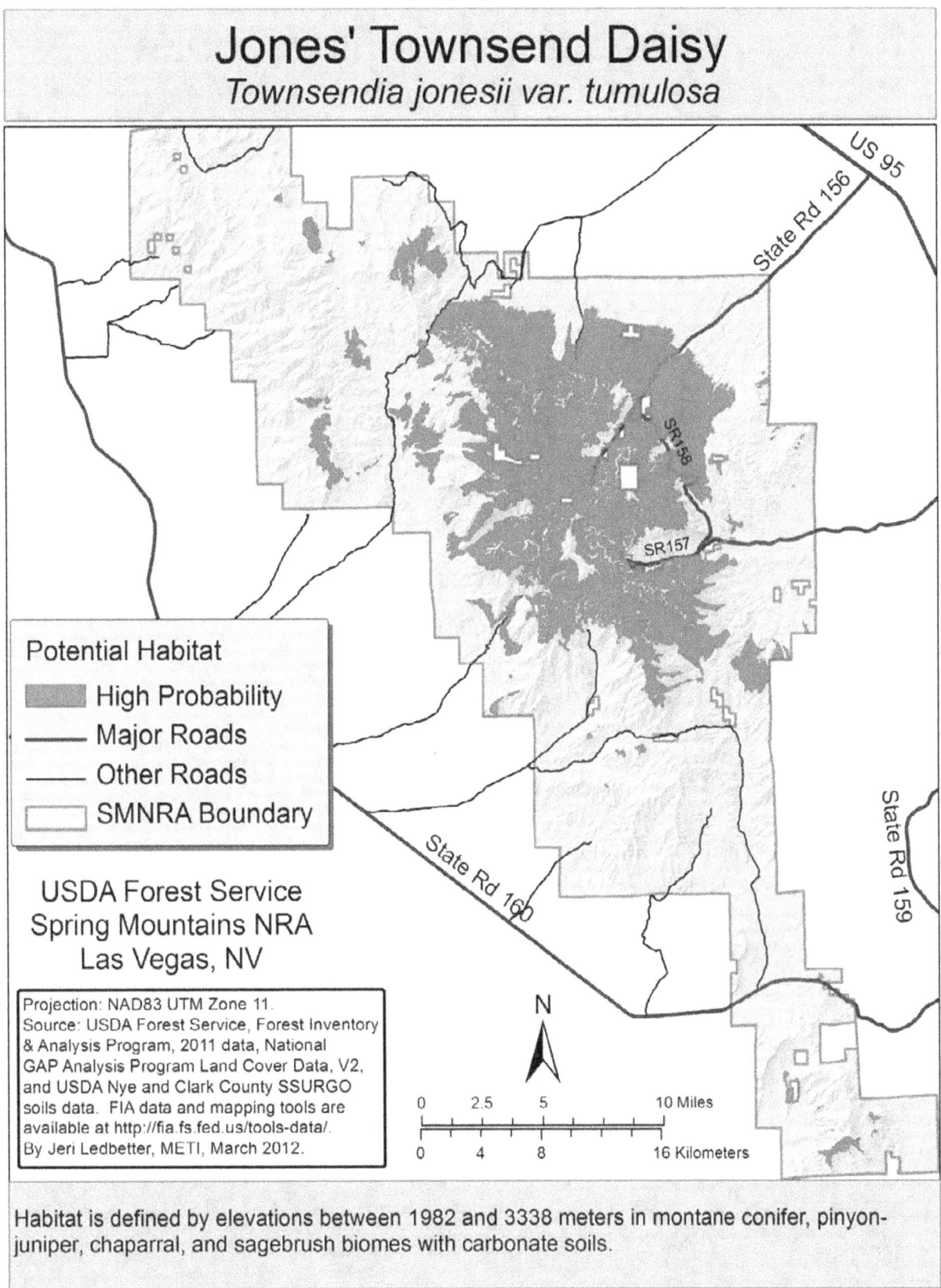

Jones' Townsend Daisy
Townsendia jonesii var. tumulosa

Potential Habitat
- High Probability
- Major Roads
- Other Roads
- SMNRA Boundary

USDA Forest Service
Spring Mountains NRA
Las Vegas, NV

Projection: NAD83 UTM Zone 11.
Source: USDA Forest Service, Forest Inventory
& Analysis Program, 2011 data, National
GAP Analysis Program Land Cover Data, V2,
and USDA Nye and Clark County SSURGO
soils data. FIA data and mapping tools are
available at http://fia.fs.fed.us/tools-data/.
By Jeri Ledbetter, METI, March 2012.

US 95
State Rd 156
SR158
SR157
State Rd 160
State Rd 159

N

0   2.5   5   10 Miles
0   4   8   16 Kilometers

Habitat is defined by elevations between 1982 and 3338 meters in montane conifer, pinyon-juniper, chaparral, and sagebrush biomes with carbonate soils.

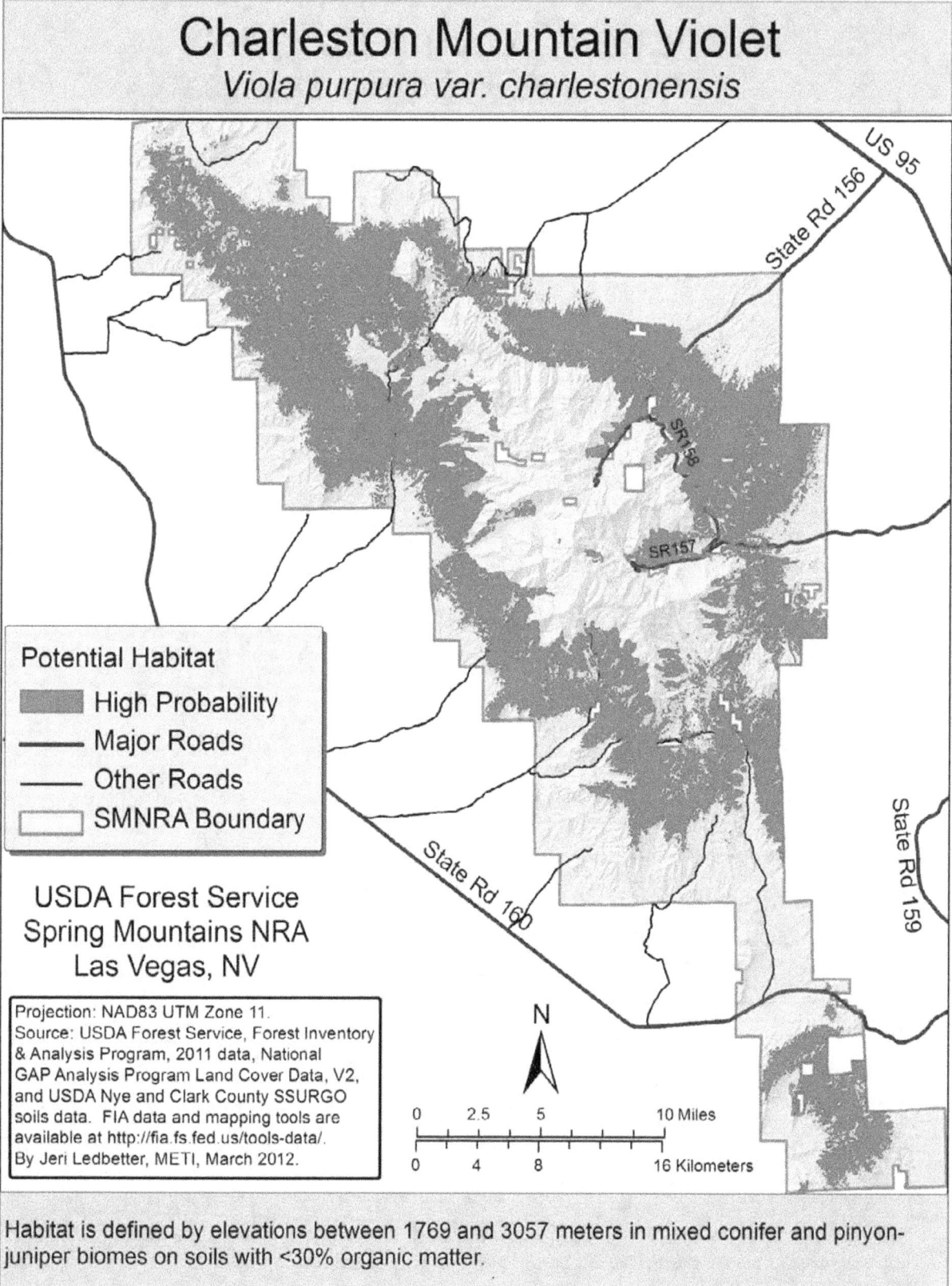

Charleston Mountain Violet
Viola purpura var. charlestonensis

Potential Habitat

- High Probability
- Major Roads
- Other Roads
- SMNRA Boundary

USDA Forest Service
Spring Mountains NRA
Las Vegas, NV

Projection: NAD83 UTM Zone 11.
Source: USDA Forest Service, Forest Inventory
& Analysis Program, 2011 data, National
GAP Analysis Program Land Cover Data, V2,
and USDA Nye and Clark County SSURGO
soils data. FIA data and mapping tools are
available at http://fia.fs.fed.us/tools-data/.
By Jeri Ledbetter, METI, March 2012.

| 0 | 2.5 | 5 | 10 Miles |
| 0 | 4 | 8 | 16 Kilometers |

Habitat is defined by elevations between 1769 and 3057 meters in mixed conifer and pinyon-juniper biomes on soils with <30% organic matter.

The *Spring Mountains National Recreation Area Inventory and Monitoring Strategy* (2006) identified three monitoring questions to be addressed using FIA data as a primary source. These questions were derived from the list of monitoring requirements identified in the Toiyabe Forest Plan.

Down/Large Woody Material (Monitoring Question 28)

Standards in the Forest Plan and GMP address habitats provided by Down/Woody Material for small mammals, reptiles, amphibians, and insects. Monitoring question 28, which is derived from Forest Plan monitoring requirements, addresses the number of downed woody logs/acre and is related to the following Forest Plan standard:

Toiyabe NF LRMP Wildlife and Fish Standard 14. Retain an average of three down logs per acre as wildlife habitat. Minimum down log size will be 15 inches in diameter at the large end and at least 15 feet in length.

The GMP establishes the following standards that can likely be monitored using FIA data by cover type and potentially seral classes within these cover types:

GMP Standard 0.37 - *(0.37) Retain a minimum of 50 linear feet/acre of downed trees with a minimum 12 inch diameter on sites being managed for late seral stage of the Pinyon/Juniper and Mixed Conifer Land Type Associations, provide ground cover for small mammals, amphibians, reptiles, and invertebrates. Trim branches and limbs as necessary. Place downed trees in such as way as to not affect drainage patterns; impede traffic or use of recreation facilities; create a public safety problem; and where consistent with "defensible space."*

GMP Standard 0.91 - *(0.91) Develop and maintain a network of shaded fuelbreaks to interrupt continuous stands of fuel. Maintain 50 linear feet/acre of downed trees with a 12 inch dbh within the shaded fuelbreak (if fuel break is being managed ecologically for the late seral stage of Pinyon/Juniper and Mixed Conifer Land Type Associations, or if managed for other seral stages within Palmers chipmunk habitat). Use existing road corridors and natural barriers.*

It is not clearly stated in the planning records whether the GMP standards are intended to supersede Forest Plan Wildlife and Fish Standard 14. However, data collected on down woody material by FIA can be used to monitor conditions related to all three of these standards. However, a crosswalk between Pinyon/Juniper and Mixed Conifer Land Type Associations as defined in Forest Plan Standard 14 and GMP Standards 0.37 and 0.91 and FIA cover types is required (see following section).

The following standard related to down and dead wood material in recreation sites cannot be monitored using FIA data and is more appropriately monitored for individual projects or sites:

GMP Standard 0.38 - *(0.38) Provide a minimum of 5 wildlife cover sites per acre within developed or primitive recreation sites by maintaining or adding dead and down wood material or rocks at appropriate locations.*

Snags (Monitoring Question 26) and Old Growth (Monitoring Question 27)

The Humboldt-Toiyabe Forest Plan identifies monitoring requirements associated with snags and old growth that were included in the SMNRA Inventory and Monitoring Strategy as monitoring questions 26 and 27.

These questions are linked to standards in the Toiyabe Forest Plan for the management of old growth habitat and habitat for cavity dwelling species using snags, which are defined as follows:

Toiyabe NF LRMP Wildlife and Fish Standard 1. *Snag management minimum requirement* ***on available productive (capable) Forest Land, when vegetative manipulation is done...***" [emphasis added]

Toiyabe NF LRMP Wildlife and Fish Standard 2. *The following standards apply to old growth habitat. Ten percent of the **available productive (capable) Forest land** will be managed as old growth habitat (by timber type-Jeffrey pine, mixed conifer, and lodgepole pine).* [emphasis added]

Available productive (capable) forest land is defined in the Forest Plan to include all lands capable of producing forest products (20 cubic feet per acre per year) that are not "reserved for timber production" (not available) by Congress or other designation. All lands within the SMNRA, including Wilderness, are reserved from timber production by statute and are not considered available for timber harvest (Toiyabe NF Plan, page C-2 and GMP, pages 1 and 72). Therefore, these standards do not apply to the SMNRA, therefore, monitoring questions 26 and 27 are not applicable to the SMNRA.

However, data gathered by FIA have been analyzed and are presented in this report to illustrate the status of old growth (see Appendix C 2.1) and snags (see Appendix C 2.2) within the SMNRA using definitions of these characteristics consistent with the Toiyabe Forest Plan. In future years, these data will not be analyzed.

GMP/Forest Plan Cover Type – FIA Cover Type Crosswalk

National and regional FIA field guides and definitions do not allow for a direct comparison of cover types used by FIA and those used in the Toiyabe Forest Plan and GMP. The following discussion provides the basis for making interpretations of cover types used in the Forest Plan and GMP standards to data sets generated using FIA inventory data.

Land Type Associations and Cover Types

The descriptions and the definitions of the different vegetation communities and Land Type Associations mentioned in the Toiyabe Forest Plan and GMP can be found on pp. 24-26 in the 1995 *Analysis of the Management Situation: Spring Mountains National Recreation Area*. Review of planning records and files has not identified the existence of a crosswalk between the GMP's Land Type Associations and the vegetation communities described in other documents Nachlinger and Reese (1996) vegetation classification, The Nature Conservancy (Provencher 2008), Clark County's 2000 MSHCP habitat models and Clark County's current work to revise their habitat models).

The following discussion and information is excerpted from the *1995 Analysis of the Management Situation: Spring Mountains National Recreation Area*:

We have identified eight major LTA's on the Spring Mountains [see the following table]. *These are characterized by elevation and major plant community components.*

We have identified eight major LTA's on the Spring Mountains [see the following table]. *These are characterized by elevation and major plant community components. There are differences in slopes, soils and suitabilities within each LTA. Suitability for development or use could be a component of the Desired Future Condition for each LTA, as suitability is not only a function of soils, landforms, plant communities, and sensitive sites (threatened, endangered and sensitive species locations and heritage resource locations), but of public perceptions and demands.*

LAND TYPE ASSOCIATIONS (LTAs)		
LTA	Elevation	Vegetation
Creosote	4000'-5000'	Creosote Bursage Red Brome
Blackbrush	5000'-6500'	Blackbrush Joshua Tree Mountain Big Sagebrush Mormon Tea Spiny Menodora
Pinyon/Juniper	6000'-8500'	Pinyon Pine Single-seed Juniper Utah Juniper Cliffrose Gambels Oak
Mixed Conifer	7500'-9500'	Ponderosa Pine Limber Pine White Fir Silk Tassel Manzanita
Bristlecone Pine	9000'-11000'	Bristlecone Pine Common Juniper Golden Currant
Alpine	11000'+	Sandberg Bluegrass Spike Trisetum Charleston Tansy Hitchcock Bladder Pod Hidden Ivesia
Lower Wash	4500'-7000'	Basin Big Sagebrush Rabbitbrush Desert Almond
Upper Wash	6000'-11000'	Woods Rose Golden Currant Desert Peach Aspen

Analysis of the Management Situation - 248

Creosote (LATR -Total Acreage in the SMNRA- 3,295. These lands are at the lowest elevations, between 4,000 and 5,000 feet on the Spring Range. They are described by a dominance of white bursage (Ambrosia dumosa) and creosote bush (Larrea tridentata). The LTA has gentle to moderate slopes (0-20%). The dominant parent material is limestone/dolomite alluvial deposits, most typically conglomerates with gravelly soils. Erosion hazard is moderate to low. The soils are typically gravelly with a desert pavement surface that protects the soil particles underneath it. If the desert pavement is disturbed, erosion increases significantly.

Blackbrush (CORA)- Total Acreage- 87,882. These lands are between 5,000 and 6,500 feet elevation. The type is described by a dominance of blackbrush (Coleogyne ramosissima) and Joshua tree (Yucca brevifolia). Other plants include mountain big sagebrush (Artemisia tridentata ssp vaseyana), mormon tea (Ephedra nevadensis, E. viridis), and spiny menodora (Menodora spinescens). The predominant underlying geologic materials are limestone/dolomite bedrock and limestone/dolomite conglomerates with gravelly, shallow soils. The LTA includes gentle rolling hills and terraces (0-20% slope) with moderate erosion potential, as well as steeper slopes (+30%) with high erosional potential if the desert pavement is disturbed.

Pinyon/Juniper (PIMO) -Total Acreage - 161,979. These lands are between 6,000 and 8,500 feet elevation. The type is described by pinyon pine (Pinus monophylla) and single-seed juniper (Juniperus osteosperma) trees. Shrubs in the type include mountain big sagebrush (Artemisia tridentata ssp vaseyana), cliffrose (Cowania mexicana), Gambel oak (Quercus gambelii) and mountain mahogany (Cercocarpus ledifolius). The underlying geologic material is predominantly limestone/dolomite bedrock and gravels. The LTA has well-drained, loamy soils on steep slopes (+20%) with highly dissected canyon bottoms. Erosion potential is moderate to high. It also includes gentle rolling hills (5-20%) with low to moderate erosion potential.

Mixed Conifer (PIPO)- Total Acreage- 25,861. This LTA occurs between 7,500 and 9,500 feet, especially in sheltered canyons. Ponderosa pine (Pinus ponderosa) and white fir (Abies concolor) predominate at the lower elevations. As the elevation increases, limber pine (Pinus flexilis) replaces ponderosa. The predominant underlying geologic material is limestone/dolomite bedrock on the hillsides, and gravels in the canyon bottoms. Slopes tend to be moderate to steep (15-40%), with moderate to high erosion potential. Soils are usually dark in color with welldeveloped horizons and covered by dead plant material.

Bristlecone (PILO)- Total Acreage- 26,942. This LTA is found between 9,000 and 11,000 feet elevation. Bristlecone pines (Pinus longaeva) predominate in this community. Herbaceous and shrub ground cover is almost lacking. Near timberline, the soils are usually shallow and slopes are extremely steep (+25%), therefore there is a high erosion potential. The underlying geologic material is predominantly limestone bedrock and gravels.

Alpine (ALPN) -Total Acreage- 6,802. This community is found above 11,000 feet to the top of Charleston Peak. Grass species include Sandberg bluegrass (Poa secunda ssp. secunda), spike trisetum (Trisetum spicatum) and bottlebrush squirreltail (Elymus elymoides). This area has the highest proportion of endemism. Conspicuous endemic plants are Hitchcock bladderpod (Lesquerella hitchcockii), hidden ivesia (Ivesia cryptocaulis), and Jaeger draba (Draba jaegeri). The underlying geologic material is limestone bedrock and gravels. Slopes tend to be steep (+25%) and soils tend to be shallow and highly erosive.

Upper Wash (UPWS) - Total Acreage - 1,200. This community is found at elevations from 6,000 to 11,000 feet. The soils are derived from limestone/dolomite gravels. The soils are cobbly and have a high erosional and depositional potential, especially during flood events. The washes tend to be steep and narrow. Water is present on an intermittent basis, especially during spring runoff from snowmelt. Water also tends to be closer to the surface in these washes and may surface as a perennial spring. The four perennial streams in the Spring Mountains are all in the Upper Wash LTA, at varying elevations. This community is characterized by woods rose (Rosa woodsii), golden currant (Ribes aureum), and desert peach (Prunus andersonii). Surrounding plant communities include the mixed conifer community with ponderosa pine, white fir and aspen, and the pinyon/juniper community.

Lower Wash (LWWS) - Total Acreage - 1,500. This community is found in washes from 4,500 to 7,000 feet elevation. It has gravelly to cobbly soils that have a high erosional and depositional potential. The *underlying geologic material is limestone/dolomite gravels. Lower washes tend to be broad and fairly flat. Water is only present during floods. This community is characterized by basin big sagebrush (Artemisia tridentata ssp tridentata) and rabbitbrush (Chrysothamnus nauseosus). Surrounding communities include the blackbrush and creosote communities.*

<u>FIA Cover Types</u>

FIA cover types suspected to occur within the SMNRA on lands capable of timber production (20 cubic feet/acre/year) or in the Pinyon/Juniper, LTA include the following groups and types:

Pinyon / Juniper Group

<u>182 Rocky Mountain juniper</u>: Rocky Mountain juniper comprises the majority of stocking. Associates – ponderosa pine, Douglas-fir, other junipers, pinyons, and oaks. Sites – often found on calcareous and somewhat alkaline soils.

<u>183 Western juniper</u>: Retired – see code 369.

<u>184 Juniper woodland</u>: includes Pinchot juniper, redberry juniper, Ashe juniper, California juniper, alligator juniper, Utah juniper, oneseed juniper and pinyon is NOT present. Associates - various woodland oaks and cercocarpus, ponderosa pine, Arizona cypress, and Douglas-fir. Sites – lower elevation with low annual precipitation.

<u>185 Pinyon-juniper woodland</u>: includes all pinyons and all junipers except Rocky Mountain and western juniper. Must have pinyon present. Associates - various woodland oaks and cercocarpus, ponderosa pine, Arizona cypress, and Douglas-fir. Sites – occurs at lower elevations with low annual precipitation.

Ponderosa Pine Group

<u>221 Ponderosa pine</u> (includes Arizona pine): Associates – Douglas-fir, lodgepole pine, grand fir, western larch, quaking aspen, Utah juniper, Gambel oak. Sites – this forest type is distributed over vast areas in the West and therefore can have great differences in environmental conditions.

<u>225 Jeffrey pine</u>: Associates - Incense-cedar, ponderosa pine, sugar pine, Douglas-fir, Port-Orford-cedar, western white pine, knobcone pine, Digger pine, red and white fir. Sites - Thrives in fairly harsh environments throughout most of its range, and is cold hardy, drought tolerant, adapted to short growing seasons, and tolerant of infertile sites. The majority of trees are found in California, although its range extends into SW Oregon and western Nevada.

Fir/Spruce/Mountain Hemlock Group

<u>261 White fir</u>: Associates – Douglas-fir, sugar pine, ponderosa pine, Jeffrey pine, incense-cedar, California red fir, blue spruce, limber pine, and aspen. Sites – deep well-drained sandy loam-covered slopes and benches with a northerly exposure.

<u>265 Engelmann spruce</u>: Associates – western white pine, western redcedar, western hemlock, Douglas-fir, western larch, grand fir, subalpine fir, and lodgepole pine. For this type to be used, if subalpine fir is at least 5% of the total stocking, the stocking of Englemann spruce must be at least 75% of the total stocking.

Lodgepole Pine Group

369 Western juniper: Associates – ponderosa pine and Jeffrey pine. Sites – found on dry sites And Ranges In Elevation From Just Above Sea Level To 6,500 Feet.

Aspen/Birch Group

901 Aspen: Associates – Engelmann spruce, lodgepole pine, ponderosa pine, Douglas-fir, subalpine fir, white fir, white spruce, balsam poplar, and paper birch. Sites – aspen has the capacity to grow on a variety of sites and soils, ranging from shallow stony soils and loamy sands to heavy clays.

Cover Type Comparison

Based on the descriptions of Land Type Associations present within the SMNRA, the following table provides information regarding the relationship of LTAs and cover types used in the Forest Plan or GMP and cover types used by FIA. This "crosswalk" was used in the following Appendices.

Forest Plan/GMP Cover Types	Land Type Association	FIA Group/Cover Type

Jeffrey pine/mixed conifer/red fir	Mixed Conifer	Ponderosa Pine Group
		   221 Ponderosa pine
		   225 Jeffrey pine
		Fir/Spruce/Mountain Hemlock Group
		   261 White fir:
		   265 Engelmann spruce
		Lodgepole Pine Group
		   369 Western juniper
		Aspen/Birch Group
		   901 Aspen

Pinyon/Juniper	Pinyon/Juniper	Pinyon/Juniper Group
		   182 Rocky Mountain juniper
		   184 Juniper woodland
		   185 Pinyon-juniper woodland
		Other Western Softwoods Group
		   369 Western juniper

Appendix C-2.1: Monitoring Question 26 – How many snangs per acre are present in mixed confifer and P-J?

DATA ANALYSIS ONGOING - ANALYSIS RESULTS WILL BE POSTED WHEN AVAILABLE

Appendix C-2.2: Monitoring Question 27 - What percentage of mixed conifer is old growth habitat?

DATA ANALYSIS ONGOING - ANALYSIS RESULTS WILL BE POSTED WHEN AVAILABLE

Appendix C-2.3: Monitoring Question 28 - What is the average number of downed woody logs per acre?

DATA ANALYSIS ONGOING - ANALYSIS RESULTS WILL BE POSTED WHEN AVAILABLE

Appendix C-2.4: Revised Monitoring Question 28 - How many linear feet/acre of downed trees with a 12-inch dbh occur within late seral stage of Pinyon/Juniper and Mixed Confiver Land Type Associations.

DATA ANALYSIS ONGOING - ANALYSIS RESULTS WILL BE POSTED WHEN AVAILABLE

Appendix D – Springs Inventory Data Reports

D-1: Springs Inventory Program

D-2: Site Reports

D-3: SMNRA-wide Summary Reports

D-4: Monitoring Question Reports

References

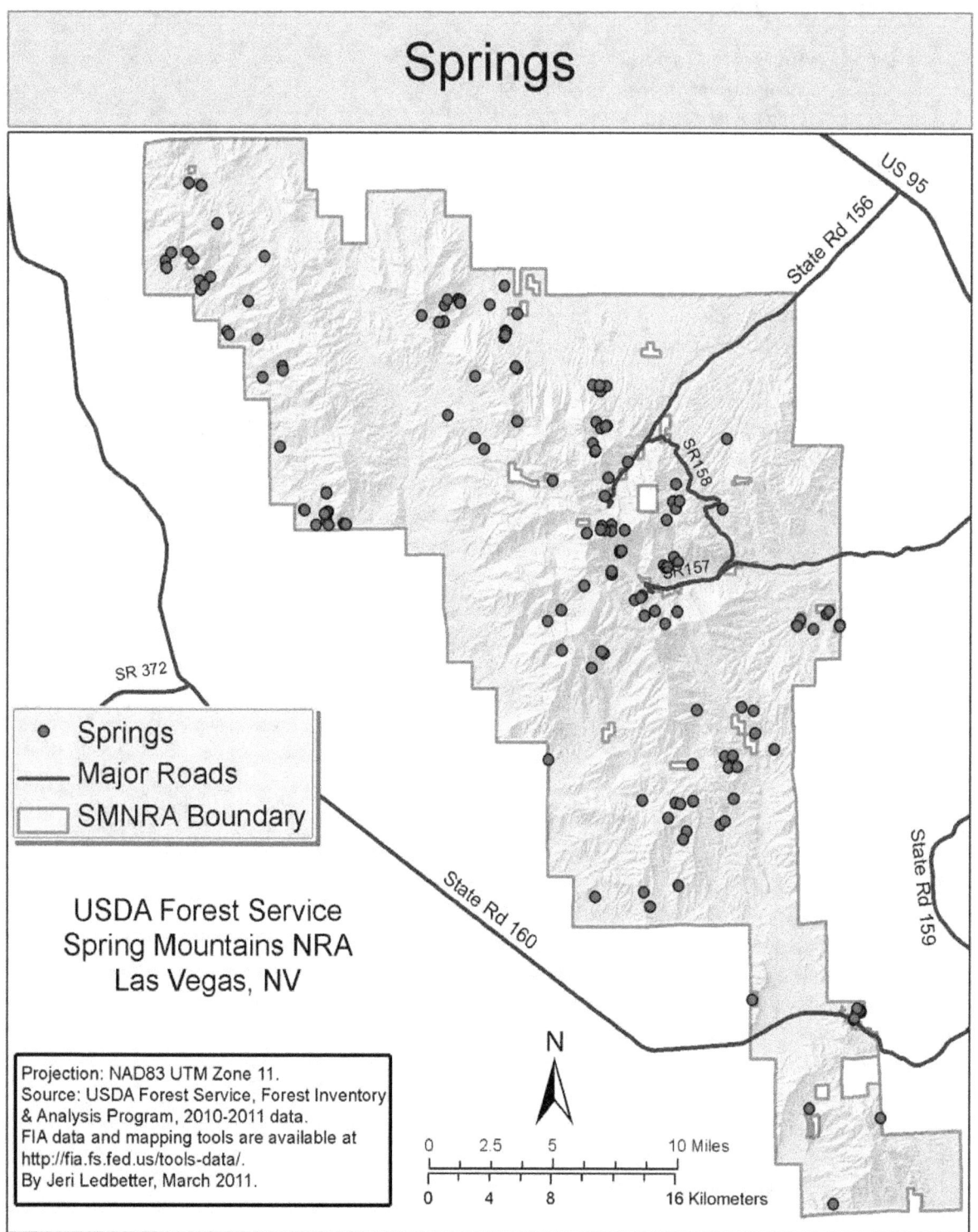

Figure 1. Springs (142) planned for sampling during the 2010-2015 inventory program

Appendix D 1.2: Springs Inventoried and Inventory Status

Site Name	Site ID	Status of Scheduled Sites (date indicates when surveyed)	Unscheduled Sites
Cane Spring 1 (No Name 165)	R4HTSMNRAH2O003	Not a spring	
Cathedral Chute Spring	R4HTSMNRAH2O199		NAU located and surveyed 7/26/2011
Cave Spring 1	R4HTSMNRAH2O136	8/1/2011	
Cave Spring 2	R4HTSMNRAH2O135	8/3/2011	
Coal Spring	R4HTSMNRAH2O153	10/29/2010	
East Mud Spring	R4HTSMNRAH2O091	7/30/2011	
Edna Grey Spring	R4HTSMNRAH2O009	7/26/2011	
Elbow Spring	R4HTSMNRAH2O204		NAU located and surveyed 9/7/2011
Falls (No Name 108)		Not a spring	
Fletcher Spring	R4HTSMNRAH2O098	7/28/2011	
Gold Spring	R4HTSMNRAH2O072	9/11/2011	
Guzzler		Not a spring	
Lower Cougar Spring	R4HTSMNRAH2O081	9/9/2011	
Lower Horse Springs (No Name 88)	R4HTSMNRAH2O115	Not a spring	
Macks Canyon 1	R4HTSMNRAH2O092	9/8/2010	
Mary Jane Falls	R4HTSMNRAH2O103	Not a spring	
Middle Mud lower spring (unnamed)			NAU located -- survey in future year
Middle Mud Spring	R4HTSMNRAH2O090	10/28/2010	
Mossfoot Seep	R4HTSMNRAH2O202		NAU located and surveyed 9/8/2011
Mummy Spring	R4HTSMNRAH2O012	7/25/2011	
Mummy View Spring	R4HTSMNRAH2O201		NAU located and surveyed 9/8/2011
No Name 114 (falls)		Not a spring	
No Name 12		Not surveyed -- not on map	
No Name 81 (Tank)		Not surveyed - not a spring	
Pahrump Spring (No Name 48)	R4HTSMNRAH2O020	Not a spring	
Pipilo Unnamed Spring	R4HTSMNRAH2O190		NAU located and surveyed 9/9/2011
Quartzite Wall Unnamed Spring	R4HTSMNRAH2O191		NAU located and surveyed 10/26/2010
Rock Spring	R4HTSMNRAH2O071	Not surveyed -- private land	
Roses Spring	R4HTSMNRAH2O137	8/2/2011	
Stanley B 1 Spring	R4HTSMNRAH2O099	7/24/2011	
Stanley B 2 Spring	R4HTSMNRAH2O100	7/24/2011	
Stanley B 3 Spring	R4HTSMNRAH2O101	9/13/2010	
Stanley B Wet Wall	R4HTSMNRAH2O200	7/24/2011	

Appendix D 1.2: Springs Inventoried and Inventory Status (Continued)

Site Name	Site ID	Status of Scheduled Sites (date indicates when surveyed)	Unscheduled Sites
Steller Spring	R4HTSMNRAH2O203		NAU located and surveyed 9/8/2011
Tank (No Name 126)		Not a spring	
Three Springs 1	R4HTSMNRAH2O122	9/11/2010	
Three Springs 2	R4HTSMNRAH2O123	9/11/2010	
Two Springs	R4HTSMNRAH2O026	9/11/2010	
Unnamed 1 Spring	R4HTSMNRAH2O027	10/21/2010	
Unnamed 19 Spring	R4HTSMNRAH2O033	Not surveyed -- secondary emergence of upstream spring	
Unnamed 20 Spring	R4HTSMNRAH2O035	9/7/2011	
Unnamed 21 Spring	R4HTSMNRAH2O126	9/12/2010	
Unnamed 27 Spring	R4HTSMNRAH2O121	9/10/2011	
Unnamed 34 Spring	R4HTSMNRAH2O082	Not surveyed -- dry	
Unnamed 41 Spring	R4HTSMNRAH2O062	10/23/2010	
Unnamed 45 Spring	R4HTSMNRAH2O112	9/14/2011	
Unnamed 47 Spring	R4HTSMNRAH2O111	Not surveyed -- dry	
Unnamed 49 Spring	R4HTSMNRAH2O117	9/13/2011	
Unnamed 55 Spring	R4HTSMNRAH2O119	9/13/2011	
Unnamed 56 Spring	R4HTSMNRAH2O048	9/13/2010	
Unnamed 59 Spring	R4HTSMNRAH2O050	7/27/2011	
Unnamed 67 Spring	R4HTSMNRAH2O095	9/12/2010	
Unnamed 74 Spring	R4HTSMNRAH2O056	Not surveyed -- secondary emergence of upstream spring	
Unnamed 75 Spring	R4HTSMNRAH2O057	8/2/2011	
Unnamed 9 Spring	R4HTSMNRAH2O061	7/29/2011	
Unnamed Spring 2 (No Name 146)	R4HTSMNRAH2O034	Not a spring	
Unnamed Spring 35 (No Name 15)	R4HTSMNRAH2O069	Not surveyed -- private land	
Unnamed Spring 37 (No Name 30)	R4HTSMNRAH2O039	Not a spring	
Upper Cougar Spring	R4HTSMNRAH2O080	10/27/2010	
Upper Horse Springs	R4HTSMNRAH2O113	10/23/2010	
Upper Lost Cabin Spring	R4HTSMNRAH2O148	10/20/2010	
Upper Sawmill Spring	R4HTSMNRAH2O024	10/27/2010	
West Mud Spring	R4HTSMNRAH2O089	7/30/2011	
Wheeler Well		Not a spring	
Willow Spring	R4HTSMNRAH2O084	9/9/2010	
Wood Canyon Spring	R4HTSMNRAH2O078	10/24/2010	
Younts Spring	R4HTSMNRAH2O149	9/12/2011	

Appendix D 2.1: Site Report Attributes List

A site report with the attributes listed in Table 1 is generated for each spring surveyed. Detailed descriptions of these attributes, their meaning, and potential uses can be found in the *Groundwater Dependent Ecosystems Level II Inventory Field Guide*.

After each field season the Northern Arizona University (NAU) field team created a report with a site report for each spring surveyed. To date there have been two of those reports; one for the 2010 field season (Springer et al. 2010) and another for the 2011 field season (Springer and Ledbetter 2011). An example of one site report from the 2011 field season is presented below Table 1. That site report was generated by an Access database designed for the GDE data, which is where the SMNRA springs data are stored and managed.

Table 1: List of attributes that are described in each site report.

Category	Attributes Summarized
Vegetation	Plant species cover Prevalence Index (based on wetland indicator status) Count of trees Basal area of trees Bryophyte cover Ground cover (bare, gravel, litter, etc.)
Soil	Depths and thicknesses of organic and mineral layers List of redoximorphic features observed Texture and color Fen characteristics present
Hydrology	Water table depth Flow (for springs and channels) Water quality - pH - Conductivity - Oxygen-reduction potential (ORP) - Dissolved oxygen - Temperature
Fauna	Species list of animals (vertebrates and invertebrates)
Disturbance	Lists of disturbances observed in these categories: - Hydrologic alteration - Soil alteration - Structures - Recreation effects - Animal effects - Other disturbances observed
Management Indicator Tool	List of indicators of management activities affecting site

Mummy Spring   ID# R4HTSMNRAH2O012

Survey Date:	7/25/2011
Ownership:	USFS
Region, Forest:	4, Humboldt-Toiyabe
District:	SMNRA
State, County:	NV, Clark

GDE Type(s): rheocrene

Aspect (TN): 36

Elevation (m): 3038

Coordinates 36 17 48.68 Latitude

-115 38 19.46 Longitude

Area: 975 square meters

Surrounding Vegetation Herbaceous/nonvascular dominated

Surficial Material: Rock (no surficial material present)

Lithology: Sedimentary , Limestone

Ground Cover	% Cover
Bare soil	3.6
Basal vegetation	3.6
Bedrock	25.0
Boulder	5.4
Bryophyte	3.6
Cobble	12.5
Gravel	8.9
Litter	32.1
Stone	3.6
Water	0.0
Wood	1.8

Vegetation Attribute	Results
Prevalence Index (based on wetland indicator status)	1.48
Prevalence Index Scale	
1 2 3 4 5	
Wetland Vegetation Upland Vegetation	
Tree basal area - live (sq m)	0.00
Tree basal area- dead (sq m)	0.00
Woody line intercept percent	23.2
Site total species count	34
Bryophyte percent cover	4.7

Hydrologic Attribute	Results
Water table type	Unknown
Inflow pattern	Groundwater inflow dominated
Outflow pattern	Both groundwater and surface water outflow significant
Surface water	Some developing channels;
Water table avg depth (cm)	Undetermined
Flow estimate (L/sec)	0.3
Water Quality (Site Average)	
pH	8.06
Specific conductance (uS/cm)	345.4
Dissolved oxygen (mg/L)	6.65
Dissolved oxygen saturation (%)	
Oxygen-reduction potential (ORP)	136.00
Temperature (C)	7.4

Tuesday, January 24, 2012   Page 1 of 5

Mummy Spring (continued)

Vegetation

Quadrat Species

Species, USDA Symbol	Native Status	% Cover
Aquilegia formosa, AQFO	N	2.1
Carex aurea, CAAU3	N	0.3
Carex subfusca, CASU6	N	1.1
Castilleja applegatei ssp. martinii, CAAPM	N	1
Cirsium eatonii var clokeyi,	N	1.6
Cystopteris fragilis, CYFR2	N	0.1
Leymus cinereus, LECI4	N	0.1
Primula fragrans, DOJER	N	12.4
Telesonix heucheriformis, TEHE5		0.1
unknown Graminoid (grass or grasslike), 2GRAM		0.4

Additional Plants

Species, USDA Symbol
Fritillaria atropurpurea, FRAT
Abies concolor, ABCO
Heuchera rubescens, HERU
Botrychium ascendens, BOAS2
Ribes cereum, RICE
Acer grandidentatum, ACGR3
Bromus ciliatus, BRCI2
Poa fendleriana, POFE
unknown Graminoid (grass or grasslike), 2GRAM
Pellaea breweri, PEBR4
Penstemon thompsoniae, PETH2
Heuchera, HEUCH
Holodiscus microphyllus var. microphyllus, HODI
Maianthemum stellatum, MAST4
Juniperus communis, JUCO6
Platanthera sparsiflora, PLSP2
Valeriana acutiloba var. pubicarpa, VAACP
Hymenoxys lemmonii, HYLE
Chenopodium, CHENO
Erysimum capitatum, ERCA14
Elymus multisetus, ELMU3

Quadrat Plant Species 10   Average % Cover/Quadrat   19.1

Woody Line-Intercept

Species, USDA Symbol	% Cover
Jamesia americana var. rosea, JAAMR	3.7
Pinus longaeva, PILO	15.1
Ribes montigenum, RIMO2	4.3

Tree Belt Transects

None

Mummy Spring (continued)

Fauna

Vertebrate Species	Detection	Comments
chipmunk, Eutamias sp	obs	
Clarks nutcracker,	obs	
Common Raven, Corvus corax	obs	
Gray Jay, Perisoreus canadensis	obs	
hummingbird, Archilochus fam	obs	
Mountain Chickadee, Poecile gambeli	call	
White-breasted Nuthatch, Sitta carolinensis	call	

Invertebrate Species	Detection	Comments
DIP Dixidae	obs	dixa
DIP Tipulidae	obs	small
TRI Limnephilidae	obs	sp 1

Mummy Spring (continued)

Disturbance

		Soils
Hydrology: No hydrologic disturbance noted	Recreational effects: Other recreational effects observed--see disturbance notes;	No soil pits were dug.
	Animal effects: Trails by animals and people;	
Soil alteration: Debris flow; Erosion (general); Trails (by people or animals);	Miscellaneous effects: No miscellaneous effects noted	
	Disturbance Notes	
	Recreational trail passed through lower part of site	
Structures: No structures noted		

Appendix D 2.2: Sample Site Report (Continued)

Mummy Spring (continued)

Management Indicators

1) Aquifer (groundwater) not altered	True
2) Watershed (surface water) not altered	True
3) Water quality changes not affecting site	True

Geomorphology and Soils

4) Landform stability not altered	True
5) Runout channel functioning naturally	True
6) Soil integrity not altered	True

Biology

7) Vegetation composition as anticipated	True	True
8) Vegetation condition is healthy	True	
9) TES, SOI/SOC, focal flora as anticipated	True	
10) Faunal species as anticipated	True	
11) TES, SOI/SOC, focal fauna as anticipated	True	
12) Invasive species not established	True	

Disturbances

13) Flow regulation not adversely affecting site	True	
14) Construction, Roads not adversely affecting	True	
15) Fencing functions properly	True	
16) Herbivory not adversely affecting site	True	
17) Recreation not adversely affecting site	False	recreational trail passes through lower part of site
18) Other disturbance not adversely affecting	True	

Administrative Context

19) Cultural values do not affect site mgmt	False	Most springs have cultural & religious significance
20) Land ownership is FS in and around site	True	
21) Other landowner actions not affecting site	True	
22) Land Management Plan provides protection	True	
23) Environmental compliance occurring	True	
24) Water uses not adversely affecting site	True	
25) Water rights filed and not outstanding	True	

Plant codes and native status are from the USDA PLANTS database web page: http://plants.usda.gov

Data from all the sites surveyed in the SMNRA were used to calculate the summary attributes listed in the table below and presented in the next section. Data definitions and attributes are described in the *Groundwater Dependent Ecosystems Level II Field Guide*.

Table 2. List of attributes that are summarized for all sites sampled in the SMNRA.

Category	Attributes Summarized
Vegetation	List of all species observed
	Species cover (averages)
	Native and introduced and invasive species cover (averages)
	Prevalence Index (average)
	Species count per site (average)
	Byrophyte cover (average)
	Ground cover (averages)
Soil	Average depths and thicknesses of organic and mineral layers
	Percent of sites with each redoximorphic feature
	Percent of sites with each soil texture and color
Hydrology	Water table depth (average)
	Flow (range and average)
	Water quality (averages)
	- pH
	- Conductivity
	- Oxygen-reduction potential (ORP)
	- Dissolved oxygen
	- Temperature
Fauna	Species list of animals (birds, mammals, insects, etc.)
	Percent of sites with various animals
Disturbance	Lists of disturbances observed
	Percentage of sites with each disturbance
Management Indicator Tool	Percent of sites with each management indicator

Appendix D 3.2: Springs Inventory Data

This section presents summarized data for all 47 springs surveyed in 2010 and 2011. The previous year's report on spring surveys of the SMNRA summarized only the 2010 data.

For all spring sites inventoried in 2010 and 2011, the average size was 331 m^2, with a range from 0.75 m^2 to 2,952 m^2.

Seven different spring types were observed in the surveys, as well as an "unknown" category. Many sites (24) had just one spring type, while 20 sites had two spring types recorded, and 3 sites had an unknown spring type generally because it did not fit the options listed (see Table 3). The most common spring type observed was rheocrene (a flowing spring that emerges directly into one or more stream channels) observed at 27 sites, and the next most observed type was hillslope (spring and/or wetland on a hillslope, generally 20- to 60-degree slope, often with indistinct or multiple sources of groundwater) observed at 20 sites. Those two spring types (hillslope and rheocrene) were often observed at the sames site (in 11 cases) which was the most frequently observed combination of spring types.

Table 3. Spring types (Springer and Stevens 2008) observed in 2010 and 2011.

Spring Types (at a site)	Sites
Cave	1
Cave, Hanging garden	1
Gushet, Hillslope	1
Hanging garden	6
Hanging garden, Rheocrene	2
Helocrene, Hillslope	2
Helocrene, Rheocrene	1
Hillslope	6
Hillslope, Rheocrene	11
Hypocrene, Rheocrene	2
Rheocrene	11
Unknown	3
Total	47

Vegetation

The combined data from 2010 and 2011 were used in this summary of the vegetation of springs of the SMNRA. There were 130 vascular plant species recorded during the sampling of the 47 spring sites. An additional 26 plants could not be identified to species. There were an average of 15.9 species per site.

Herbaceous wetland species that were most abundant were scented shootingstar (*Primula fragrans*, also known as *Dodecatheon redolens,* sometimes referred to as *Primula fragans)*) with 5.7% cover, Western Columbine (*Aquilegia formosa*) with 2.5% cover, stinging nettle (*Urtica dioica*) with 1.4% cover, desert baccharis (*Baccharis sergiloides*) with 1.3% cover, and onerow yellowcress (*Nasturtium microphyllum*) with 0.9% cover. Moss (Byrophyte) cover averaged 7.6%.

The shrub species that were most abundant were Woods' rose (*Rosa woodsii*) with 6.3% cover, arroyo willow (*Salix lasiolepis*) with 3.2% cover, desert baccharis (*Baccharis sergiloides*) with 2.6% cover, canyon grape (*Vitis arizonica*) with 2.2% cover, and fivepetal cliffbush (*Jamesia americana*) with 1.0% cover.

The tree species that were most abundant were white fir (*Abies concolor*) with 5.2% cover, Rocky Mountain juniper (*Juniperus scopulorum*) with 4.3% cover, ponderosa pine (*Pinus ponderosa*) with 2.4% cover, quaking aspen (*Populus tremuloides*) with 1.5% cover, and Gambel oak (*Quercus gambelii*) with 1.2% cover. In terms of tree counts, nine sites (19%) had trees (greater than 5 cm in diameter) within the site, and each of those sites had just 1 to 11 individual trees. The total basal area of trees, at sites with trees, ranged from 0.0009 m^2 to 1.8 m^2. Some sites had cover from trees that were just outside the site, but had no trees within the site. Two sites had a single standing dead tree.

There were 14 non-native species observed among all the sites. The average cover of non-native species at a site was 2.5%. Invasive species observed included saltcedar, (*Tamarix ramosissima*), red brome (*Bromus rubens*), cheatgrass (*Bromus tectorum*), dandylion (*Taraxicum officianale*), yellow sweetclover (*Melilotus officianalis*), water speedwell (*Veronica anagallis aquatica*), and annual rabbitsfoot grass (*Polypogon monspeliensis*). These invasive species were observed at between one and ten sites.

The only CA species encountered in the 2010 and 2011 surveys was Charleston Mountain angelica (*Angelica scabrida*) at one site.

Vegetation data were used to calculate a "prevalence index" which is a commonly used method to describe the abundance of wetland vegetation for a site and to determine if a site is a wetland (National Research Council 1995). The prevalence index has been described as a way of characterizing the "wetlandness" of a site (Tiner 1999). The prevalence index is calculated using a weighted average of the species abundance (cover in this case) and the wetland indicator status value (Reed 1988) to characterize a site's vegetation on a scale of 1 (all obligate wetland species) to 5 (all upland species). A value below three is generally considered to be a wetland. For the 46 SMNRA spring sites where vegetation data were collected the range in the prevalence index values was 1.0 to 4.1, and the average for all sites was 2.5.

Vegetation data for each site were compared to vegetation described in community type classifications by Manning and Padgett (1995), Nachlinger and Reese (1996), and Weixelman et al. (1996). The dominant vegetation for each site matched relatively well with a community type described in the classifications. The number of sites with each community types is presented in the table below.

Table 5. Community types of the springs inventoried in the SMNRA in 2010 and 2011. Six sites had little or no vegetation, and are therefore not included in this table.

Published Community Type	2010	2011	TOTAL
Dodecatheon redolens-Aquilegia formosa Series (Nachlinger and Reese (1996)	4	5	9
Rosa woodsii var. ultramontana Association (Nachlinger and Reese (1996)	6	8	14
Salix lasiolepis/Rosa woodsii var. ultramontana Community Type (Manning and Padgett 1995)	2	4	6
Urtica dioica Community Type (Weixelman et al. 1996)	0	1	1
Baccharis sergiloides Association (Nachlinger and Reese (1996)	3	2	5
Jamesia americana/Petrophytum caespitosum-Ivesia jaegeri Association (Nachlinger and Reese 1996)	0	5	5

Ground cover data describe what is on the ground surface, which is summarized here as litter (dead plant material), rock (including gravel, cobble, boulder and bedrock), bryophytes, water, or basal vegetation (where the plant emerges from the ground). If there was none of those ground cover types then it was recorded as bare ground. Significant bare ground at a spring could be an indicator of excessive disturbance. The average ground cover for the springs of the SMNRA is represented in Figure 2, with litter and wood being the most abundant type.

Figure 2. Average ground cover data for the 47 spring sites sampled in 2010 and 2011.

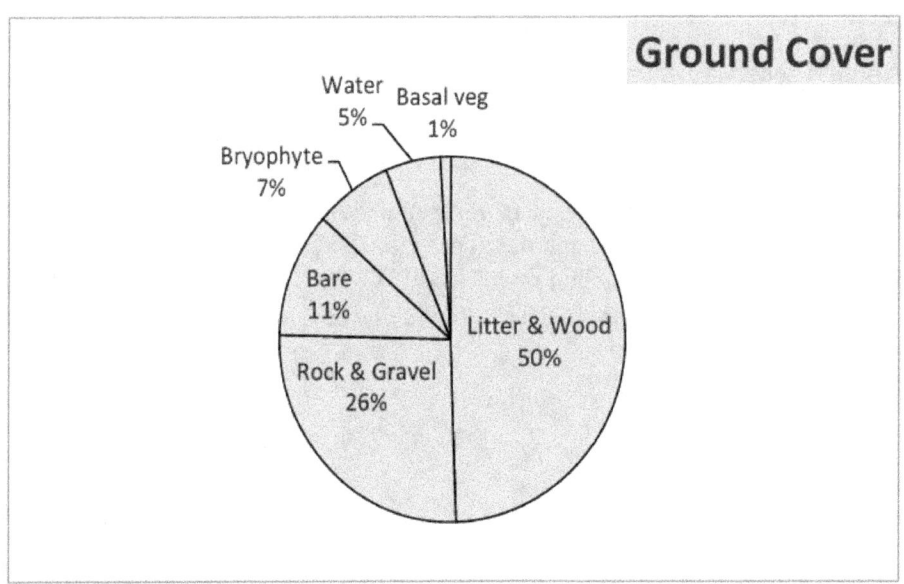

Soil

Most sites in the SMNRA did not have organic soil. At four sites a peat layer was recorded that was 4 to 20 cm thick. Two sites had redoximorphic features. Among all the sites surveyed, the soil texture was commonly sand and silt and soil colors were 10Y, 10YR, 5G, 5Y, and 5YR. A hydrogen sulfide odor was detected in the soil at two sites (Mack's Canyon 1 and Unnamed 45). No soils reacted to HCL. Holes dug for sampling averaged 10.8 cm in depth.

Hydrology

Measurement of water table depth is primarily intended for wetlands, not for springs, therefore that was generally not measured at the SMNRA sites.

Flow was measured at springs or runout channels of wetlands at 42 sites (89%). The median flow was 0.17 L/second, with a range of 0.002 to 103 L/second. At the other sites there was either no discernible flow or the flow was diffuse and could not be measured.

Data on water quality are presented in Table 6 and Figures 3-7.

Table 6. Water quality data from springs sampled in 2010 and 2011.

Attribute	Minimum	Median	Average	Maximum	Sites Measured
Temperature (centigrade)	3.0	11.2	11.36	19.5	n=43
pH	6.5	7.45	7.5	8.6	n=45
Specific Conductance (microsiemens/centimeter)	136	496	550	1011	n=43
Oxygen-reduction potential (mV)	-33.2	123.2	105.5	221.9	n=25
Dissolved oxygen (mg/L)	2.3	5.5	5.4	9.7	n=25

Analysis of these data will be provided in the 2012 Annual Report.

Box and whisker plots are presented in the figures below to show the distribution of the hydrologic data for all spring sites sampled in 2010 and 2011.

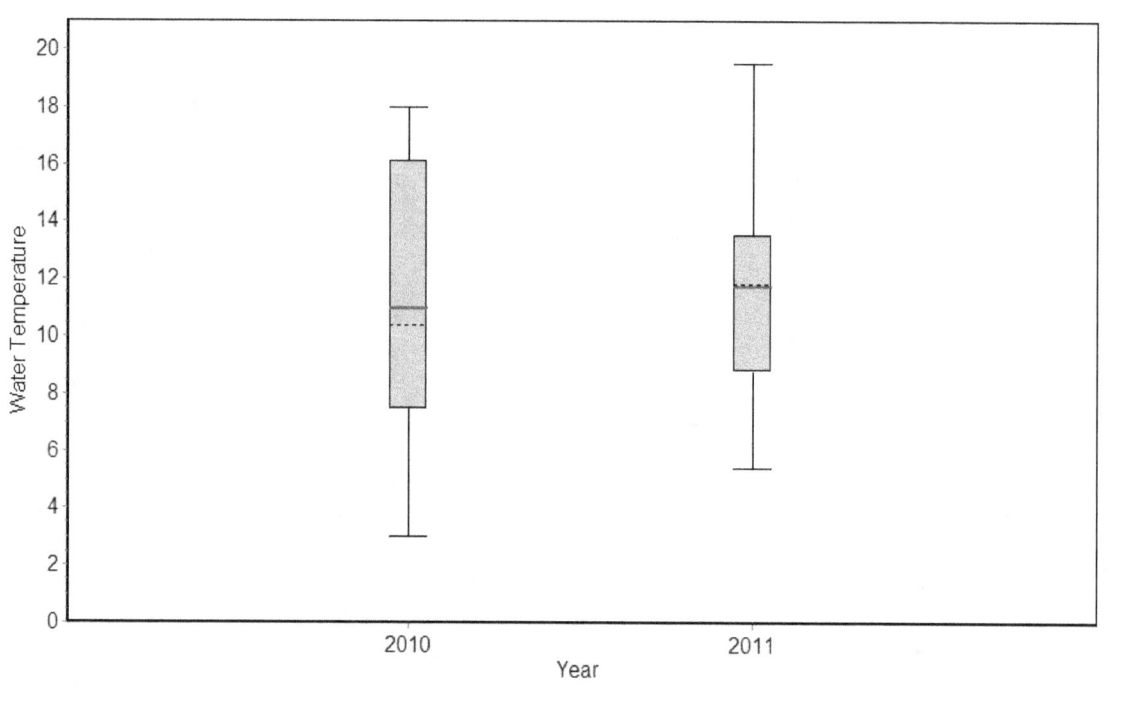

Figure 3. Distribution of the water temperature (centigrade) for springs sampled in 2010 and 2011. Mean value is solid blue line and median value is dashed blue line.

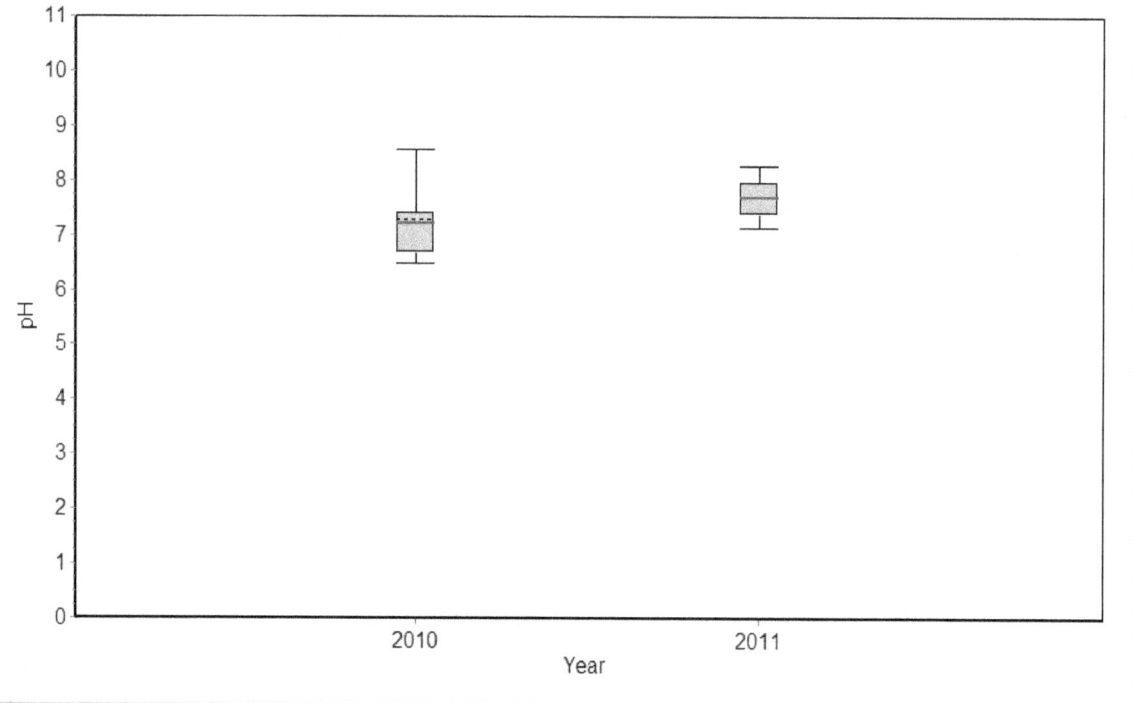

Figure 4. Distribution of pH values for springs sampled in 2010 and 2011. Mean value is solid blue line and median value is dashed blue line.

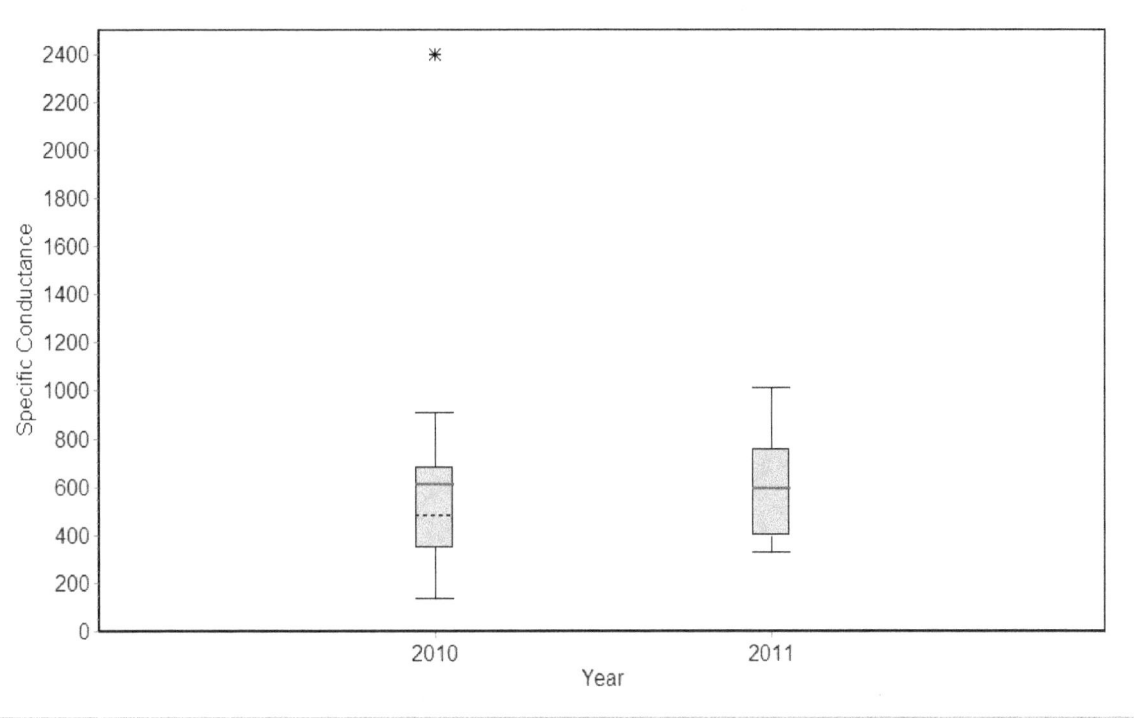

Figure 5. Distribution of specific conductance (microsiemens/centimeter) in water sampled at springs in 2010 and 2011. Mean value is solid blue line and median value is dashed blue line.

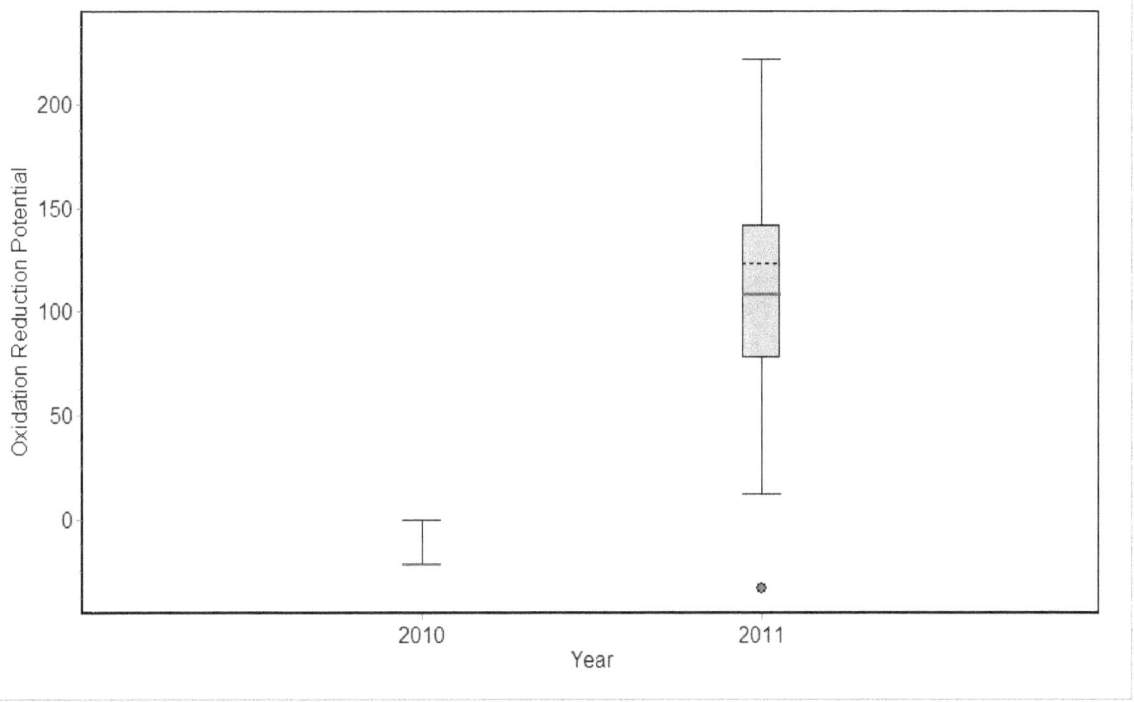

Figure 6. Distribution of oxidation-reduction potential (ORP) in water sampled at springs in 2010 (only one site had ORP data) and 2011. Mean value is solid blue line and median value is dashed blue line.

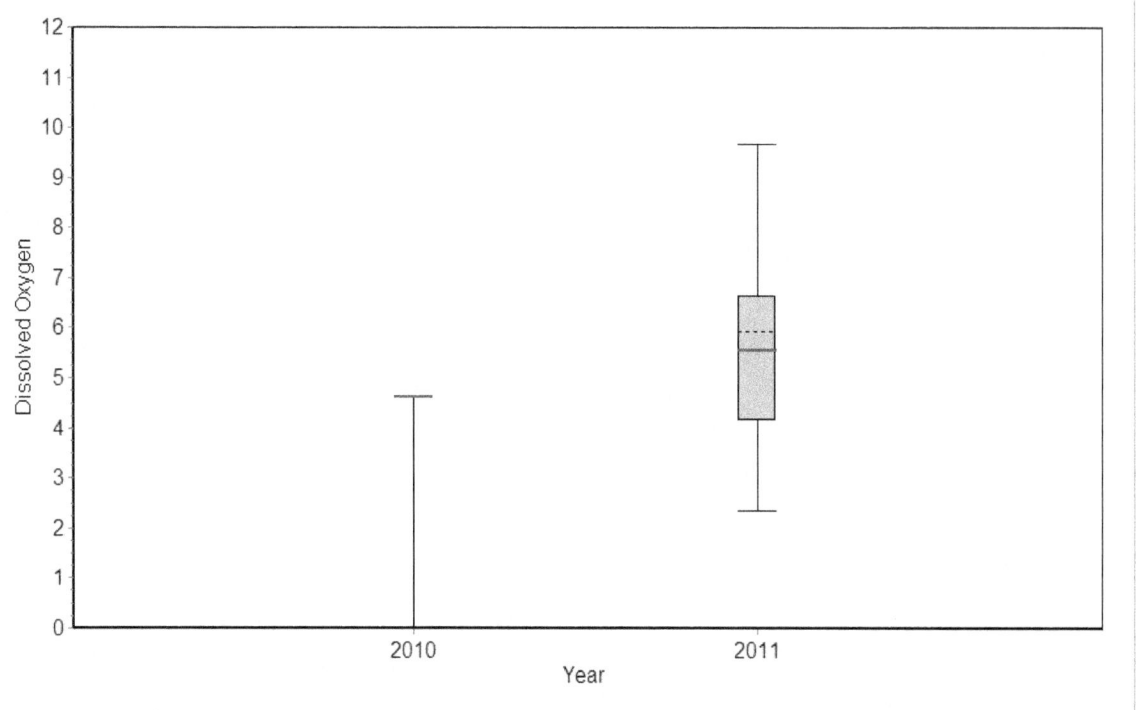

Figure 7. Distribution of dissolved oxygen for springs sampled in 2010 (only 1 site had dissolved oxygen data) and 2011. Mean value is solid blue line and median value is dashed blue line.

Fauna

Aquatic macroinvertebrates were found through spot searches at the spring sites. The macroinvertebrates that were found at the most sites were the following taxa: caddisflies, order *Trichoptera*, family *Limnephilidae* (26% of sites); flatworms, class Turbellaria (21% of sites); mayflies, order Ephemeroptera, family Baetidae (15% of sites); damselflies, order *Odonata*, family Coenagrionidae (15% of sites); midges, order *Diptera*, family Chironomidae (13% of sites). It is noteworthy that springsnails (genus Pyrgulopsis, family Hydrobiidae) were found at 5 of 47 (11%) springs (all had genetic samples unless noted): Unnamed 49 Spring, Standley B 3 Spring (no genetic sample), Upper Horse Springs, Willow Spring, and Wood Canyon Spring.

Terrestrial vertebrates were observed at a number of sites, through observation and spot searches. A total of 75 animal species were observed. The animals that were most commonly observed are listed in the figure below, while an additional 52 vertebrate species (mostly birds) were observed at less than 10% of sites per year.

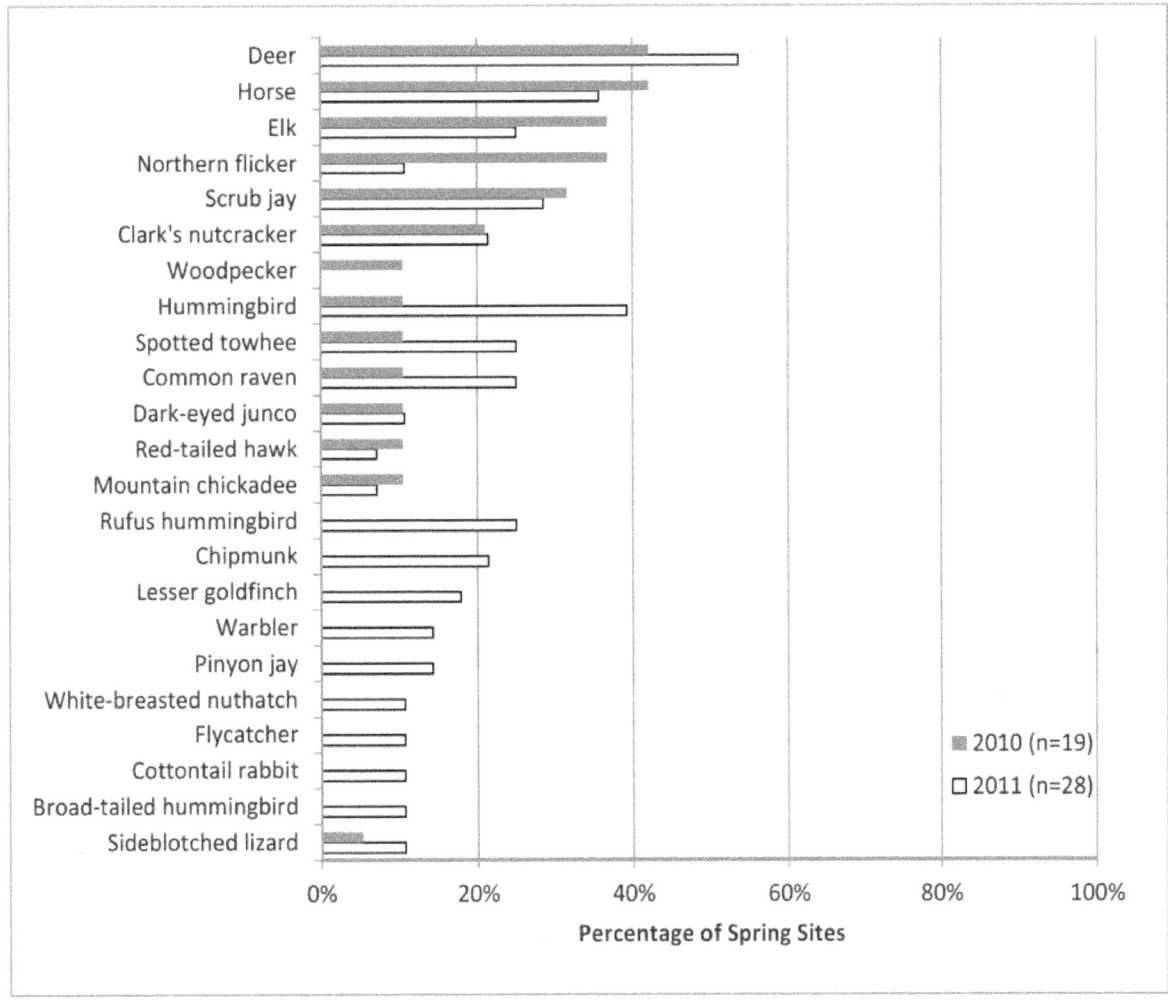

Figure 8: Percentage of spring sites where the most common terrestrial vertebrates were observed during surveys in 2010 and 2011. Note: Species observed at less than 10% of sites are not included in this figure.

Disturbances

At each site the disturbances observed were noted, and a summary of the most commonly observed disturbances is presented in Figure 9. An additional 37 disturbance types were noted at less than 15% of sites.

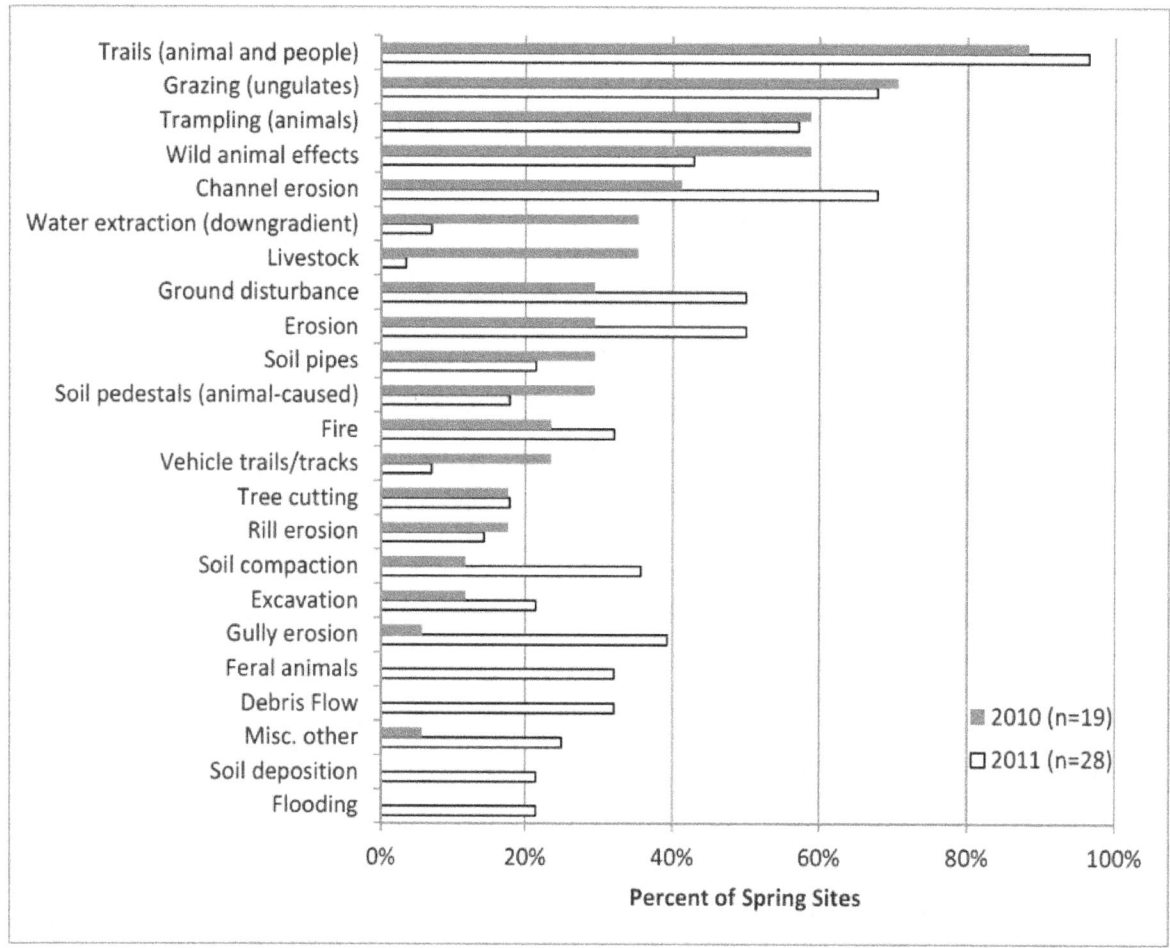

Figure 9: Percent of spring sites where the listed disturbances were observed during sampling in 2010 and 2011. Note: Disturbances observed at less than 15% of sites are not included in this figure.

A summary of the responses to the 25 questions in the Management Indicator Tool are presented in Figure 10. The responses represented by the bars generally indicate adverse alteration to spring sites. In 2011 additional categories were added, which is why some categories have a bar for 2011 but not for 2010. The categories in the lower part of the graph, where neither year has a bar, all had the same response because the SMNRA does not vary much for those management indicators.

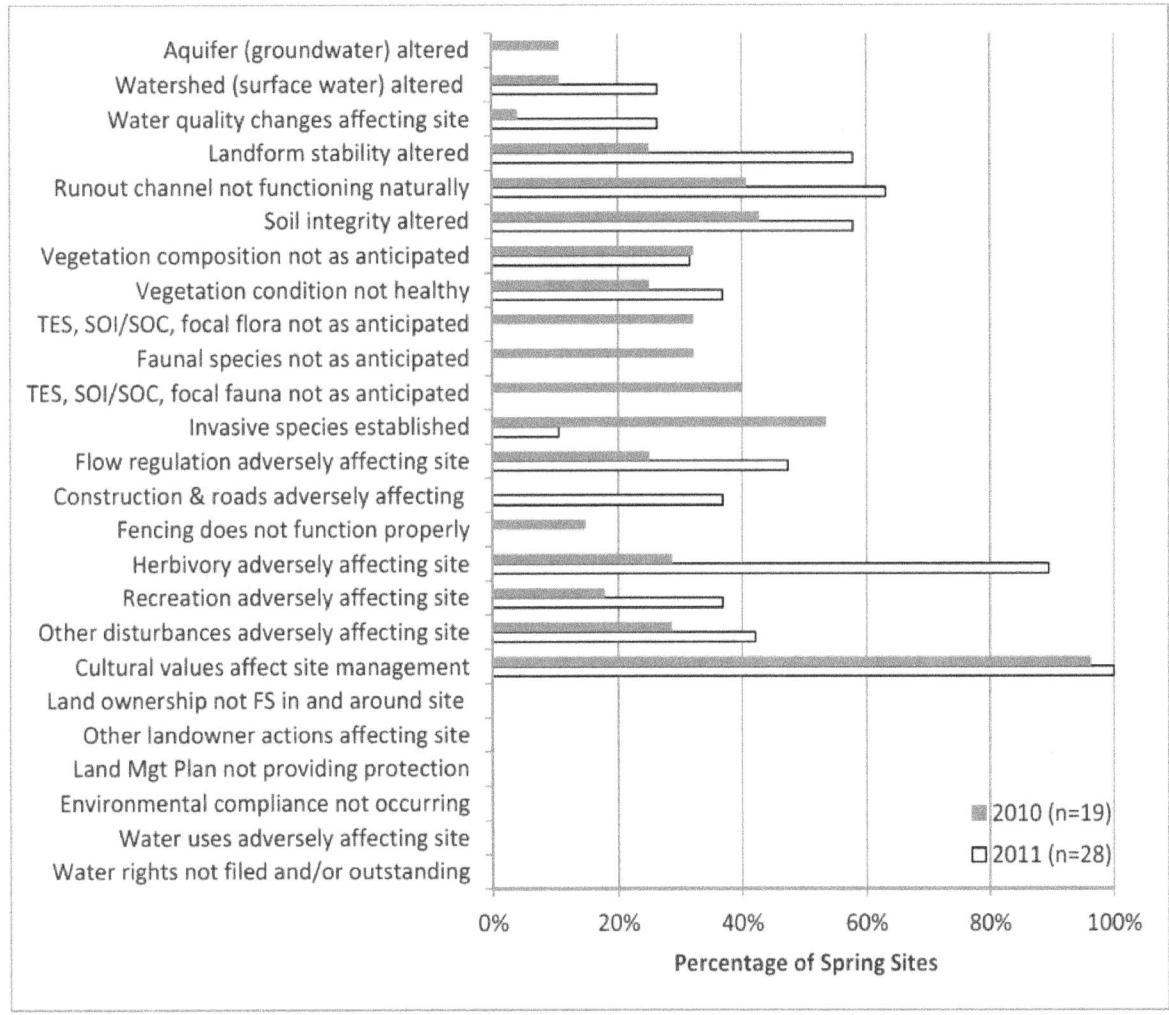

Figure 10: Percent of sites where management indicators were observed based on the sampling of spring sites during 2010 and 2011.

Appendix D 4.1: Supporting data for Monitoring Question 53 – What is the ecological status of riparian areas?

2010 Sites

Site Name	Site ID	Size (m²)	Vegetation composition not as anticipated	Vegetation condition not healthy and vigorous	Faunal species not as anticipated	Invasive flora and fauna established	Introduced Species Cover (%)	Prevalence Index (1=wetland; 5=upland)	Bryophyte Cover (%) (more is generally good)	Vegetation Cover (%) in herbaceous layer	Vegetation Cover (%) in shrub and tree layer
Coal Spring	R4HTSMNRAH2O153	140			Unavailable		41	1.5	1	60	10
Macks Canyon 1	R4HTSMNRAH2O092	745	X		Unavailable		0	1.8	30	81	20
Middle Mud Spring	R4HTSMNRAH2O090	233	X	X	X	X	0	1.9	0	38	21
Quartzite Wall Unnamed Spring	R4HTSMNRAH2O191	270			Unavailable		0	3.1	10	39	3
Stanley B 3 Spring	R4HTSMNRAH2O101	95			Unavailable		0	3.2	3	14	95
Three Springs 1	R4HTSMNRAH2O122	180	X		Unavailable		0	3.0	18	4	0
Three Springs 2	R4HTSMNRAH2O123	101			Unavailable		1	1.1	17	45	2
Two Springs	R4HTSMNRAH2O026	15			Unavailable		0	1.0	30	25	0
Unnamed 1 Spring	R4HTSMNRAH2O027	78			Unavailable	X	10	2.8	17	36	5
Unnamed 21 Spring	R4HTSMNRAH2O126	1	X	X	Unavailable		cement tank (no data)	Unavailable	Unavailable	Unavailable	Unavailable
Unnamed 41 Spring	R4HTSMNRAH2O062	1		X	Unavailable		0	3.9	22	30	0
Unnamed 56 Spring	R4HTSMNRAH2O048	5		X	Unavailable		0	2.6	48	7	0
Unnamed 67 Spring	R4HTSMNRAH2O095	352		X	Unavailable		0	2.9	3	34	11
Upper Cougar Spring	R4HTSMNRAH2O080	12	X	X	Unavailable		hardly any veg	0.0	0	0	9
Upper Horse Springs	R4HTSMNRAH2O113	80			Unavailable		3	2.5	0	63	0
Upper Lost Cabin	R4HTSMNRAH2O148	88			Unavailable		3	3.9	5	37	4
Upper Sawmill Spring	R4HTSMNRAH2O024	14	X	X	Unavailable		0	3.3	0	23	11
Willow Spring	R4HTSMNRAH2O084	462			Unavailable		0	3.0	0	43	68
Wood Canyon Spring	R4HTSMNRAH2O078	137			UA		1	3.3	0	72	20

2011 Sites

Site Name	Site ID	Size (m²)	Vegetation composition not as anticipated	Vegetation condition not healthy and vigorous	Faunal species not as anticipated	Invasive flora and fauna established	Introduced Species Cover (%)	Prevalence Index (1=wetland; 5=upland)	Bryophyte Cover (%) (more is generally good)	Vegetation Cover (%) in herbaceous layer	Vegetation Cover (%) in shrub and tree layer
Cathedral Chute Spring	R4HTSMNRAH2O199	444					0	2.2	8	48	71
Cave Spring 1	R4HTSMNRAH2O136	202	X			X	0	1.4	2	23	109
Cave Spring 2	R4HTSMNRAH2O135	508				X	2	2.2	2	45	24
East Mud Spring	R4HTSMNRAH2O091	1104	X		X	X	0	2.6	3	59	21
Edna Grey Spring	R4HTSMNRAH2O009	320		X	X	X	0	2.5	3	29	53
Elbow Spring	R4HTSMNRAH2O204	18					0	1.7	0	43	29
Fletcher Spring	R4HTSMNRAH2O098	288				X	0	2.3	15	36	8
Gold Spring	R4HTSMNRAH2O072	25	X	X	X		0	0.0	0	0	39
Lower Cougar Spring	R4HTSMNRAH2O081	24	X	X	X	X	0	4.1	10	4	37
Mossfoot Seep	R4HTSMNRAH2O202	45					0	1.0	26	2	0
Mummy Spring	R4HTSMNRAH2O012	975					0	1.5	5	19	23
Mummy View Spring	R4HTSMNRAH2O201	56					0	1.0	0	19	35
Pipilo Unnamed Spring	R4HTSMNRAH2O190	102				X	12	2.3	0	45	58
Roses Spring	R4HTSMNRAH2O137	36	X		X	X	2	2.3	1	5	29
Stanley B 1 Spring	R4HTSMNRAH2O099	60					0	3.2	2	7	63
Stanley B 2 Spring	R4HTSMNRAH2O100	16					0	2.8	0	2	127
Stanley B Wet Wall	R4HTSMNRAH2O200	222					0	2.8	19	7	12
Steller Spring	R4HTSMNRAH2O203	169					0	1.3	2	51	16
Unnamed 20 Spring	R4HTSMNRAH2O035	332					0	1.6	9	73	14
Unnamed 27 Spring	R4HTSMNRAH2O121	25		X	X	X	7	3.5	5	11	100
Unnamed 45 Spring	R4HTSMNRAH2O112	552	X	X	X	X	0	1.3	0	15	27
Unnamed 49 Spring	R4HTSMNRAH2O117	846	X	X		X	2	1.7	0	22	48
Unnamed 55 Spring	R4HTSMNRAH2O119	2952					0	4.0	0	1	96
Unnamed 59 Spring	R4HTSMNRAH2O050	122				X	0	2.0	12	41	17

Site Name	Site ID	Size (m²)	Vegetation composition not as anticipated	Vegetation condition not healthy and vigorous	Faunal species not as anticipated	Invasive flora and fauna established	Introduced Species Cover (%)	Prevalence Index (1=wetland; 5=upland)	Bryophyte Cover (%) (more is generally good)	Vegetation Cover (%) in herbaceous layer	Vegetation Cover (%) in shrub and tree layer
Unnamed 75 Spring	R4HTSMNRAH2O057	188	X			X	8	3.2	4	27	3
Unnamed 9 Spring	R4HTSMNRAH2O061	15					0	4.0	13	2	40
West Mud Spring	R4HTSMNRAH2O089	1940		X	X	X	0	2.4	4	66	7
Younts Spring	R4HTSMNRAH2O149	638	X		X	X	26	3.1	0	46	1

Appendix D 4.2: Supporting data for Monitoring Question 57 – Are soil disturbing activities creating excessive sedimentation or soil loss?

2010 Sites

Site Name	Site ID	Size (m²)	Disturbances				Management Indicators				Bare Ground (%)
			Erosion	Deposition	Trails & Tracks	Excavation or Other Ground Disturbance	Soil Integrity Altered	Landform Stability Altered	Construction and Roads Adversely Affecting Site	Recreational Uses Adversely Affecting Site	
Coal Spring	R4HTSMNRAH2O153	140	X		X			X		X	13
Macks Canyon 1	R4HTSMNRAH2O092	745			X		X			X	1
Middle Mud Spring	R4HTSMNRAH2O090	233	X		X	X	X	X	X		5
Quartzite Wall Unnamed Spring	R4HTSMNRAH2O191	270			X		X				1
Stanley B 3 Spring	R4HTSMNRAH2O101	95	X		X	X		X			8
Three Springs 1	R4HTSMNRAH2O122	180					X				0
Three Springs 2	R4HTSMNRAH2O123	101			X						1
Two Springs	R4HTSMNRAH2O026	15			X	X			X	X	0
Unnamed 1 Spring	R4HTSMNRAH2O027	78	Unavailable	Unavailable	Unavailable	Unavailable					13
Unnamed 21 Spring	R4HTSMNRAH2O126	1			X	X	X		X		UA
Unnamed 41 Spring	R4HTSMNRAH2O062	1			X		X	X			21
Unnamed 56 Spring	R4HTSMNRAH2O048	5					X	X		X	0
Unnamed 67 Spring	R4HTSMNRAH2O095	352	Unavailable	Unavailable	X	X	X	X	X	X	12
Upper Cougar Spring	R4HTSMNRAH2O080	12	Unavailable	Unavailable	Unavailable	Unavailable		X	X	X	3
Upper Horse Springs	R4HTSMNRAH2O113	80			X			X			23
Upper Lost Cabin	R4HTSMNRAH2O148	88			X						12
Upper Sawmill Spring	R4HTSMNRAH2O024	14	X		X		X	X	X		3
Willow Spring	R4HTSMNRAH2O084	462			X		X	X	X	X	0
Wood Canyon Spring	R4HTSMNRAH2O078	137			X	X	X	X	X		4

2011 Sites

Site Name	Site ID	Size (m²)	Disturbances: Erosion	Deposition	Trails & Tracks	Excavation or Other Ground Disturbance	Management Indicators: Soil Integrity Altered	Landform Stability Altered	Construction and Roads adversely affecting site	Recreational uses adversely affecting site	Bare Ground (%)
Cathedral Chute Spring	R4HTSMNRAH2O199	444		X	X			X		X	4
Cave Spring 1	R4HTSMNRAH2O136	202			X						0
Cave Spring 2	R4HTSMNRAH2O135	508	X		X						3
East Mud Spring	R4HTSMNRAH2O091	1104	X		X	X					20
Edna Grey Spring	R4HTSMNRAH2O009	320	X		X	X	X				22
Elbow Spring	R4HTSMNRAH2O204	18									8
Fletcher Spring	R4HTSMNRAH2O098	288			X					X	4
Gold Spring	R4HTSMNRAH2O072	25	X		X	X	X	X			46
Lower Cougar Spring	R4HTSMNRAH2O081	24			X						4
Mossfoot Seep	R4HTSMNRAH2O202	45			X		X	X		X	25
Mummy Spring	R4HTSMNRAH2O012	975	X		X					X	4
Mummy View Spring	R4HTSMNRAH2O201	56			X		X				7
Pipilo Unnamed Spring	R4HTSMNRAH2O190	102			X	X					28
Roses Spring	R4HTSMNRAH2O137	36			X	X	X				25
Stanley B 1 Spring	R4HTSMNRAH2O099	60	X	X	X	X		X			9
Stanley B 2 Spring	R4HTSMNRAH2O100	16	X	X	X	X				X	6
Stanley B Wet Wall	R4HTSMNRAH2O200	222			X	X					1
Steller Spring	R4HTSMNRAH2O203	169			X						13
Unnamed 20 Spring	R4HTSMNRAH2O035	332			X						7
Unnamed 27 Spring	R4HTSMNRAH2O121	25			X		X				0
Unnamed 45 Spring	R4HTSMNRAH2O112	552	X	X	X	X	X				36
Unnamed 49 Spring	R4HTSMNRAH2O117	846	X		X	X	X	X			33
Unnamed 55 Spring	R4HTSMNRAH2O119	2952	X	X	X	X					2
Unnamed 59 Spring	R4HTSMNRAH2O050	122			X	X	X				2
Unnamed 75 Spring	R4HTSMNRAH2O057	188	X		X	X					14
Unnamed 9 Spring	R4HTSMNRAH2O061	15	X		X	X	X				0
West Mud Spring	R4HTSMNRAH2O089	1940	X		X	X	X	X			19
Younts Spring	R4HTSMNRAH2O149	638	X	X	X	X	X	X			50

Spring Mountains National Recreation Area
2011 Inventory and Monitoring Analysis and Evaluation Report - 5/11/12

Appendix D 4.3: Supporting data for MQ 59 – Is recreation use or grazing by wild horses/burros or recreational livestock impacting bank stability?

2010 Sites

Site Name	Site ID	Size (m2)	Disturbances			Management Indicators		
			Animal Trails	Channel Erosion	Runout Channel Substantially Altered	Flow Regulation Adversely Affects Site	Herbivores Adversely Affects Site	Recreational Uses Adversely Affects Site
Coal Spring	R4HTSMNRAH2O153	140	X	X	X	X	X	X
Macks Canyon 1	R4HTSMNRAH2O092	745	X		X	X	X	X
Middle Mud Spring	R4HTSMNRAH2O090	233	X	X	X	X	X	
Quartzite Wall Unnamed Spring	R4HTSMNRAH2O191	270	X			X	X	
Stanley B 3 Spring	R4HTSMNRAH2O101	95	X	X	X		X	
Three Springs 1	R4HTSMNRAH2O122	180						
Three Springs 2	R4HTSMNRAH2O123	101	X				X	
Two Springs	R4HTSMNRAH2O026	15	X		X	X	X	X
Unnamed 1 Spring	R4HTSMNRAH2O027	78	Unavailable	Unavailable				
Unnamed 21 Spring	R4HTSMNRAH2O126	1	X		X	X	X	
Unnamed 41 Spring	R4HTSMNRAH2O062	1	X	X	X		X	
Unnamed 56 Spring	R4HTSMNRAH2O048	5					X	X
Unnamed 67 Spring	R4HTSMNRAH2O095	352	X	X	X	X	X	X
Upper Cougar Spring	R4HTSMNRAH2O080	12	Unavailable	Unavailable	X		X	X
Upper Horse Springs	R4HTSMNRAH2O113	80	X		X		X	
Upper Lost Cabin	R4HTSMNRAH2O148	88	X				X	
Upper Sawmill Spring	R4HTSMNRAH2O024	14	X	X	X	X	X	
Willow Spring	R4HTSMNRAH2O084	462	X			X	X	X
Wood Canyon Spring	R4HTSMNRAH2O078	137	X	X	X	X	X	

2011 Sites

Site Name	Site ID	Size (m²)	Animal Trails	Channel Erosion	Runout Channel Substantially Altered	Flow Regulation Adversely Affects Site	Herbivores Adversely Affect Site	Recreational Uses Adversely Affect Site
Cathedral Chute Spring	R4HTSMNRAH2O199	444	X	X				X
Cave Spring 1	R4HTSMNRAH2O136	202	X					
Cave Spring 2	R4HTSMNRAH2O135	508	X					
East Mud Spring	R4HTSMNRAH2O091	1104	X	X	X	X	X	
Edna Grey Spring	R4HTSMNRAH2O009	320	X	X	X	X	X	
Elbow Spring	R4HTSMNRAH2O204	18		X				
Fletcher Spring	R4HTSMNRAH2O098	288	X					X
Gold Spring	R4HTSMNRAH2O072	25	X	X	X	X	X	
Lower Cougar Spring	R4HTSMNRAH2O081	24	X	X				
Mossfoot Seep	R4HTSMNRAH2O202	45	X					X
Mummy Spring	R4HTSMNRAH2O012	975	X	X				X
Mummy View Spring	R4HTSMNRAH2O201	56	X	X				
Pipilo Unnamed Spring	R4HTSMNRAH2O190	102	X	X	X		X	
Roses Spring	R4HTSMNRAH2O137	36	X	X	X		X	
Stanley B 1 Spring	R4HTSMNRAH2O099	60	X	X		X		X
Stanley B 2 Spring	R4HTSMNRAH2O100	16	X		X			
Stanley B Wet Wall	R4HTSMNRAH2O200	222	X		Unavailable			
Steller Spring	R4HTSMNRAH2O203	169	X	X				
Unnamed 20 Spring	R4HTSMNRAH2O035	332	X	X				
Unnamed 27 Spring	R4HTSMNRAH2O121	25	X	X		X		
Unnamed 45 Spring	R4HTSMNRAH2O112	552	X	X	X		X	
Unnamed 49 Spring	R4HTSMNRAH2O117	846	X	X	X	X	X	
Unnamed 55 Spring	R4HTSMNRAH2O119	2952	X	X				
Unnamed 59 Spring	R4HTSMNRAH2O050	122	X		X			
Unnamed 75 Spring	R4HTSMNRAH2O057	188	X	X				
Unnamed 9 Spring	R4HTSMNRAH2O061	15	X	X				
West Mud Spring	R4HTSMNRAH2O089	1940	X	X	X		X	

Younts Spring	R4HTSMNRAH2O149	638	X	X	X		X

References

Nachlinger, J. and G. A. Reese. 1996. Plant Community Classification of the Spring Mountains National Recreation Area Clark and Nye Counties, Nevada. The Nature Conservancy, Reno, NV.

National Research Council. 1995. Wetlands: Characteristics and Boundaries. National Academy Press, Washington, DC.

Manning, M. E. and W. G. Padgett. 1995. Riparian Community Type Classification for Humboldt and Toiyabe National Forests, Nevada and Eastern California. USDA Forest Service, Intermountain Region, Ogden, UT.

Reed, P. B., Jr. 1988. National list of plant species that occur in wetlands: Intermountain (Region 8). USDI Fish and Wildlife Service, Washington, DC.

Springer, A. E., L. Stevens, and J. Ledbetter. 2010. Spring Mountain Springs Inventory: 20-30 October 2010 Draft Trip Report. Northern Arizona University (NAU), Flagstaff, Arizona.

Springer, A. E. and J. Ledbetter. 2011. Spring Mountains National Recreation Area Springs Inventory: 2011 Final Annual Report. Northern Arizona University (NAU), Flagstaff, Arizona.

Springer, A. E. and L. Stevens. 2008. Spheres of discharge of springs. Hydrogeology Journal 17:83-93.

Tiner, R. W. 1999. Wetland Indicators: A Guide to Wetland Identification, Delineation, Classification, and Mapping. Lewis Publishers, Boca Raton, Florida

Weixelman, D. A., D. C. Zamudio, and K. A. Zamudio. 1996. Central Nevada Riparian Field Guide. Toiyabe National Forest, Sparks, NV.

The 2010 and 2011 IM Audits provide a basis for evaluating the effectiveness of management practice design and mitigation that can serve as a foundation for future management proposals. The following management response "frameworks" can be used as a starting point for the development of future project proposals and the identification of modifications to on-going actions. They define the management situation (current conditions/desired outcomes or objectives) and best practices for achieving those outcomes/objectives based on evaluation of the application and effectiveness of those practices in the SMNRA. Priorities for action can also be used to integrate proposed actions into resource management and conservation program budget requests.

E-1: Wildland Fire Suppression and Restoration Framework

The following recommendations apply to future wildland fire suppression and restoration actions and are based on observations noted in both the implementation and effectiveness monitoring discussions described in the 2010 IM Audit.

1. **Suppression Planning and Direction**

   a) State the specific direction for suppression and fire impacts described in the Forest Plan and the Fire Management Plan. Clearly identify the important values needing protection and the specific expectations of the agency administrator(s) to help the IMT successfully accomplish all objectives.

   b) Adopt and describe modified Minimum Impact Suppression Technique (MIST) guidelines outside wilderness. Use of MIST guidelines outside wilderness may be required to protect sensitive sites and resources.

   c) Prepare templates for the Delegation of Authority that are specific to the SMNRA and support the General Management Plan (Forest Plan Amendment) and Forest Fire Management Plan. Properly reflect the full range of fire management options available (protection & beneficial objectives). Continue utilizing WFDSS to assist in development of future Delegation of Authority letters.

   d) Develop an annual WFDSS fire exercise to stay current with the process and any future changes. Conduct annual training prior to fire season that includes exercises in WFDSS, and involves all SMNRA staff.

   e) Preload as much information as possible into WFDSS so important information is readily available when future wildland fires occur. Every wildland fire is different so direction, objectives, and expectations need to be specifically thought out, developed and communicated to the responsible fire management organization for each incident.

   f) Analyze past fire history in the Spring Mountains. There have been numerous large fires throughout the area. Understanding fire's history in the area helps to effectively and efficiently manage future wildfires.

2. Coordination

g) Improve communication, operational understanding, and relationships among all the entities involved in wildland fire suppression by developing patterned and rehearsed responses. Focus on understanding responsibilities for decisions on evacuations, suppression activities, communications with agencies at other levels/locations and the public, and interagency requirements. All parties need to share an understanding of who is responsible for what, under what circumstances, and the roles of different jurisdictions. This understanding is particularly important when transitioning from initial attack responsibilities to Incident Management Team and Unified Command responsibilities.

h) In the absence of appropriate pre-suppression planning and coordination, the District runs the risk of committing resources needed to advise agency administrators on the management of the incident vs. participating in and directing initial attack on site.

3. Resource Protection

i) Provide more trained Resource Advisors and include them in more fire training to improve their skills. Hold a pre-season meeting or some other session to discuss what they are looking for and what is important. Along with this, brainstorm any other issues that might be a problem in managing a fire, such as situations where springs might be used as water sources. Build a GIS layer showing this information and make it available to incoming IMT's.

j) Develop GIS layers for all values at risk that can be readily accessed at the time of a fire. This should be put on a disk or portable drive that could be given to in-coming IMT's to help them understand location of all values at risk within and surrounding the planning area on a wildfire. An example of values at risk includes (not intended to be all inclusive): Sensitive plant habitat or known locations, critical habitat for any important species, past and present fuel/fire breaks, private and FS structure location, any improvements or infrastructure that needs protection (cell towers, power transmission lines, campgrounds, picnic areas, organization sites and camps, heritage sites, trailheads, bridges, etc.). This information would also greatly assist in the development of WFDSS and incident specific letters of delegation.

4. Managing Fire Behavior

k) Locate past fuel breaks and treatments on-the-ground and record them in GIS. Assess their current condition and effectiveness. Develop maintenance plans and schedules.

l) Conduct fire behavior modeling to generate fire behavior runs under different fuel and weather conditions. This will show different fire spread/intensities and will begin to show the critical thresholds when various objectives may or may not be able to be met. Validate these runs with local fire behavior knowledge and experience.

E-2: Hazardous Fuel Treatment Prescription Framework

Design measures used in the 2007 Spring Mountains Hazardous Fuels Reduction Project EA provided the basis for developing a consistent approach or framework for developing hazardous fuel reduction treatment prescriptions. References to specific design measures refer to those used in the 2007 EA.

1. Design Features Common to All Treatment Proposals

With regard to specific design measures or groups of design measures, future proposals should consider the results of this audit and consensus of participants. Specific groups of design measures and rationale common to potential treatments include:

a) Design measures that are not necessary to obtain the objective of keeping flame lengths and fire behavior within the limits expected for direct attack by hand crews:

   1) Pruning (S9)- In all cases, drop design measures that specify pruning because they are not needed when surface fuel continuity has been disrupted and stands are thinned. Resulting wounds provide a vector for insects and disease that may actually increase fuel hazards.

   2) Tree/Shrub Removal (S11-13, S15) - Do not remove black brush. Its size and fire behavior are within fire behavior objectives. Retention of mountain mahogany should use clumps similar to those used in the "Old Kyle" fuel break treatment example.

b) Design measures better addressed through proposed treatment design:

   1) Visual Effects (V 1 through V18) - Visual design measures should be built into proposed actions as opposed to being identified as design measures. They cannot be effectively translated to contract terms and are more appropriately dealt with during project design.

c) Design measures determined to be effective that should be retained in future proposals and necessary modifications include:

   1) Botany – improve the source of GIS information used to develop contract specifications and designate areas of concern on the ground closer to the timing of actual treatment.

   2) Cultural and Historic Sites –no changes.

   3) Riparian and Streambank Protection –no changes.

   4) Soil Protection – no changes.

d) Fuel Treatment and Activity Fuel Disposal Descriptions – Desired conditions and options for disposal of activity fuels need to be better described and linked to sites that can serve as examples of desired results (e.g., Old Kyle, Stimson LDS Camp, Lee/Foxtail) and describe the specifications for activity fuel disposal and removal of materials.

e) Do not propose actions that should be addressed as part of the annual operating plan or maintenance requirements under the terms and conditions of existing authorizations that are the responsibility of the permit holder or grantee. These include highway and powerline rights-of-way, permitted areas for recreation residences, ski areas, organization camps, and other authorized uses.

f) Do not create expectations for resource specialists in environmental documents that are inconsistent with contract relationships.

2. Potential Treatment Prescriptions

SMNRA Staff identified six potential treatment sites and discussed current conditions, need and purpose of treatments, desired outcomes, and the type of treatment associated with different vegetation cover types. The following tables describe the treatment prescriptions for different treatment areas based upon current vegetation and need/purpose associated with each site. (See the 2010 IM Audit Report for specific treatment area locations and past treatment areas referenced).

Treatment Prescription A (North Lee Canyon)

Current vegetation	Mixed conifer on moist north-facing slopes; Pinyon-juniper, brush, and mountain mahogany on dry south-facing slopes
Desired Condition	Fuel loading (crown spacing, ladder fuels, and surface continuity) should be reduced to allow for direct attack by hand crews. Flame lengths reduced to 2 feet or less.
Need and purpose	- Slow fire spread - Facilitate reintroduction of fire into Wilderness, by preventing spread of fire from the west into Lee Canyon, which could threaten private land. -No ingress/egress issue
Treatment	Mixed conifer: - Favor ponderosa pine, - Thin to preferred spacing, do not prune Pinyon/Juniper: - Shaded fuel break similar to the "Old Kyle" fuel break - Whole tree removal - Leave individual trees and mountain mahogany clumps - No pruning - Retain some low-height brush in between retained trees, do not remove black brush - Hand pile and burn activity fuels. Chip and masticate only when needed to protect structures or key CA Species habitats.

Treatment Prescription B (Deer Creek Road - Lee Canyon Grade)

Current vegetation	Pinyon/juniper and mountain mahogany, some mixed conifer on lower end
Desired Condition	Fuel loading (crown spacing, ladder fuels, and surface continuity) should be reduced to allow for direct attack by hand crews. Flame lengths reduced to 2 feet or less.
Need and purpose	- Ingress/egress - Reducing the rate of spread to allow for more effective and efficient response time, reducing fire intensity to allow for safer fire control operations.
Treatment	Same as recent Stimson/LDS Camp treatment w/o pruning Hand pile and burn activity fuels. Chip and masticate only when needed to protect structures or key CA Species habitats.

Treatment Prescription C (Angel Peak Road – north side of road)

Current vegetation	Pinyon/juniper and mountain mahogany
Desired Condition	Fuel loading (crown spacing, ladder fuels, and surface continuity) should be reduced to allow for direct attack by hand crews. Flame lengths reduced to 2 feet or less.
Need and purpose	- Provide for the protection of workers and residents at the Angel site to safely shelter in place and for ingress and egress to the Deer Creek road. - Coordinate treatment with power line right of way fuel treatment for protection of air traffic control and youth camp facilities and operations.
Treatment	Same as recent Stimson/LDS Camp treatment w/o pruning Hand pile and burn activity fuels. Chip and masticate only when needed to protect structures or key CA Species habitats.

Treatment Prescription D (Deer Creek-Kyle Canyon Grade)

Current vegetation	Pinyon/juniper or brush	
Desired Condition	Fuel loading (crown spacing, ladder fuels, and surface continuity) should be reduced to allow for direct attack by hand crews. Flame lengths reduced to 2 feet or less.	
Need and purpose	-	Buy time to get resources on site
	-	Prevent and/or slow spread from starts along the road
	-	Provide for ingress/egress for residents
Treatment	-	Shaded fuel break similar to the "Old Kyle" fuel break
	-	Whole tree removal, leave individual trees and clumps
	-	No pruning
	-	Some low-height brush in between retained trees
	-	Consider multiple entry treatments
	-	Hand pile and burn activity fuels. Chip and masticate only when needed to protect structures or key CA Species habitats.

Treatment Prescription E (Fletcher Fire)

Current vegetation	Chaparral, mesquite, scattered pinyon trees	
Desired Condition	Fuel loading (crown spacing, ladder fuels, and surface continuity) should be reduced to allow for direct attack by hand crews. Flame lengths reduced to 2 foot or less.	
Need and purpose	-	Reintroduction of fire
	-	Moderate to low intensity fire behavior
Treatment	-	Tie into Robbers Fire/topographic barrier
	-	Shaded fuel break similar to the "Old Kyle" fuel break
	-	Whole tree removal, leave individual trees and clumps
	-	No pruning
	-	Some low-height brush in between retained trees
	-	Hand pile and burn activity fuels. Chip and masticate only when needed to protect structures or key CA Species habitats.

Treatment Prescription F (Forest Service Corridor Road behind NDF Station)

Current vegetation	Mixed conifer, ponderosa pine	
Desired Condition	Fuel loading (crown spacing, ladder fuels, and surface continuity) should be reduced to allow for direct attack by hand crews. Flame lengths reduced to 2 feet or less.	
Need and purpose	-	Provide for ingress/egress for resident
Treatment	-	Similar to the Lee/Foxtail fuel break
	-	No pruning
	-	Hand pile and burn activity fuels. Chip and masticate only when needed to protect structures or key CA Species habitats.

E-3: Springs/Riparian Area Management Framework

A key factor in determining when and how to establish riparian exclosure fences and initiating other management actions is the ecological significance of the spring/riparian area. Ecological significance is determined by a combination of factors and can be determined using the information and data being collected in the springs inventory program. Preliminary discussions indicate the following elements should contribute to the determination of ecological significance:

- o Spring Type
- o Riparian Area/Feature Size

- o Surface Flow
- o Vegetation Community
- o Presence of CA Species

The potential for disturbance or damage by wild horses/burros, elk and recreation use are other factors to be considered. In some instances, drift fences established in lower portions of canyons are a more effective alternative to reducing potential effects from wild horses/burros and should be considered before fencing individual sites.

Elk use effects at springs are related to the distribution of the elk population across the SMNRA. Fences that effectively exclude elk are expensive to build and maintain. Use of external water sources is likely more effective in reducing use by elk than more elaborate fencing designs.

Recreation use effects can often be effectively managed by a combination of restricting use by establishing physical barriers and designation of access routes and interpretive signing/visitor education.

Forest Plan standards and guidelines provide a starting point for developing a framework for managing recreation use at springs and in riparian areas. They also provide guidance for determining when fencing should be used to protect CA species and their habitats, as well as exclosure design. The following Forest Plan/GMP standards apply design elements included in this framework:

Forest Plan/GMP Standards

- If a riparian area within a wild horse and burro territory is fenced, pipe water out of riparian areas for wild horse and burro use. (0.2)
- When developing water sources, pipe water from a point downstream of the source if snails or other sensitive species are present, or if the spring source has not been previously developed. (0.8)
- Remove existing water developments and debris from springs, providing they no longer serve their original purpose, are not critical to wildlife, and the items are not of historical significance. (0.13)
- Prohibit parking and camping within riparian areas. (0.2)
- MA 11 - Provide protection of the riparian areas (in accordance with NV Revised Statute 503.660) at Cold and Willow Creeks through the use of new road alignments, vehicle barriers, and/or signage. Redirect parking and camping away from riparian corridors. Allow only day-use, walk-in activities to occur within the riparian corridor. (11.1)
- MA 13 - Develop low standard recreation facilities, including small campsites or restrooms, in Carpenter Canyon as a resource protection measure. Close the last section of road to prevent vehicle access through the stream and riparian area. Make campsites walk-in access only. (13.17)

The following decision framework is recommended to determine proposed actions associated with springs/riparian management and is designed to reduce the effects of uses and disturbance on springs and riparian areas.

Springs/Riparian Management Framework

Common Design Features

- <u>Drift Fences</u> – Evaluate opportunities to establish drift fences to control access to springs by wild horses/burros before proposing fencing at individual sites.
- <u>Perimeter</u> – Consider fencing areas larger than the spring riparian area to provide better anchor points and screening. At a minimum, exclosure fences and management efforts should approximate the perimeter of the spring riparian area. Slope breaks and vegetation should be the primary factors used to determine the perimeter and location of fences and delimiting areas of use.
- <u>Existing Developments</u> - Remove existing water developments and debris from springs, providing they no longer serve their original purpose, are not critical to wildlife, and the items are not of cultural significance. Restore and re-vegetate areas associated with these improvements.
- <u>Maintenance and Monitoring</u> – Adhere to maintenance schedules established for each fencing design and associated monitoring schedules and focus.

High Ecological Significance Wild Horses & Burros Present/Elk Use High – Moderate Recreation Use	High Ecological Significance No Wild Horses & Burros/Elk Use High – Moderate Recreation Use
Priority A - Establish and maintain a post/wire rope exclosure - Exclude <u>all</u> wild horses and burros - Do not allow elk access - Provide external water source(s) - Restrict and manage recreation use/access using physical barriers/trail locations - Provide interpretive and recreation signing	Priority C - Restrict and manage recreation use/access using physical barriers/trail locations - Interpretive and recreation signing
Moderate Ecological Significance Wild Horses & Burros Present/Elk Use Moderate – Low Recreation Use	Moderate Ecological Significance No Wild Horses & Burros/Elk Moderate – Low Recreation Use
Priority B - Establish and maintain a t-post/barbed wire exclosure - Provide external water source - Restrict and manage recreation use/access using physical barriers/trail locations - Provide interpretive and recreation signing	Priority D - Restrict and manage recreation use/access using physical barriers/trail locations - Provide interpretive signing
Low Ecological Significance Wild Horses & Burros Present Low Recreation Use	Low Ecological Significance No Wild Horses & Burros/Elk Low Recreation Use
Priority D - No exclosure fence warranted. Site-specific exceptions may occur - Provide interpretive signing	Priority E - No exclosure fence warranted - No interpretive or recreation signing

Given the complexity associated with the management of motorized use within the SMNRA and limited staff resources available, it is essential that management actions be focused on those areas where they are necessary to minimize effects to CA Species and their habitats. Key factors in setting management priorities include:

Level and Type of Recreation Use – The level and type of use potentially affecting CA Species and their habitats needs to be described and mapped using a qualitative approach to assist in setting management priorities.

Ecological Significance of CA Species Habitats and Life Cycle Events – Information on CA Species habitat and information on the species' life history are important factors in managing recreation use. A combination of habitat extent and timing associated with key life history events need to be considered. Information being developed as part of the I&M program will address these needs by providing current life history information and potential habitat models. A current example is provided by the UNLV study of the Mount Charleston Blue Butterfly, which has identified limited habitat for this species located in the vicinity of West Mud Springs, Cold Creek and Willow Spring. These habitats are critical during key life cycle stages and may warrant seasonal restrictions on some uses.

Forest Plan/GMP standards provide a starting point for developing a framework for managing motorized recreation. The following apply to design elements included in this framework:

Forest Plan/GMP Standards

- Prohibit parking and camping within riparian areas. (0.2)
- Existing roads and trails should remain open to current use unless site-specific constraints dictate a need for closure or seasonal restrictions. (0.24).
- Provide for public safety in management of recreation. Cooperate with and support other agencies to ensure safety. (0.28).
- Work cooperatively with federal, state, local agencies, tribal governments, and others to increase public education and awareness of resource values and interpretation opportunities throughout the SMNRA. (0.30).
- Manage for a variety of road types, including limited maintenance roads that offer recreational opportunities for OHV's and other users. (0.36).
- Allow motorized vehicle use only on designated roads and trails, except for snowmobile use in approved areas. Close washes to motorized use. (0.65).
- Sign all designated forest system roads to identify the route names/number and to indicate the ends of roads and parking areas. (0.120).
- MA 11 - Provide protection of the riparian areas (in accordance with NV Revised Statute 503.660) at Cold and Willow Creeks through the use of new road alignments, vehicle barriers, and/or signage. Redirect parking and camping away from riparian corridors. Allow only day-use, walk-in activities to occur within the riparian corridor. (11.1)
- MA 13 - Develop low standard recreation facilities, including small campsites or restrooms, in Carpenter Canyon as a resource protection measure. Close the last section of road to prevent vehicle access through stream and riparian area. Make campsites walk-in access only. (13.17)

Management practices and techniques appropriate for managing motorized recreation use in the SMNRA that have been proven to be effective serve as a basis for future proposals.

The following management framework is a recommended for determining proposed actions associated motorized recreation management designed to reduce the effects on CA Species and their habitats.

Motorized Recreation Management Framework

Common Design Features

- <u>Visitor Education, Signing and Maps</u> – Improve and maintain visitor information/signing, update and improve the Motorized Vehicle Use Map, and increase partnership programs.
- <u>Wilderness Trespass Enforcement</u> – Monitor and enforce prohibitions on motorized travel within designated Wildernesses.
- <u>Route Closure and Restoration Practices</u> – Develop and refine practices used for restoring and rehabilitating user-created routes and closed roads based on the work done at Mountain Springs.
- <u>Monitoring and Enforcement</u> – Implement programmatic recommendations listed in Section 3 of the 2011 IM Audit report regarding monitoring and cooperative law enforcement.

High Ecological Significance **High Motorized Recreation Use**	**High Ecological Significance** **Mod. Motorized Recreation Use**	**High Ecological Significance** **Low Motorized Recreation Use**
<u>Priority A</u> • Restrict and manage recreation use/access using physical barriers/trail locations • Site designation in Infra • Site Master Plan and OHV Trail System Plan • Interpretive and recreation signing	<u>Priority B</u> • Restrict and manage recreation use/access using physical barriers/trail locations • Evaluate "connections" with other OHV system components • Interpretive and recreation signing	<u>Priority C</u> • Restrict and manage recreation use/access using physical barriers/trail locations • Evaluate "connections" with other OHV system components • Interpretive and recreation signing
Moderate Ecological Significance **High Motorized Recreation Use**	**Moderate Ecological Significance** **Mod. Motorized Recreation Use**	**Moderate Ecological Significance** **Low Motorized Recreation Use**
<u>Priority B</u> • Restrict and manage recreation use/access using physical barriers/trail locations • Evaluate "connections" with other OHV system components • Provide interpretive and recreation signing	<u>Priority C</u> • Restrict and manage recreation use/access using physical barriers/trail locations • Evaluate "connections" with other OHV system components • Provide interpretive signing	<u>Priority D</u>
Low Ecological Significance **High Motorized Recreation Use**	**Low Ecological Significance** **Mod. Motorized Recreation Use**	**Low Ecological Significance** **Low Motorized Recreation Use**
<u>Priority C</u> • Restrict and manage recreation use/access using physical barriers/trail locations • Evaluate "connections" with other OHV system components • Provide interpretative signing	<u>Priority D</u>	<u>Priority E</u>